The Bookman

William Troy on Literature and Criticism, 1927–1950

The Bookman

William Troy on Literature and Criticism, 1927–1950

JAMES R. RUSSO

sussex
ACADEMIC
PRESS
Brighton • Chicago • Toronto

Introduction and organization of this volume copyright © James R. Russo 2022.
Further information regarding the original publication of the Reviews &
Reports is provided in the Acknowledgments

2 4 6 8 10 9 7 5 3 1

First published 2022 in Great Britain by
SUSSEX ACADEMIC PRESS
PO Box 139
Eastbourne BN24 9BP

Distributed in North America by
SUSSEX ACADEMIC PRESS
Independent Publishers Group
814 N. Franklin Street, Chicago, IL 60610

British Library Cataloguing in Publication Data
A CIP catalogue record for this book is available from the British Library.

Library of Congress Cataloging-in-Publication Data
To be applied for.

Paperback ISBN 978-1-78976-172-6

Typeset & designed by Sussex Academic Press, Brighton & Eastbourne.

Contents

Acknowledgements   ix

Introduction   1

Reviews & Reports
 1. White Lightning (1927)   18
    Hippolytus Temporizes, by H.D.

 2. Crisis in the Novel (1927)   19

 3. Gusto and Literature (1928)   24

 4. Comedy of Time (1928)   31
    Orlando: A Biography, by Virginia Woolf

 5. The Position of Liam O'Flaherty (1929)   33

 6. The Story of the Little Magazines (1930–32)   39

 7. Proof Positive (1930)   60
    The Proof, by Yvor Winters

 8. Nathan's Testament (1931)   61
    Testament of a Critic, by George Jean Nathan

 9. Symbolism as a Generating Force in Contemporary   64
    Literature (1931)
    Axel's Castle, by Edmund Wilson

10. Henry James and Young Writers (1931)   67

11. Rimbaud, "The Literaturicide" (1931)   78
    A Season in Hell: The Life of Arthur Rimbaud,
    by Jean-Marie Carré

                                                                     ⌄

CONTENTS

12. The New Intellectual (1932)   81

13. Cummings' Non-Land of Un- (1933)   89
Eimi, by E. E. Cummings

14. Fragmentary Ends (1933)   91
Death in the Woods, by Sherwood Anderson

15. Newer Novelist (1933)   92
Miss Lonelyhearts, by Nathanael West

16. Bundles of Fragments   94
The Best Short Stories of 1933, edited by Edward J. O'Brien
Twentieth-Century Short Stories, edited by Sylvia Chatfield Bates

17. Literary Trapezist (1933)   96
Orphée, by Jean Cocteau

18. Hemingway's Opium (1933)   97
Winner Take Nothing, by Ernest Hemingway

19. Sean O'Faolain (1934)   99
A Nest of Simple Folk, by Sean O'Faolain

20. Studs Lonigan's World (1934)   102
The Young Manhood of Studs Lonigan, by James T. Farrell

21. T. S. Eliot, Grand Inquisitor (1934)   104
After Strange Gods: A Primer of Modern Heresy,
by T. S. Eliot

22. The Worm i' the Bud (1934)   107
Tender Is the Night, by F. Scott Fitzgerald

23. Flower of Manhattan (1934)   109
A Backward Glance, by Edith Wharton

24. The Conversion of André Gide (1934)   111

25. Romains's Progress (1934)   116
The Proud and the Meek, by Jules Romains

26. Priapus in Georgia (1935)   119
    Journeyman, by Erskine Caldwell

27. New Country (1935)   121
    Collected Poems, 1929–1933, by C. Day-Lewis
    Vienna: A Poem, by Stephen Spender
    Cry of Time, by Hazel Hall

28. And Tomorrow (1935)   124
    Pylon, by William Faulkner

29. Portrait of an Age (1935)   125
    Judgment Day, by James T. Farrell

30. Radix Malorum (1935)   128
    The Treasure of the Sierra Madre, by B. Traven

31. Footprints in Cement (1935)   129
    Lucy Gayheart, by Willa Cather

32. A Matter of Quality (1935)   131
    Flowering Judas and Other Stories, by Katherine Anne Porter

33. The Critic's Job (1935)   133
    The Double Agent: Essays in Craft and Elucidation,
    by R. P. Blackmur

34. On Being Contemporary (1936)   135

35. The Comic View (1936)   139
    Bones of Contention and Other Stories,
    by Frank O'Connor

36. Huxley Agonistes (1936)   140
    Eyeless in Gaza, by Aldous Huxley

37. Aragon's Novel of Pre-War Europe (1936)   143
    The Bells of Basel, by Louis Aragon

38. New Rhetoric for Old (1936)   146
    The Philosophy of Rhetoric, by I. A. Richards

39. The Poetry of Doom (1936)   149
Absalom, Absalom!, by William Faulkner

40. Two Small Books (1937)   151
The Sacrilege of Alan Kent, by Erskine Caldwell
Three Times Three, by William Saroyan

41. Revolution by Poetic Justice (1937)   153
On This Island, by W. H. Auden
Forward from Liberalism, by Stephen Spender

42. Gloried from Within (1937)   157
The Notebooks and Papers of Gerard Manley Hopkins,
edited by Humphry House

43. The Symbolism of Zola (1937)   159
Germinal, by Émile Zola

44. Quintessence of Dust (1943)   162
Shakespeare and the Nature of Man, by Theodore Spencer

45. The New Parnassianism and Recent Poetry (1944)   164

46. Stephen Dedalus—in the Rough (1945)   176
Stephen Hero, by James Joyce

47. The Passion and the Task (1948)   178
The Notebooks of Henry James, edited by F. O. Matthiessen &
Kenneth B. Murdock

48. The Rebirth of Allegory (1949)   180
The Plague, by Albert Camus
Caligula and *Cross Purpose*, by Albert Camus
The Blood of Others, by Simone de Beauvoir
Modern French Short Stories, edited by John Lehmann

49. Poetry and "The Non-Euclidian Predicament" (1949)   184
Collected Poems of William Empson, by William Empson

50. Limits of the Intrinsic (1950)   186
Theory of Literature, by René Wellek & Austin Warren

Bibliography & Index   189–217

Acknowledgements

For their permission to reprint, I would like to extend my gratitude to the publishers of the still-extant magazines in which William Troy's essays and reviews originally appeared: the *Nation*, *New York Times*, *North American Review*, *New Republic*, *Hudson Review*, and *Poetry*. My thanks go out, in addition, to Moira Fitzgerald of the Beinecke Rare Book and Manuscript Library of Yale University (New Haven, Connecticut), where the Léonie Adams and William Troy Papers are housed, for her cooperation and assistance; and to Dolores Colon, also of Yale's Beinecke Rare Book and Manuscript Library, for locating the photograph of William Troy and giving me the permission to reproduce it.

Introduction

William Troy was born in Chicago, Illinois, on July 11, 1903, and grew up in the nearby suburb of Oak Park, attending high school at Loyola Academy, a Jesuit institution. At fifteen, he sold his first review to a newspaper. Upon graduating from Yale University in 1925, he taught for one year at the University of New Hampshire and then enrolled in graduate school at Columbia University. From 1929 to 1930 Troy studied at the Sorbonne and the University of Grenoble in France on an American Field Service fellowship; in order to do so he took a year off from a teaching position at New York University, where he worked from 1926 to 1935.

He married the poet Léonie Adams (1899–1988) in 1933 and, in 1935, the two moved to Bennington, Vermont, to take up teaching positions at Bennington College, where Troy also chaired the Department of Literature and Humanities. Throughout the 1930s, he was a regular literary and film reviewer for the *Nation*, and during the 1940s he published essays, reviews, and a few poems in various literary journals. As a result of illness, he published almost nothing in the 1950s: a few afterwords to earlier essays being reprinted, and an introduction to a paperback edition of Shakespeare's *Antony and Cleopatra* (1607). From 1945 to 1960, except for one year as a Fulbright Lecturer at France's University of Bordeaux and University of Rennes in 1955 and 1956, Troy taught at the New School for Social Research in New York, focusing on Joyce and Shakespeare. He was a popular teacher among his students and was remembered among them as a great lecturer. Cancer of the larynx and a subsequent throat operation forced him to leave teaching in March of 1960. He died in New Milford, Connecticut, on May 26, 1961. Troy's *Selected Essays*, containing twenty-one of his literary articles and reviews, was published posthumously in 1967 and won the National Book Award in 1968 in the category of Arts and Letters.

Those are the facts of William Troy's life, necessary here because few people today know anything about him. Nonetheless, Troy was a highly regarded literary critic during the 1930s and 1940s. This was the period of the independent man of letters such as H. L. Mencken,

Van Wyck Brooks, Lewis Mumford, Paul Rosenfeld, and Malcolm Cowley—men who gradually disappeared with the boom in higher education after the Second World War. With that boom, criticism migrated into the American university, first as the New Criticism, doing battle against the old *belles lettres* and scholarly pedantry; then, starting in the 1970s, as critical theory (including, but not limited to, post-structuralism, semiotics, deconstruction, post-colonialism, and new historicism), which challenged the humanistic curriculum that had been transformed by New Critics such as John Crowe Ransom, Cleanth Brooks, and William K. Wimsatt into a close study of selected literary masterpieces.

Among his (independent) critical contemporaries, William Troy himself ranked with Edmund Wilson, Kenneth Burke, and F. O. Matthiessen. His work also justified the admiration of critics somewhat younger, like R. W. B. Lewis and Joseph Frank, who acknowledged his importance as an influence. Indeed, in a memoir included in *Selected Essays*, Allen Tate placed Troy "among the handful of the best critics of this century" (Troy, 1967: xi). Yet Troy was not so much a seminal critic as a usable one. That he should have been forgotten is the mark of his achievement; in the excitement of urging the reader back to the text, good criticism is *meant* to be forgotten. As for his teaching (untenured or freelance, and therefore independent) at Bennington College, the New School for Social Research, and New York University—teaching that was itself, of course, a form of criticism—his Bennington colleague Stanley Edgar Hyman, the editor of *Selected Essays*, concurred with Troy's students in citing him as "the finest lecturer on literature" (Troy, 1967: 4) that he had ever heard.

The Bookman: William Troy on Literature and Criticism, 1927–1950 collects a selection of his remaining writings on such major literary figures as Henry James, E. E. Cummings, Ernest Hemingway, Edith Wharton, F. Scott Fitzgerald, T. S. Eliot, André Gide, William Faulkner, James Joyce, Albert Camus, Jean Cocteau, Willa Cather, W. H. Auden, and Émile Zola. In the essays and reviews gathered here, Troy provides further evidence that he produced a body of work that is timeless, permanent, and exemplary—perhaps as much as, if not more so than, the work of such critical contemporaries of his as the Anglo-Americans Yvor Winters, I. A. Richards, William Empson, George Jean Nathan, and R. P. Blackmur (all of whom he addresses in this new volume). "Great poetry," Troy once wrote, "impresses us with genuineness through its concreteness, its definiteness, and the exact correspondence between the object evoked and the full linguistic apparatus used to evoke it" (Troy, 1967: 16). The same could be said for great criticism—like William Troy's. He must now assume his proper role as one of the foremost literary critics of his age.

The Usable Critic

When Troy was writing for several magazines, including the *Nation*, Proust had just been translated, the novels of Malraux were coming out, and *Finnegans Wake* (1939) was not yet complete. Little wonder that criticism today seems puny by comparison. Coming from that age of great literature and seminal criticism, a figure like Troy, who wrote around a hundred critical pieces but no book during his lifetime, is easily forgotten. He could not bring himself to gather them into a book because of a mad Irish perfectionism: they were not good enough, his mind had changed on this or that matter, he could see more clearly now, he would re-write them better. Troy never did. It was all that he could do to write them at all in his later years, since writing came hard to him—he was so purely a talker, an actor or performer.

Lacking the theoretical brilliance of a critic like Burke (also a Bennington colleague), or even the exemplary methods of William Empson or Lionel Trilling, William Troy was too eclectic for easy labeling and thus for packaging in histories of criticism. His attempts at theory were both loose and unoriginal; his most suggestive theoretical statements were likely to have been tossed off in the heat of battle, in more practical pieces. Nor was he great by virtue of extent of interest or influence: neither protean like Edmund Wilson nor messianic like F. R. Leavis. Yet Troy is eminently worth reviving, just as he was dangerous to forget.

Indeed, because of their very distinctiveness, the methods and gifts of more famous critics have hardened into tools or commandments. (And their epigones are not only lesser, they are also likely to be more doctrinaire.) With his lucid sensibility and freedom from restrictive categories, Troy may prove a more fruitful model than those great critics who begin to seem larger than creative writers and have thus become distractions from literature itself. In its range and resourcefulness, as well as in the fineness of its discriminations and evaluations, Troy's criticism is a model of excellence for his and our time. In fact, there is hardly a method of literary criticism that he does not demonstrate on one occasion or another. "The problem," Troy writes in "The Lawrence Myth" in 1938, "is always to discover the approach that will do least violence to the object before us, that will reconcile the greatest number of the innumerable aspects that every object presents to the understanding" (Troy, 1967: 121).

Though Troy was not a theoretician, his criticism was informed by an intelligence so balanced that, where many theoreticians took up positions that inadvertently placed them in logical traps, Troy easily avoids them. Neither a mover nor a shaker in scope and intensity, when confronted with a text, he analyzed it with a firm sense of its inherent meaning and of its cultural implications, in a style that expresses seriousness of commitment clearly and precisely. Thus at the very moment—the 1930s—when scholars and critics were either treating literature like polemics or investigating ideas as if *belles lettres* were a sub-category of history or philosophy (only rather effete and somewhat unreliable), Troy was able to acknowledge both the centrality of literary ideas and their distinction from ideas in other forms. On the question of form's relationship to content, for example—a subject that threatened to turn some twentieth-century critics into secular mystics—Troy is eminently sensible. Recognizing that the art of poetry has always been the maintenance of the proper harmony between the sound and meaning of words, he falls neither into an irresponsible fixation on form (as found in the criticism of Susan Sontag) or that exaltation of content which characterized his own epoch—overtly in Marxist criticism, covertly in the disguised religiousness of the Southern (Agrarian) critics Donald Davidson, Stark Young, and Robert Penn Warren.

Sometimes Troy focuses on minute particulars, but always with a larger goal in mind. In a review of *Tender Is the Night* (1934), he studies the occurrence of the word "glamor" in Fitzgerald's fiction, as perhaps a key to the author's sensibility. With strategic brilliance, he makes use of the poetic jottings of Paul Valéry to insist that in poetry, form and content are engaged in an intense conflict with each other, on an equal plane, to produce a poem. Or rather, this conflict is itself the poem— *la forme sensible*. Armed with this subtle definition, Troy attacks the triumph of style over content in Virginia Woolf (among others), which he rightly predicted would harm the novel's subsequent growth. Free, nonetheless, from that specious philistinism which infects defenders of naturalistic, "content-heavy" fiction, Troy never embraced the obverse fetish: the "poetic" or mannered novel. Thus, confronted with the Romantic penumbra and ironic prose style of Stendhal, he can still prefer the documentary amplitude of Balzac, showing that Balzac's details are always subordinated to his grasp of truth.

Troy was perhaps too free from an emphasis on textual analysis; he seldom peers very closely through the lens of a writer's prose. Too often, his intense regard for literature makes him ask it for salvation (but in this he merely partakes in the widespread inflation without which the age's great criticism would probably not have been possible). Still, he is to be praised for his originality, which is impressive. More impressive is the enduring rightness of Troy's judgment. He was early, for example, in taking Thomas Mann seriously and analyzing *The Magic Mountain* (1924) in a long, brilliant essay published in three parts in 1938, though it is more thrilling to see him finally realize, in 1956 (in New School lecture notes on Mann later incorporated into the same long piece, "Thomas Mann: Myth and Reason," in *Selected Essays*), that Mann's intellectual richness is shallow, that he is not, in the last analysis, *un homme sérieux* (Troy, 1967: 241).

Moreover, Troy's balanced dismissals of Virginia Woolf and Gertrude Stein have become standard, as has his partial retraction in Woolf's case. After attacking Woolf, in essays published in 1932 and 1937, for "limiting herself to purely formal variations on the same old dirge-like tune" (Troy, 1967: 86), he apologized in a 1952 afterword: "Since her tragic death Woolf's work has found its own secure and appropriate place in the literature of our time. That place has turned out to be neither so small nor so inconsequential as the prevailing tone here [in "Virginia Woolf and the Novel of Sensibility," from 1932, but which, as anthologized in *Selected Essays*, appends the 1937 piece "Variations on a Theme"] tends to predict" (Troy, 1967: 87). Honor is due Troy, as well, for being the first to recognize that "Absolution" (1924) is Fitzgerald's finest story, but more honor is due him for recognizing it at all. It's true that, through selfless devotion to the work at hand, Troy seldom attains the distinctive prose style of asserted personality. Nor is he notably witty. Yet when a sharp definition is needed, he can be felicitous. It was Troy, after all, who dubbed Fitzgerald the "Authority of Failure" (Troy, 1967: 140).

William Troy's central interest was in prose fiction. He seems to have acquired his wide background, his exigent sense of form, and his passionate concern for humanistic values at the beginning of his career. He had a deep affinity for James Joyce, because of his own Irish Catholic upbringing and certain common traits of temperament and intellect. Like Joyce, Troy left the Church in his youth (*unlike* his sister Camilla, who became a nun), never to return; but—again like Joyce— he never lost the humanistic wisdom that the Catholic tradition may possess at its best. That saved him from shallow infatuations with any of the intellectual gadgetries of the moment, and helped to keep alive his sympathy for the classics of Greece and the heritage of the Middle Ages. He was, for instance, fascinated with the medieval fourfold approach to literary interpretation (literal, allegorical, moral, and anagogical), and toyed several times with the possibility that it might be adapted for the purposes of modern criticism.

French fiction was also very important to Troy for a number of years, as it was for so many Americans of his generation; yet few, if any, could see it in so wide a perspective. French literature, and behind that the Mediterranean tradition in general, seems to have been for Troy a dependable source of insight and discipline. (Henry James, whom Troy was among the first to hail as a master, also went to school to the French.) Troy was observing an Irish tradition in turning toward France rather than England. Following his undergraduate years at Yale, remember, he studied at the Sorbonne rather than in an American graduate school; for the French *doctorat d'université*, he had even chosen a thesis topic on the symbolist poet Albert Mockel. His essays on Stendhal, Balzac, and Valéry, in particular, pointed the way, when they first appeared in the 1940s, to critical methods later designated in France as structuralist, sociological, thematic, and psychoanalytical.

In fact, William Troy anticipated much that later critics became famous for discovering. He opposed Jamesian form to the "large loose baggy monsters" (Troy, 1967: 52) of the novel in 1936—quite a few years before R. P. Blackmur did so (1951); and he insisted on the influence of the senior Henry James on his son's work two decades before Quentin Anderson discovered it in 1957. Troy reviewed André Malraux's *Man's Fate* (1933) when the English translation appeared in 1934, and pointed out what others painfully discovered only in the 1950s: that it is not revolutionary or Marxist, but tragic. Leslie Fiedler, for his part, wrote in the *New Leader* in April of 1951: "And yet the *essential* appeal of Fitzgerald is elsewhere—astonishingly enough, in his *failure*" (Fiedler, 1955: 175). This was a brilliant observation when William Troy made it—in 1945 (in the autumn issue of *Accent*), more elegantly and restraining his astonishment, in the aforementioned "Scott Fitzgerald: The Authority of Failure."

Myth was as important to Troy as literature in general and French literature in particular. Beginning in the 1930s, along with Francis Fergusson and Kenneth Burke, he was writing a form of criticism based on the use of myth and ritual in literature. The myth-cult in literary criticism once came in for some justified mockery because it so easily lent itself to pretentious obscurity. Yet there is nothing obscure in Troy's careful exposition of the uses that Joyce, Eliot, Valéry, and others made of myth for their very different purposes. For instance, in "The Symbolism of Zola" (included here), a 1937 article occasioned by the re-issue in English of *Germinal* (1885), Troy writes that the scene in the collapsed mine "brings us back to an atmosphere and a meaning at least as old as the story of Orpheus and Eurydice." In Mann's *Death in Venice* (1912), he analyzed the fundamental patterns of the ancient male initiation rite; in *The Magic Mountain*, he found the sanitarium to be a kind of Mount Olympus. In Stendhal's *The Red and the Black* (1830), Troy viewed Julien Sorel's death in terms of the ritualistic stages underlying ancient Greek tragedy. And in Fitzgerald's *The Great Gatsby* (1925), he considered the eponymous protagonist as a truly mythological creation, with the novel itself taking on the pattern and meaning of a Grail romance; while in *The Last Tycoon* (1941), Monroe Stahr is, from Troy's perspective, the image of the modern Icarus soaring to disaster.

Troy's knowledge of myth in our time was both empirical and exact—and urgent. As he wrote in 1945 in "Myth, Method, and the Future":

> If we are to be saved, which also assumes that we wish to be saved, it can only be through some reintegration of Myth in terms of the heartbreaking concerns of the times. "The times are nightfall," [Gerard Manley] Hopkins said long ago, and they grow worse from hour to hour. Yet, when really everything has been said, are the most overwhelming problems of our age ultimately different from what have been the greatest problems of the race from its dark beginnings—love and justice? And it is exactly with these two problems above all else that Myth is concerned. It is the cartograph of the perennial human situation, the more appealing for being concrete, the more persuasive for being not subject to final analysis. Myth provides us not merely with illustrations of destiny but with a guide to its better control and mastery—the anagogical. "We must love one another or die," as [W. H.] Auden warns us. In a regenerated Myth alone we may hope to find a beckoning image of the successful alliance of the twin virtues of love and justice. (Troy, 1967: 42)

Sometimes Troy moves from myth criticism to metaphysical concerns. He uses this term literally, since, as he says in an unpublished lecture, "Man in the Nineteenth Century," delivered at Bennington College in 1941, "it is impossible for the human animal to dispense with metaphysics." Troy expounds on this subject in "The Lawrence Myth":

> Both in his life and in his works Lawrence illustrates what Nietzsche, in his well-known analysis of the Dionysus myth, calls

"the agony of individuation." This will have an unpleasantly metaphysical sound to modern ears; but it must be recalled that to the generation to which Lawrence belonged life still presented itself in terms of metaphysical problems. To these problems any serious discussion of Gide, Proust, Mann, and Joyce must likewise sooner or later be conducted. No matter into what unpopularity metaphysics has fallen, it is the only relevant approach to these writers. (Troy, 1967: 123–124)

In another lecture, "Time and Space Conceptions in Modern Literature," delivered at Bennington College in 1936 and unpublished in his lifetime (but subsequently published in *Selected Essays*), Troy writes: "Of the various approaches to literature—the technical or aesthetic, the historical, the socio-economic—the metaphysical alone has the advantage of throwing light at one and the same time on both the form and the content of a work" (Troy, 1967: 19). He goes on to give his fullest definition of the method:

When we speak of a metaphysical approach to literature, therefore, we do not mean that critical exercise which consists of summarizing a set of ideas and then showing how they have been applied or demonstrated in particular works. It is rather that approach which consists in showing the similarity of the problems consciously dealt with by metaphysics with those consciously or unconsciously expressed in literature. In brief, criticism, lacking a language of its own, turns to metaphysics as the only other realm of abstract thought having one at all useful for its purpose of definition and interpretation. (Troy, 1967: 21)

For other works, Troy uses other methods. In 1943 he writes in "The Altar of Henry James": "The great works of the last period, *The Ambassadors* [1903] and *The Golden Bowl* [1904], are put together, if not like a vastly exfoliated lyric, like one of the final plays of Shakespeare. And to approach them in the manner of Caroline Spurgeon and G. Wilson Knight on Shakespeare is almost certainly to uncover conflicts of feeling that are more often than not belied by the overt urbanity of style" (Troy, 1967: 59). This symbolic approach to James leads him to study the symbol of the garden in James's fiction, with all its Edenic and other associations. At other times, Troy focuses not on symbolism but on literary archetypes: the Marked Man (Mann); the Noble Brigand and the Man of Sensibility (Balzac); the Man of Feeling combined with the Satanic Hero (Stendhal).

Troy was always something of a Freudian, as well, although in his later work he tended to prefer Jung. It is hard to say how much of Freud's writing he had read, since he invariably paraphrases instead of quoting directly from Freud, and he never names specific works. Still, he reads a handful of Stendhal's books as expressions of the Oedipus complex in which the assertions of the superego are successfully drowned out by the protests of the id—and Troy hazards the guess that as a result of this complex Stendhal himself was impotent. He discusses the idea of the role of the artist in Joyce's *Portrait of the Artist as a Young Man* (1916) as one of the projections of the Freudian superego. He finds Freudian symbols in *The Magic Mountain,* including a hypodermic syringe that, as scientifically described, proves to be identical in mechanism with the phallus. In Mann's four-part *Joseph and His Brothers* (1943), moreover, Troy relates the whole pattern of Joseph's adventures in Egypt to the Freudian description of the relations of the individual ego to the world. And in the 1944 essay "The New Parnassianism and Recent Poetry" (included in *The Bookman*), he writes that the new poets make deliberate use of what the Freudians call the "traumatic experience" and the "genetic history of the individual."

In 1939 Troy was still a Freudian, expressing serious reservations about Jung. He writes in an unpublished letter:

Freud and his school in our time have devoted themselves to what we may call the myth of the individual. The description of Freud is so well known that it needs no elaboration. The individual is born with a shock into a world that turns out to be so hostile that when he reaches adolescence, he has to make a great decision whether or not he wishes to accept its terms. In childhood the world of the individual is lonely, exclusive, and conservative; that is to say it tends to maintain the status quo of infantile security against the revolution of adolescence. The struggle at that period is a heroic one: it leaves many vanquished. Unless the individual transcends the self-centered childish world by finding a proper object of love and authority in the external world, he is lost. This object may not be a person, but a cause, an abstract belief, a vocation. If he discovers such an object, he achieves maturity, of which the token is some kind of creative social activity.

The particular pattern of this whole experience is such that it has led Jung and others to the conviction that the great heroic stories of all races are simply the concrete and objective projection of this essential individual experience. It has led Jung also

. . . into the undemonstrable hypothesis that every individual carries around with him the memory of these heroic stories in what he calls the "collective unconscious," a kind of second memory older and vaster than that of the individual. But this is turning us around in a vicious circle, for we cannot have it both that the stories are determined in their form by the psychology of the individual and the form of the individual by the psychology of the story. The importance of Jung's theory, however, is that it enables us to relate the myth of the individual to the myth of the tribe. We may say that a culture, too, has need of an object of love or authority by means of which it can transcend its merely selfish and practical interests and achieve an equilibrium between these interests and its obligations.

By 1941, however, Troy had turned sharply to Jung and away from Freud, whom he sums up sadly in the unpublished "Man in the Nineteenth Century" as a "man of the imagination who lacked the courage of the imagination." In some other unpublished lecture notes dating from the 1940s, Troy writes further: "Freud failed sufficiently to realize that the symbolism of dreams was an attempt of the unconscious to return to a more integrated experience than is allowed the individual in the modern bourgeois world: Jung is right in enabling us to relate the myth of the individual to the myth of the tribe." In his previously referenced 1956 New School lecture notes on Thomas Mann later incorporated into the piece "Myth and Reason" in *Selected Essays,* Troy now directs his hearer not to psychoanalysis for aid with the Joseph series but to analytic psychology, explaining: "For myths come out of the unconscious processes of mankind. The symbols on which they are based have more meanings or layers of meaning than the conscious mind can ever grasp" (Troy, 1967: 241).

Nobody's Perfect

If Troy's learning was not encyclopedic, it was more extensive, both within literature and outside it, than that of most critics of the twentieth century. He drew extensively in his work on J. G. Frazer and *The Golden Bough* (1890), on Pico della Mirandola, Giordano Bruno, and Giambattista Vico, on Ramon Fernandez and Ernest Seillière. In a 1940 essay on Balzac, he speaks (in reference to the novel *César Birotteau* [1837]) of the promise of the harmonization of the most advanced biochemistry with the most advanced modern physics, quotes Marx and Brunetière, compares Balzac with Meissonier and Delacroix, and contrasts Balzac with Dante and Blake. Troy's wealth of learning, together with his range of method, would have been nothing, however, without his sensibility and scrupulousness, his respect and love for literature.

In the 1938 piece "A Further Note on Myth," for example, Troy writes: "For it must be repeated that the real objection to the application of science to art and literature is not to science as such but to its fundamental inappropriateness in these realms. Unfortunately, it is much less difficult to say what literature is not than to say what it is: the anatomy of the imagination will probably remain the last challenge to the scientific mind" (Troy, 1967: 36). In a review ("New Country," anthologized here) of C. Day-Lewis's *Collected Poems* (1935), he tartly declares: "Lewis is so intent on being articulate at all costs that he does not permit himself to have any of the feelings which usually confuse and retard the poet. Among these rejected feelings must be included the distrust of rhetoric, the fear of repetition, and the sense of the difficulty of the craft in which he is working." And in his answer to a questionnaire ("What Is Americanism?") in the *Partisan Review* of April 1936, Troy rejects Marxism because "in the ultimate description of his role that it offers the individual, it leaves no place for the moral imagination" (Troy, 1936: 12).

Troy's primary concern, finally, was with the present health of literature. When he studied Stendhal, or when he meditated on medieval techniques of interpretation, he was looking for light on the practice of literature *now*. That is why his essays are indispensable to anyone   interested in the two decades between the world wars, when so much of our present understanding of literature was being constructed. But Troy's significance goes far beyond his time: he never wrote merely fashionably; his respect for reason and form was much too strict for that. He is not likely to be fashionable at this moment, either, when the arbiters of our taste—arbiters who have not inherited the methods of their great predecessors, let alone their genius, their sensibility, or their commitment to literature—reject form and meaning in favor of identity politics (connected with race, ethnicity, gender, and sexuality), victimology, and even pornography. Troy is for those who enjoy the passionate and witty play of a first-rate mind upon the perennial mysteries of human conduct, and upon the beautiful forms that literature may take now or in any age.

Indeed, he never failed to point out some of the relationships that exist between the writer and his age, particularly if the writer has the genius of Henry James—or of Virginia Woolf or Thomas Mann. Yet

Troy seemed to be more concerned with the way in which a genius went beyond his age, the way in which the genius would survive his age. Troy was more interested in the work itself than in its temporal situation. The literary work is a world by itself, and differs from the world by what it includes and excludes. The artist creates a *special* world of his own, organized in accordance with laws that are peculiar to it, a complete if microscopic world where all the complexity of life is recapitulated. The critic is not the man who preemptively judges this strange world of the artist, but the one who first seeks to penetrate it, to observe its functioning, to follow its order.

And the critic, in the understanding that William Troy gave to the task of the critic, will discover that the key to opening any artistic world sometimes includes biography, for there is an important type of modern writer—Poe, Rimbaud, even Melville—in whom the life and the work are so mutually indispensable that the latter does not yield up its real interest or significance when taken alone. The effort of Troy's thought thus always strives to dissipate the confusions in a writer's work *and* his life, by discovering the principle presiding over the life and the work. His critical analysis is the search for the center of the psychic unity in Balzac or Proust, Malraux or Stendhal. Troy held with Ramon Fernandez, one of the French critics he especially admired, the belief that literary criticism joins with the creative movement of the work being criticized and assimilates, on an intellectual level, the characteristics of the work if not the man himself. Troy's pages on Joyce, for example, reveal an unusual affinity with the mind and the sensibility of the Irish writer. And his work on Fitzgerald is heavily biographical, discussing two aspects with which Troy himself identified: the large and positive influence of Fitzgerald's Celtic inheritance, especially in his feeling for language, and the permanent effects of his early exposure to Catholicism.

In the end, William Troy wrote with style and eloquence. He could be scathing, however, as in a 1949 review of French existentialist fiction that concludes: "Of all the members of the group Sartre is least endowed with the narrative gift, coldest in feeling, and most expert in sophistry" (Troy, 1967: 14). In a review of Glenn Hughes's *Imagism and the Imagists* (1931), Troy says flatly and dismissively: "About [Amy] Lowell the conviction becomes stronger that she will be remembered less for her poetry than for her berserk personality" (Troy, 1931: 9). At other times he is pungent as well as persuasive, as in his aforementioned review of Zola's *Germinal*: "Irony is an uncomfortable mode for the doctrinaire; having blundered into it, Zola retraces his steps as quickly as possible" (Troy, 1937: 65).

Related to the matter of irony, Troy writes in 1939 in some unpublished lecture notes:

> Pathos is to be applied to human life only when we are referring to that inherent suffering common to all nature; death in battle (when the aims of the battle are not integrated closely to the hero), death from starvation, the kitten crying in the wilderness. It is touching, because it is the touch of earth that makes the whole world kin. The modern world is pathetic because loud with the reverberations of innumerable kittens each crying in his private wilderness.

He adds wryly, "Irony is the form that pathos takes to the detached mind."

I do not mean to suggest that Troy was a perfect critic. He had weaknesses and made mistakes of judgment, some of which I describe above. I think that his shift from Freud to Jung was such a mistake, and I do not share, for example, Troy's low estimate of Hemingway's short stories, or his high opinion of Yvor Winters' verse (see "Hemingway's Opium" and the review of Winters' *The Proof* in the current volume). But in his hundred-odd essays—fifty of which are reproduced in *The Bookman*—William Troy produced a body of work that is ageless, enduring, a model of literary criticism, and a challenge to us all.

Coda

In addition to being a foremost literary critic, Troy was one of America's first full-time professional film critics—for *The Nation* from 1933 to 1935. This, of course, was a significant period in the history of cinema, as the medium made the transition from silence to sound. And Troy's reviews—of such films as Buñuel's *L'Âge d'or* (1930), Dreyer's *The Passion of Joan of Arc* (1928), Renoir's *Madame Bovary* (1934), Lang's *M* (1931), and Pudovkin's *Mother* (1926)—acutely reflect this transition. In conjunction with the publication of *The Bookman: William Troy on Literature and Criticism, 1927–1950*, therefore, Sussex Academic Press is also publishing the first collection of Troy's film criticism, titled *Film Nation: William Troy on the Cinema, 1933–1935*.

Works Cited & Bibliography

Anderson, Quentin. *The American Henry James*. New Brunswick, N.J.: Rutgers University Press. 1957.

Blackmur, R. P. *The Double Agent: Essays in Craft and Elucidation*. New York: Arrow Editions, 1935.

——. "The Loose and Baggy Monsters of Henry James: Notes on the Underlying Classic Form in the Novel." *Accent*, 11 (Summer 1951): 129–146. Reprinted in Blackmur's *Studies in Henry James*. Ed. Veronica A. Makowsky. New York: New Directions, 1983. 125–146.

Brooks, Cleanth. *The Well Wrought Urn: Studies in the Structure of Poetry*. New York: Harcourt Brace, 1947.

Burke, Kenneth. *The Philosophy of Literary Form: Studies in Symbolic Action*. Baton Rouge: Louisiana State University Press, 1941.

Davidson, Donald, et al. *I'll Take My Stand: The South and the Agrarian Tradition*. New York: Harper & Brothers, 1930.

Empson, William. *Seven Types of Ambiguity: A Study of Its Effects on English Verse*. London: Chatto & Windus, 1930.

Fergusson, Francis. *The Idea of a Theater: A Study of Ten Plays; The Art of Drama in a Changing Perspective*. Princeton, N.J.: Princeton University Press, 1949.

Fernandez, Ramon. *Moralisme et littérature*. Paris: Éditions Corrêa, 1932.

Fiedler, Leslie. "Some Notes on F. Scott Fitzgerald." In Fiedler's *An End to Innocence: Essays on Culture and Politics*. Boston: Beacon Press, 1955. 174–182. Originally published in two parts in *The New Leader*, 34 (April 9, 1951): 20–21; 34 (April 16, 1951): 23–24.

Frank, Joseph. *Dostoevsky: A Writer in His Time*. 5 vols., 1976–2003. Princeton, N.J.: Princeton University Press, 2010.

Goldsmith, Arnold L. *American Literary Criticism*. Vol. 3: 1905–1965. Boston: Twayne, 1979.

Hyman, Stanley Edgar. *The Armed Vision: A Study in the Methods of Modern Literary Criticism*. New York: Alfred A. Knopf, 1947.

Leavis, F. R. *Revaluation: Tradition and Development in English Poetry*. London: Chatto & Windus, 1936.

Leitsch, Vincent B. *American Literary Criticism since the 1930s*. 1988. New York: Routledge, 2010.

Lewis, R. W. B. *The American Adam: Innocence, Tragedy, and Tradition in the Nineteenth Century*. Chicago: University of Chicago Press, 1955.

Matthiessen, F. O. *The Achievement of T. S. Eliot: An Essay on the Nature of Poetry*. London: Oxford University Press, 1935.

Ransom, John Crowe. *The New Criticism*. New York: New Directions, 1941.

Richards, I. A. *Practical Criticism: A Study Of Literary Judgment*. London: Kegan Paul, Trench, Trubner, 1929.

Seillière, Ernest. *Psychoanalyse freudienne ou psychologie impérialiste?* Paris: Vrin, 1928.

Sontag, Susan. *"Against Interpretation" and Other Essays*. New York: Farrar, Straus, and Giroux, 1966.

Tate, Allen. *On the Limits of Poetry: Selected Essays, 1928–1948*. New York: Swallow Press/William Morrow, 1948.

Trilling, Lionel. *The Liberal Imagination: Essays on Literature and Society*. New York: Viking Press, 1950.

Troy, William. "A Study of the Imagist Group of Poets: *Imagism and the Imagists*, by Glenn Hughes." *The New York Times Book Review* (April 19, 1931): 9.

——. "New Country: C. Day-Lewis & Stephen Spender." *The Nation*, 140.3636 (March 13, 1935): 311–312.

——. "What Is Americanism?" *Partisan Review*, 3.3 (April 1936): 12–13. (Other respondents to this questionnaire, published on pages 3–16 of the issue in question, include Theodore Dreiser, Josephine Herbst, Matthew Josephson, Kenneth Burke, and William Carlos Williams.)

——. "The Symbolism of Zola: *Germinal*, by Émile Zola." *The Partisan Review*, 4.1 (December 1937): 64–66.

——. "Thomas Mann: Myth and Reason." *Partisan Review*, 5.1 (June 1938): 24–32, and 5.2 (July 1938): 51–64; "A Further Note on Myth," *Partisan Review*, 6.1 (Fall 1938): 95–100.

——. *Selected Essays*. Ed. Stanley Edgar Hyman. New Brunswick, N.J.: Rutgers University Press, 1967.

——. Unpublished writings, lectures, teaching materials, correspondence, and other papers, 1903–1961. In the Léonie Adams and William Troy Papers (1902–1980) from the Yale Collection of American Literature. New Haven, Conn.: Beinecke Rare Book and Manuscript Library, Yale University.

Wilson, Edmund. *Axel's Castle: A Study in the Imaginative Literature of 1870–1930*. New York: Charles Scribner's Sons, 1931.

Wimsatt, William K. *The Verbal Icon: Studies in the Meaning of Poetry*. Lexington: University of Kentucky Press, 1954.

Winters, Yvor. *Primitivism and Decadence: A Study of American Experimental Poetry*. New York: Arrow Editions, 1937.

Reviews & Reports

1. "White Lightning" (1927)
Hippolytus Temporizes, by H.D.

The classicism implied in the title of this little drama, by one of the most distinguished of living lyrical poets, need not intimidate any modern reader. Myths, genealogical exercises, all the stiff paraphernalia of official classicism, are altogether secondary: the dry light of erudition pales before the brightness of this fervid personality that can evoke a dead world through the sharp apprehension of the senses. H.D. [Hilda Doolittle, 1886–1961] is Alexandrian rather than Augustan. That is to say, almost alone among English-language poets, she has tried to probe beneath the scattered surface to "the very form, the very scent" ["At Baia" (1921)] of a beautiful and half-forgotten antiquity. Alexandrian, also, in that the mood is nostalgic, the passion charged with a kind of fierce desperation. Discarding the attractions of lexicon and atlas, she has depended on intuition to bring her ever closer to that central essence, "fire and ice" from ["Fire and Ice" (1920)] of what we are accustomed to call the Greek spirit. There is a sense, striking one now for the first time, in which she seems even more intimately allied to that spirit than some of the later Greeks themselves— Euripides, for example, who likewise wrote a drama on the story of Hippolytus.

It is appropriate that this legend should be specially favored, already in H.D.'s lyrics and now in this play, by one whose theme has so frequently been the strife between the beauty of austerity and the energy of passion. The chaste Hippolytus and the dark Cretan princess become universalized figures, pitted against each other in an antagonism that is inevitable as well as fatal. Artemis represents an ideal of spiritual perfection that even her most devoted worshiper realizes he may never attain:

> Nay wild and sweet,
> but song may yet entrap you,
> fire and rhythm
> may yet contain the ecstasy
> and the heat—
> cold like white lightning.

The final note of the play is something like the conviction implicit in these lines: that perfection may best be sought in the cold beauty and high loneliness of poetry.

The drama is not, as may be supposed, based on the strict pattern of Greek tragedy. Although H.D. has borrowed much from the past, she has always found her forms in the present, an idiosyncrasy that has probably rendered her suspect in both camps. The device of stichomythia, effectively used throughout, is, of course, a loan from the Greek. But, on the whole, the affinity is modern, W. B. Yeats or Francis Vielé-Griffin, the French poet whose resemblance to H.D. is so extraordinary. In treating the material, she follows previous models, except that Phaedra seduces Hippolytus by means of a ruse instead of the usual love-potion. The characterization is slight, every syllable strained in the effort to extract and amplify the lyrical deposit of each scene. For, to this poet, the principal appeal of the legend is as a medium for lyrical enunciation, as to Euripides it was a convenient frame for dialectic, or to Racine a natural vehicle for the rhetoric of his age.

To be questioned, however, is how much H.D. has gained by turning to this ineffectual type of poetic drama. Her lyrics on the same subject, one of which is here reprinted, possessed a superior evenness and solidity. The tenuous thought and fastidious precision of phrase produce a peculiar effect of feebleness in the mouths of dramatic characters. This is accentuated by the arrangement of the lines and also by the expensive format, which seems to magnify the few faults.

2. "Crisis in the Novel" (1927)

In literature, as in the other arts, imitation begins as soon as a form has attained a stage of transparent perfection in the hands of a first-rate artist. When a form has been once fully realized, the lesser talent is able to analyze its elements and absorb its effects sufficiently to reproduce something that shall bear at least an emotive resemblance to the original.

Today the process is rather naïvely at work in many efforts to employ what is perhaps the most important single literary form that has crystallized in our generation—the subjective novel. The naïveté is increased by the existence of an extraordinary feat of the creative mind that includes development and perfection within the compass of a single work. The anomalous result has been a great deal of futile experimentation after the main achievement. For of all recent novelists who have manifestly gone to school to James Joyce, Virginia Woolf alone has shown any inclination to transcend his method and adapt it to the needs of an individual expression; the others have been content to lag behind in a spirit of unabashed emulation that scarcely condones their ineptitude. It may not be entirely unprofitable, therefore, to review the method in terms of their failure and at the same time indicate limitations inherent in a method that makes such failure seem preordained in the future.

It is necessary to correct two current aberrations: that the method was discovered by Joyce, and that it is an outgrowth, or by-product, of psychoanalysis. In all essentials the method first appears in literature in a novel by Édouard Dujardin, *Les Lauriers sont coupés* [*The Laurels Are Cut*], published in 1887. We may account for the date by regarding the book as representing a mild protest against the sterility that the objective novel had then reached, by a writer whose technical ingenuity exceeded his imaginative resources. As fiction it is feeble and unreal, comparable only with current endeavors in the same field, and throws into even greater relief the accomplishment of Joyce. The following extract is characteristic:

> The waiter. The table. My hat to the coat-rack. Let's take off our gloves; they must be thrown carelessly onto the table, beside the plate; rather, placed on the shelf above the table; no, onto the table; these little things are part of the general layout. My overcoat to the coat-rack; I sit; phew! I was tired. I will put my gloves into the pocket of my overcoat. Illuminated, golden, red, with ice, this sparkling—what?—coffee; the coffee where I am. Oh! I was tired.

The idiom of psychoanalysis is naturally absent here, although the process is as evident as in most works of the imagination. Since the method plainly existed before the advent of either Joyce or Sigmund Freud, we must regard whatever features of psychoanalysis adhere to it in *Ulysses* [1922] as a later and subordinate addition. As a method it is primarily literary in origin and purpose, and not the product of any science or pseudo-science.

To understand why the most ambitious writer of his age should have selected this particular vehicle of expression, we must look to causes other than the availability of a popular and unstable theory of psychology. These were, and in about the following order, the exhaustion of the objective method; the appropriateness of the subjective method for Joyce's individual temperament and equipment; and the peculiarly modern character of the latter method. There should hardly be need to amplify the first of these causes: the French naturalists had already hastened the purely objective novel to its logical *cul-de-sac*, and Henry James had pretty thoroughly dissipated its metaphysical possibilities. The simple law of reaction, which functions as strongly in the arts as elsewhere, swung the pendulum in the opposite direction. It is likewise easy to realize, now that we possess the accomplished fact, how perfect an instrument the method afforded for the recording of a mind primarily sensory and dissociative in its operation (Dionysian, rather than Apollonian, in the Nietzschean distinction). To this temperament, so preoccupied with the parity between the ideal and the actual, a temperament whose incapacity for resignation relieved itself by every sort of irony, satire, perverse self-mockery, the subjective offered the most satisfactory, because the most intimate and unimpeded, mode of expression.

It will be noted that of the causes suggested this is the most personal in its application, offering us an instance of how a method may become identical with a style. This suggests the inquiry as to whether Joyce has not made every feature of the method so distinctly his own that any attempt by others to use it amounts simply to an imitation of his style. At any rate, every such attempt that has since been made sounds more like an echo of the consciousness behind *Ulysses* than like the record a fresh consciousness: to give a single instance, the frequent snatches of song or poetry, a habit of mind that seems native in Joyce but acquired in his successors. Similarly, the vocabulary of implicit speech, the kind of imagery and its associations, is strangely uniform in all later subjective fiction, although one would be surprised if this were true for all minds in actual life. The anatomy of consciousness presented by Joyce has been accepted by such writers as definitive; the idiosyncrasies of one mind have become, at the moment, universal conventions. The result is the same as that which has always rewarded any effort to appropriate something as personal, as Remy de Gourmont remarks, as the color of the eyes or the sound of the voice.

The modernity of the method, which made perhaps the greatest appeal to Joyce, exists in more than the superficial sense. For a time it must have seemed a vehicle of expression as inevitable and characteristic for this age as the blank-verse tragedy to the Elizabethans or the formal essay to the eighteenth century. It seemed appropriate because it was the single method on the aesthetic horizon that might possibly serve to communicate the horde of dissociated ideas, checked responses, and frustrated energies which make up the modern mind. The multiplicity of that mind, to adopt a current philosophical label, might hope to become articulate only on the condition that no invalid unity be superimposed. ("Tradition as unity is not contemporary," writes Allen Tate [in issues 1–3 (1927) of the experimental literary journal *transition*, edited by Eugene Jolas].)

The subjective method as employed by Joyce laid its stress on character, on the implicit life of a character, rather than on plot or the relationships occasioned by the explicit life of a character. The absence of plot in *Ulysses*, and its general waning importance in modern narrative, must be ascribed not so much to a lack of ingenuity as to an instinctive distrust in any design of life based on absolute values of conduct. With the collapse of morals came the collapse of the moral, which was more truly responsible for the pattern of fiction in the past than is generally recognized. This does not mean that the method necessarily prohibits structure, or that *Ulysses* itself is without structure of a certain kind; but such structure is and must be independent of the actions of the characters. It is externally imposed—in the case of *Ulysses*, by the introduction of an already existent design that has no purpose other than affording chronological order. (It is not irrelevant to recall that the design which Joyce borrowed, the design of the *Odyssey* [ca. 700 B.C.], was determined not by the author of that poem but by some later intelligence who put their separate fragments together.) What the subjective method made possible, however, was a direct and uninterrupted transcription of the dissociated consciousness, which has made any unified system of thought or behavior untenable for our generation.

Although we assume the above causes to have operated actively in Joyce's selection of an appropriate means of expression, we need not assume that all of them operated in the case of his followers. We have noted how the method in his hands tends to merge into style and how all subsequent experiments with it retain the imprint of his personal temperament. We also must consider the extraordinary demand that the method makes upon the consciousness of a writer. Not only is a particular kind of consciousness required, but also a consciousness whose richness of ideas and image is great enough to commend our interest and possess a more than individual significance. Unfortunately, those writers who have been attracted to the method, either by its novelty or by its deceptive appearance of freedom, have manifested a singular poverty of inner experience. No intervening skill or cleverness was possible to save them from an exhibition of feebleness or banality. It is the unusual consciousness alone that should risk the humiliations of a public confession.

For the future, some recognition of the limitations inherent in the method may be helpful. While we may admit its freedom in one sense, in another we should see that it seriously narrows the scope of what has always been the principal concern of the novel. Characterization in the subjective novel is necessarily limited to the character of the writer himself, since the process of projection into the mind of another is as precarious as it is ambitious. Even in the work of Virginia Woolf, the most distinguished that has followed in the path of *Ulysses,* the consciousness tends to remain essentially the same for all the characters, young or old, male or female, so that her work has come gradually to take on a monotonous unreality of surface. It is true that Joyce is more successful; but Leopold Bloom is never quite as real as Stephen Dedalus [in Joyce's *A Portrait of the Artist as a Young Man* (1916)]. The presentation of Bloom's mind is not so much Bloom's actual mind as it is Joyce's conception of what that mind must really be like. Since it is patently impossible to register purely and entirely the interior life of another, the subjective writer can never expect to create more than one full character, that character remaining at all times and under all disguises basically his own.

In the second place, one may question whether the subjective, even with the finest use of the means at its disposal, is a very valuable mode of characterization. Its value is uncertain because it shows us a character solely as he exists within his own mind, without allowance for the refractions occurring upon contact with the external world. It happens that the reality of a character to himself is not always the same as his reality to the world, the actual reality perhaps lying somewhere between the two; the interior life of a child or an idiot, for example, would be a poor index to his personality. For that reason it is essential to know a character's position in relation to his environment, as well as his private sense of that environment, if we wish to see him in true perspective. By placing too much value on the implicit life, the subjective novel has come to the same impasse as the objective novel at the close of the last century. But an appraisal of both methods, based on the intensive exploitation that has been separately accomplished, might possibly result in a new and altogether more satisfactory approach to the problem.

Further questions center around the assaults of the method upon the aesthetic integrity of the novel: the enforced contraction of the time element; the absence of any sort of progressive unity; the elimination of prose as a potential unit. To consider only the last of these, subjective prose at its best (the monologue of Molly Bloom, for example) is indistinguishable from its content. We cannot imagine the given thought or image expressed in any other way than it is first expressed in consciousness merged with its attendant word-association: "I was just beginning to yawn with nerves thinking he was trying to make a fool of me when I knew his tattarrattat at the door he must have been a bit late because it was 1/4 after 3 when I saw the 2 Dedalus girls" [*Ulysses*]. Language, as we have been taught to believe, here determines the thought more often than thought the language. What is lost is the purely aesthetic value of prose, that is, the value to the emotions over and above the burden of its intellectual content. In this single loss we may observe how the subjective surrender to life tends to leave less and less quarter to the pretensions of art. The creative will, *der schaffende Geist*, with its function of transcending and adapting material to its own uses, is rendered impotent. In slightly different terms, it is the triumph of matter over mind.

Prophecy is scarcely within the province of criticism; but some opinion may be hazarded as to the probable direction of the novel in the near future. That direction, we may say, will be toward less rather than greater restriction of its possibilities. The next step need not be toward any more unified tranquility of vision; but there should at least be some effort to express our contemporary predicament with more variety, with a greater sense of the magnitude of the theme. All the resources of the novel will need to be combined in the production of a whole that shall possess an artistic, in place of the former ethical or philosophical, unity. The task may be undertaken not without a certain degree of irony. For the crowning mockery of this generation would be a work whose perfection of form should surmount the confusion and renunciation of its only available material—a work that should represent the triumph of the mind over the forces that are tending to destroy its ancient aspirations.

3. "Gusto and Literature" (1928)

People often complain that what is preeminently lacking in our modern writers is the quality of "gusto." We are asked to think of Dante Alighieri, of the Elizabethans, of Victor Hugo. We are asked to consider, in fact, all the great literary figures of the past whose genius can be matched only by their largesse. Beside the bright plenty that these men offered, our modern candidates for greatness are made to look very parsimonious indeed. They have accustomed us to remain satisfied with the slightest and most infrequent examples of art. If it takes T. S. Eliot a long time to confirm his poetic reputation with *The Waste Land* [1922], it promises to take him an even longer time to recover from it. For although our poets may still possess the secrets of the great lyre, they are inclined to employ them very rarely, or with too little fire, and their fingers grow too soon weary at the strings. We have thus been brought back, in every field of writing, to the fragment, the improvisation, the *abbozzo* [preliminary sketch or outline]. "Give back the glamour to our will," writes a modern poet [H.D., in the poem "Prayer" (1921)], invoking that spirit which once sowed masterpieces through the world. Once we wrought things not unworthy; but today we seem to have lost the energy, the compulsion, or whatever it is that was responsible for their accomplishment.

As most of those who deplore its loss are literary critics, it is not surprising that gusto should always be mentioned as a kind of literary quality, like any other that has been permitted to disappear or dwindle in our day. For the literary critic, like the laboratory specialist, is so blinded by discoveries in his own field as to ignore their simultaneity with discoveries in other fields. But if this were not such a necessary condition of research, we should never hear gusto spoken of as a loss sustained by literature alone. We should be shown that the same loss is shared by other expressions of life as far removed from aesthetics as ethics or morality, and that the mistake is to mourn the blight of one branch without examining the roots that nourish the whole tree.

Gusto is a word with a precarious breadth of connotation, but what is usually meant by it is a certain energy of feeling. I should extend this definition to include the positive convictions on which any such energy must finally rest. Accordingly, gusto would be defined as an energy of feeling based on some conviction or system of convictions. Ordinarily we make use of the word to indicate the degree of emotional intensity with which we take up a given piece of work, and measure its presence in an individual on the testimony offered by his work. For its application to the special kind of work that is writing, we may weigh this remark from Gustave Flaubert's correspondence: "One has to feel strongly, so as to think, and to think, so as to express" [letter to George Sand (a.k.a. Amantine Lucile Aurore Dupin), March 9, 1876]. In other words, for some persons the spectacle of the visible world acts upon the emotions as a stimulus of such force as to cause the mind to reflect and then to exert itself toward finding its proper means of expression.

But Flaubert does not begin far enough back in his progression to explain what is the nature and what are the causes of those feelings that the visible world is thus able to set into operation. These feelings, as we know, are as numerous and varied as the potentialities of the human mind itself, corresponding in fact to the whole gamut of human aspirations and despairs, from the ecstasies of the mystic to the darkest forebodings of the skeptic. What we are not always ready to recognize is that every such feeling has its real origin in the mind, since we can perceive the world only through our own mind and react to it only in terms of our own vision. Thought, in this view, is as often the cause as it is the effect of feeling; we think before we feel in as true a sense as we feel before we think.

Psychologically, thought may be regarded as either stimulus or response, and in each case may be positive or negative. When we refer to thought as a *positive* stimulus, that is, as a stimulus which owes its force to being tied up with the emotions, we explain all the opinions, beliefs, convictions, and even prejudices that in fact have harassed and diverted mankind since the beginning of time. The concept of democracy, to take but one example, is something that was first arrived at intellectually through the mind, and then identified with its corresponding emotions so powerfully as to generate energy that released itself in a wide variety of ways—in oratory, in government, in literature, in revolution.

The characteristic of our generation is that we can no longer make this affiliation between our thoughts and our emotions. We can no longer give to our ideas that emotional authorization which enables them to become convictions. We have lost the secret, the ability, or the desire. We have by no means lost the capacity for feeling, or the capacity for thinking, but we have lost the habit of combined thinking and feeling that promotes the formation of convictions. And without convictions we can scarcely be agitated by the urge or the necessity to relieve ourselves through expression. Literature and the other arts are in this way being deprived of the impulse that created and maintained them. Poets find it increasingly more difficult to write lyrics based on emotions that have been stripped of all mystery in their minds; dramatists cannot build their plays around moral conflicts toward whose issues they are indifferent; and prophets cannot reveal to us apocalypses [in this sense, eschatological visions of heavenly, divine, or spiritual secrets that can make sense of earthly realities] that they have not themselves enjoyed.

These are conclusions that for obvious reasons few people have been willing to acknowledge. Certainly, literature has not come to a prompt halt at the behest of logic. Literature has acquired through its centuries of existence sufficient momentum to ensure a leisurely demise, and its pursuit has become an incorrigible habit for a large part of mankind. In the meantime, the more helpful can point to the immense quantity of written matter still being produced as evidence of a clean bill of health. But they will refrain from the observation that all this writing which is not manifestly insincere or banal is either lacking in force or direction or else cast in distinctly elegiac molds.

We may discover a precedent for the last in the great body of philosophical poetry written in England after the collapse of the religious dogma of the nineteenth century. Doubt here provides the theme, an exceptionally plastic theme, but the emotion, affixed to such feeble and uncertain support, is not strong enough to survive. Unable to achieve any higher moods than those of resignation or simple melancholy, this work also disappoints through its lack of gusto. For the last few decades we have been offered an even larger and more insubstantial literature of disillusion and despair. Needless to say, the disordered consciousness, and the confusion of aim behind its composition, have prevented the writers of this literature from realizing their theme in any full and artistic form. I can think of only two for whom the objection is not valid, and they are of sufficient interest to invite more extended examination, if only that we may persuade ourselves of the further *cul-de-sac* to which their theme has separately brought them.

Both the *Ulysses* [1922] of James Joyce and *The Waste Land* of Eliot have most of the attributes that we like to associate with masterpieces. Both of them possess the requisite breadth, scale, completeness, even size; and both of them present the one theme that is possible for the generation in which they have been written. In *Ulysses*, the theme is expressed as the irreconcilable dualism existing between dream and reality, between the emotion and the fact, between whatever is the subjective mind wishes for itself and the objective world provides. Even the pattern of the book depends for its unity on the implied contrast between an idealized past and an insupportable present. The result achieved is an exhaustion of all the known modes of irony; and the problem suggested by the achievement is an exploration of its source of energy.

We can do no better than to pursue the modern method of attempting to divine a writer's psychology from the solid implications of his work. It is not difficult; for here everything testifies that toward his particular world this writer feels nothing but the most profound resentment. *Ulysses* may be taken in one sense as a massive rebuke against a world that has betrayed every belief and illusion that its author once held sacred; in a narrower sense, it might be taken as no more than the satisfaction of a private grudge against a particular community. In either case, the motive must appear singularly negative and perverse. While Joyce imposes on his contemporaries an even more refined revenge than Dante by subjecting them to the subtler flames of his satire, he has not written a *Paradiso* [1320, third and final part of *The Divine Comedy*].

Such a masterpiece of literature is like a fact in nature, which comes to be not only more important than all those who view it but also more important even than the one who created it. *Ulysses*, not attaining to this impersonality, never rises above the significance of an individual statement, the assertion of a special case. This becomes more apparent when we recall that the conditions which produced it are not the characteristic conditions of this age. Not many have paralleled in early life the depths of religious experience necessary before Joyce could write his work; one must have once believed with passion in order finally to doubt with passion. The spring of faith that indirectly supplied the energy for *Ulysses* cannot be tapped again.

In Eliot's *The Waste Land*, the approach to the theme is more direct. The theme becomes identical with the subject. As a result, *The Waste Land,* despite its surface obscurity of style, is the clearest and most definitive expression of the modern consciousness that we have yet received. But it is in the nature of the impact that this poem leaves on the mind that it will not be a source of emulation or influence for the poets of our time. It is improbable, because it is illogical, that poets should continue indefinitely to lead their readers into the same waste land whose boundaries Eliot has once and for all defined, or that readers should in any case be persuaded to follow them there. It is somewhat inconsistent with first principles, then, to see in Eliot and Joyce the precursors of a robust literature, even of a robust literature of despair. We should look upon the appearance of another *Ulysses* or another *Waste Land* as unlikely as it would be unnecessary.

The response to a situation that has made literature seem more and more of an anachronism in our modern world has been varied and ominous. Those still attracted to its pursuit write without any settled recognition of their motives or their aims. There has arisen in consequence the vast literature of confusion already mentioned, a literature whose superficial confusion of form is but a reflection of the confused motives and aims behind its composition; and, side by side with this, there has arisen a smaller and rather more aristocratic literature of indifference. No better representative of the latter is to be found than Paul Valéry, whose attitude toward his art will also help explain the poverty of his output. The unique reputation that this writer enjoys is rather as a phenomenon of modern culture than as a writer of books. An amateur, in his own words, of "intellectual comedy," he has striven throughout his career to abstract himself as much as possible from the concerns of life, from those concerns that were once thought the legitimate province of the literary artist. [Valéry said, in "Note and Digression" (1919), that after Dante's *Divine Comedy* (1320) and Balzac's *Human Comedy* (1799–1850), it was time to start a third, "intellectual" comedy treating the adventures and transformations of human thought.] In his retirement into the eternity of pure thought, he has refused to allow himself to be distracted by the problems of existence presented by this or any other epoch, on this or any other planet.

Valéry's acceptance of literature as a game widens even further the breach between literature and reality adumbrated by his predecessors, the symbolists; for he substitutes a mathematical for the emotional center that kept their poetry still within the traditional confines of literature. Although his theory of poetry is impersonal in many respects, it is extremely personal in its range of appeal. It offers its rarest satisfaction to the player, not to the spectator; for the player receives enjoyment from the process as well as from the solution. Valéry's interest is likewise directed exclusively toward the object before him, not to the effect of the object upon others; he perceives in writing, not a medium, but an end. I think this should explain the slender bulk of Valéry's poetry and prose. The most essential feature of his talent appears to be indifference. He is indifferent to the world's possible interest in his work, as he is indifferent, in the first place, to the claims of the world upon his own interest. This is what we may understand by his statement that once he has brought a problem to its proper solution, he feels no need to give it expression in writing.

We may also recall here Valéry's little note to his *Variétés* [1924], which protests that all the essays in the collection were written only on some definite assignment. If this attitude had been carried to its logical conclusion, if he had not yielded to the entreaties of his friends, we should have had nothing from his pen. And what is more significant is that there is no reason to assume that this attitude is not widespread among other writers and philosophers, perhaps the equals or superiors of Valéry in high and fastidious thinking, who have given us nothing because the accidents that called forth his work did not happen to them.

To consider fully the great mass of work resulting from the other failure on the part of modern writers, to relate their motives with their aims, would be to risk a confusion as enormous as the total confusion of their works. We may say that this confusion has shown itself in two different ways: a lack of unity within works that have nevertheless achieved a certain unity of form; and a complete absence of unity, both of subject matter and of form. We have seen extraordinary examples of the first kind in the novel by Joyce and the poem by Eliot; and for examples of the second kind, we have only to look about at the fruits of the various literary movements of the past few decades.

In France, the successive schools of unanimism, neo-Catholicism, and surrealism have failed to produce a single work of sufficient dimensions to justify either its own tenets or its inclusion in the main literary tradition. The fiction has consisted mainly of technical exercises, autobiographical fragments, or variegated *pastiche*; the poetry has never expanded beyond the cleverly epigrammatic or the narrowly lyrical. Now it is customary to apologize for the failure of new schools to fulfill themselves on the ground that they are merely experimental. But the number and the rapid mortality of most modern schools suggest that they have been no more than diverse and random gestures from a disrupted central source. Dadaism, in this view, would be the most legitimate of them all to the extent that it aimed and did manage to express this central disruption with considerable success.

The recent poetic renaissance in the United States [the "little renaissance" of the 1920s] likewise foundered through its inability to progress beyond the trivial, the fragmentary, the incidental. John Livingston Lowes [in *Convention and Revolt in Poetry* (1919), reissued in 1924] characterized the weakness of all this poetry several years ago when he pointed out its almost complete lack of ideas. He did not make clear, however, whether he believed a poetry of ideas would be possible today. The great poetic masterpieces of the past were constructed around ideas that were affirmed not only by the mind but by the whole emotional makeup of the poet and the audience for whom he wrote. The idea and the emotion become so inseparable in these older works that it is impossible to dissociate them: not until Goethe [who, in *Dichtung und Wahrheit* (*Poetry and Truth*, 1811–33), saw that something had occurred since the time of the ancient Greeks (rather like Eliot's dissociation of sensibility) to separate thought and feeling] are we made aware that they have their existence apart.

In recent years, poetry has completely forsworn adherence to any one set of universally affirmed emotions, or ideas, and limited itself to the enunciation of individual, sometimes highly specialized, emotions. The poem thus becomes no more than an approximation of an isolated moment of experience. The poet abandons his vatic role in society, he exists solely for himself, and he finds his arch-prototype in such men as Charles Baudelaire and Arthur Rimbaud. He becomes the connoisseur of emotions, of distinct, intense, and usually very esoteric emotions. The obscurity and perversity that often result are not voluntary, as many would like to think, but imposed by the conditions of the dominant mind of his time, of which mind he himself is the inevitable product. What is responsible, therefore, for the unsatisfactory character of the recent American poetic movement and similar movements in the arts is once again traceable to the general disappearance of palpable convictions in our time.

I am aware that the total feeling that these reflections must leave with the reader is not the most pleasant that might be desired. But it should be realized that such conclusions as are reached are not offered as final, since that would be equivalent to admitting that one's conclusions about life could be final; for literature and life have identified themselves in an indissoluble way through the long period of their association. Pessimism is a state of feeling as invalid for the critic as optimism; and pessimism concerning the future of literature would be more defensible in the poet than in the critic. The effort has been rather to adhere to that part of the critical function which aims toward diagnosis. It is enough to inquire whether we are not using old terms for a new situation; whether the attitude of writers toward their art is not perhaps moving in the wrong direction; whether we are not losing sight of the old relationship between literature and life. Diagnosis does not always include prognosis, and no more can be reasonably vouchsafed in the present case than to suggest that the remedy must be found outside the body under examination. If literature is sick, it is too much to ask that it be its own physician.

The trouble is not so much with literature or with writers, as with the conditions of life that produce both literature and writers. We shall owe whatever renaissance the future may hold in store, not to a revolution in literature, but to a revolution in life. This may take the form, as the more hopeful and intelligent in all countries are fond of believing, of a new synthesis of all the possibilities of human life on this planet. But such a synthesis will justify its name by drawing not upon one, or a few, but upon all the expressions of thought that our ingenuity or desperation has devised. We must not make the mistake of expecting too much from literature alone; for literature, which has given us so many things, has never yet granted us an apocalypse.

4. "Comedy of Time" (1928)
Orlando: A Biography, by Virginia Woolf

This is the comedy that Virginia Woolf has made out of one of the antic discoveries of the new philosophers. Not too much surprise need be allowed us: Woolf has before this shown a quiet aptitude for harnessing the random intellectual currents of the age to the uses of literature; no modern writer has betrayed a more restless necessity for progression than is to be traced throughout her work. Nor should we stress too much the novelty of a design that has been suspended in the contemporary air for some time, a design derived from a rather simple metaphysical idea that has served Gertrude Stein for years and is now at the bottom of James Joyce's feats of legerdemain with the Aryan family of languages.

All this makes it nonetheless notable that Woolf should now expand where formerly she contracted the time element in human affairs; nonetheless extraordinary that her hero was born during the reign of Elizabeth, lived on through the reigns of James and Charles, changed sex one night in Constantinople some time in the seventeenth century, and is living this moment in England, a very up-to-date young woman of thirty six. These are anomalies out of which Woolf weaves something at once grander and finer than anything she has yet done: a fresco of a whole race through one of its members, almost of all history through a single mind and heart. She makes of our notions of time as serviceable a yardstick for plumbing illusions as Swift made of our notions of stature.

Some will indeed insist that the author has not made the richest use of her possibilities (the alteration of sex, for example); that opportunities for instruction, for satire, for fun even, are ruthlessly ignored; that the book should be twice or three times its length [134 pages]. Others (the question is more pointed) may inquire whether Woolf has not abandoned her long pursuit of reality and sought refuge in a hypothesis. Never once, these may protest, with all her chattering about life, of what life is and is not made, of its strange and unpredictable chemistry— never once does she create for us the living tissue itself. For these it may not be sufficient to remark that Woolf is a poet with a sense of humor. If she does not achieve that which the major line of writers often have the appearance of achieving, it may not be entirely that the power is denied her. It may be that an intellect schooled in several centuries of skepticism is wary of the eager affirmations of the heart.

For Virginia Woolf's intellect is ever glittering through the page, bowing, parrying, arranging the flowers of her perception with a grace that forestalls all objections even as it discourages all praise. The product of such a mind can be neither quite fiction nor quite criticism. It is for that reason difficult to apply to *Orlando* any of the traditional critical canons; the book is unusual in a deeper sense than the mere novelty of its pattern. If it belongs to any tradition, it is to the small secret tradition that harbors such works as *Gulliver's Travels* [1726, Jonathan Swift], *Tristram Shandy* [1759, Laurence Sterne], and *Candide* [1759, Voltaire (a.k.a. François-Marie Arouet)]—among which works it may finally stand, to the almost certain amusement of Orlando's biographer, as a masterpiece.

5. "The Position of Liam O'Flaherty" (1929)

Liam O'Flaherty [1896–1984], at the age of thirty-two, has written five novels, four volumes of short stories, a biography, and a large number of sketches and short stories soon to be gathered together in another collection. His reputation, however, is commensurate neither with this record of sustained creative energy nor with the easily recognizable distinction of his work. Literary popularity is never a matter of significance in speaking about a serious artist; but the reasons behind the critical apathy in the present instance are more interesting than usual. To consider them is to discover something about the mechanism of literary popularity at any time. It is also one excellent means of approaching certain of the essential features of this writer's contribution to the literature of our age. For the two things that are responsible for the neglect of O'Flaherty are at the same time inseparable from the deepest meaning and value of his work: his nationality and his fondness for melodrama.

The disadvantages of being an Irish writer today would be numerous even were it possible for the English reviews to be less loyal to their country and their class. Liam O'Flaherty has had at least as much to overcome in detaching himself from the settled mist of the "Celtic Revival" as the writers of that movement had in detaching themselves from the earlier schools of Charles Lever and Dion Boucicault. The unfortunate result is that O'Flaherty has perhaps suffered more than he has gained by the association. It would also seem pretty definite that the critical portion of the public is as avid of novelty as the common reader; and both certainly have had reason of late to become rather stalely habituated to the periodic emergence of ambitious talent in Ireland.

At any rate an unmistakable tone of weariness has become the custom in whatever is written about this writer in the few literary journals that do not altogether ignore him. Actually, O'Flaherty's relationship to the double tradition of Anglo-Irish literature is unique and distinct. He is on the side of J. M. Synge and James Joyce, as against the side of Swift and Shaw; but he does not belong unreservedly with either of those writers. Neither intellectual refinement nor the impedimenta of culture and religion operate to confuse the complete identification with nature that is the predominant feature of his work. He is closer to the unknown writers of early Gaelic folk literature than to any of his contemporaries. He is less the product of any modern school than of that period when European culture had not yet entirely lost its innocence.

33

There can be no question that all the novels of O'Flaherty belong to the category of melodrama; there can be equally little doubt that judgment of their value has been affected by the prevailing distrust of this mode. The objections to the mode have never been clearly formulated, although adherence to it has often been enough to discredit much of the work of Joseph Conrad and Fyodor Dostoevsky in the eyes of some critics. In the Greek sense, a melodrama meant simply a play with music; but the term was never used to differentiate such entertainment from a tragedy by Aeschylus, for instance, which nevertheless has most of the objectionable features of a modern melodrama. Today we signify by the term any composition in which the element of action seems exaggerated or strained beyond certain vaguely determined limits. What we probably mean is the extension of action beyond the boundaries to which we are accustomed in normal social experience. This restriction may apply with considerable justice to certain works of drama and fiction of inferior merit; but applied to other more pretentious works of the imagination it seems to involve an inconsistency. Perhaps the misconception rests on a failure to determine the nature of the relationship between action and theme, on the failure to recognize that the treatment of certain themes requires the extension of action on a more strenuous and heroic plane than the normal.

Melodrama, so considered, might be accepted as the elaboration of human motives on a grand scale, against immense backgrounds, and to the accompaniment of enormous music. In terms of function, one might discover in this form the most appropriate medium for the working out of certain crises or highly intensified human situations, the proper conditions for which depend on a heightening of the common laws of circumstance. However, any such defense of melodrama as a legitimate mode has nothing to do with its value in comparison with other recognized modes or with any possible system of values of its own. It is possible to write *good* melodramas, like *Macbeth* [1606] or John Webster's *The Duchess of Malfi* [1614]; it is also possible to write *bad* melodramas, like any number of plays written in Shakespeare's time or like any number of books written in our own. It is part of O'Flaherty's distinction as a novelist that he has had the courage, throughout all his five novels, to adopt what is at once the most dangerous and the most unpopular of literary modes.

The fact that all of O'Flaherty's novels, from *Thy Neighbour's Wife* [1923] to *The Assassin* [1928], adhere to the one mode suggests that it is inevitable for the particular pattern of life that has shaped itself in his imagination. His themes dictate the choice, themes that resolve themselves always into the larger and more violent conflicts of melodrama.

Should this explanation prove insufficient, there remains the exceptional nature of the background against which these themes are represented. Modern Ireland is a portion of the earth's surface that it would be necessary to imagine if it did not exist. The Aran Islands, where O'Flaherty was born, are not unlike those western islands around which Odysseus sailed and adventured; and Dublin, in the civilized modern mind, often takes on the colors of the Elizabethan version of the Italian cities of the Renaissance. It is clear that whatever temperamental predilection O'Flaherty may have had toward the writing of melodrama was strengthened by the inherent conditions of his environment.

For convenience, O'Flaherty's work may be divided into those novels and tales that have Dublin, and those that have his native Aran, for their setting. Of the Dublin group, *The Informer* [1925], *The Assassin*, and two earlier stories, "The Sniper" [1923] and "Civil War [1925]," are based on real or imagined circumstances of the period of insurrection and disorder through which that city has passed in the last twelve years. As a whole they constitute the most remarkable record of the period that we are likely to receive: the most complete because derived largely from personal observation and participation; the most reliable because written without any other bias than that of artistic selection.

The Informer, as the title suggests, is a novel of the revolutionary half-world, the story of Gypo Nolan, who betrays his friend to the police for twenty pounds. Less than one page is devoted to the actual capture and death of the betrayed man. All the interest is centered on the subsequent psychological history of the informer; his failure to liberate himself from the consciousness of the crime, except through the expiation of death, affords the theme. To appreciate his state of soul it is always necessary to remember the peculiar ambient of shame and horror that surrounds his crime in Ireland. Although low enough down on the moral scale of society, Gypo Nolan proves himself at bottom hopelessly loyal to the one code of morality that he can understand. How his guilt makes him give himself away at every turn, at every word, every movement, until he is finally shot down on his own doorstep, is told with a profound command of the Judas psychology. *The Informer* is a study in conscience; it might even be described as a melodrama of the conscience.

In *The Assassin*, his last published novel, O'Flaherty essays the most ambitious study of the revolutionist psychology yet attempted in fiction. Here the object of the action, its specific political or social aspects, is completely ignored. Also, the whole explicit action is subordinated to the conflict of motives, sometimes clear, sometimes strangely obscure, operating in the mind of the chief conspirator. Every step in Michael McDara's procedure from the moment of his return to Dublin—his selection of confederates, his preparations for the deed, his conduct after the deed—is described in a minute and exciting manner. At the beginning he is presented as the perfect and idealized archetype of the tyrannicide. As such he is thoroughly contrasted with each of his colleagues: Ketch, the professional thug, expert in murder as a trade; Tumulty, a mouthy sentimentalist, an inveterate patriot of the old order. Neither is able to rise to the hard purity of McDara's own philosophy of revolution. "Nobody had the *idea*," he explains, referring to the past. "Without an idea behind it, every political act becomes immoral and unnecessary. Such an act as this should be done in cold blood, not for motives of revenge or greed or for the purpose of seizing power or for anything else. Merely to cut off the head that is blocking the forward movement of the mass. . . . This act must also be directed against the idea of God."

In such speeches as this McDara is sustained by his reason and his eloquence; but at other moments he reverts to his peasant origin, remembering his own mother and the creed of his childhood, feeling suddenly terrified at the enormity of the gesture he is making against society. In the finest scene of the book, the contrasted mental states of the three conspirators are shown as they sit about in a cheap furnished room on the eve of the murder. Here the closeness of observation is consummate; no movement, no vibration of the tense atmosphere, is left unobserved as a possible source of intimate revelation. The style is attuned to the mood of the situation with a precision calculated to make the reader also share in the physical suspense. Ketch lies stretched out on the bed; Tumulty moves about nervously, talking foolishly to conceal his terror; but McDara, at the climax of his dream, ruminates on the sordidness of his surroundings, the cowardice and worthlessness of his companions, the essential waste and futility of his scheme.

If *The Informer* was a melodrama of the soul, with conscience as the principal protagonist, this last novel of O'Flaherty's is a melodrama of the intellect, founded on the immemorial strife between the will and the memory, between what the mind would determine and what life has decreed. At the end McDara is not strong enough to unbind the cords of tradition and sentiment that chain him to his emotional past, to whose aggregate symbol, on bended knees, he finally succumbs: "Mother, forgive me!" He has been clever enough to make his escape after the assassination quite certain; but the train that hastens him away from Ireland, of whose every beauty he is now made suddenly aware, bears an outcast and a failure. Suicide awaits him as soon as he reaches London.

Mr. Gilhooley [1926] represents an interesting effort on the part of O'Flaherty to extend his range of interest into a new sphere of Dublin society, the more quiescent, distinctly more bourgeois, society that is now forming out of the old. Gilhooley is a successful, middle-aged engineer who has come back to Ireland to recover his health after twenty years spent in South America. His is a full-length portrait of *l'homme moyen sensuel.* The sure sense of a wasted capacity for strong feeling, the depression of autumnal yearning, make him ripe for his affair with the girl whom he picks up one night on the pavements. The differences in age and sensibility make the relationship impossible from the beginning. Tragedy becomes certain when Gilhooley's affection burns gradually into the fierce passion of middle-age. Perhaps the meaning of their last terrible scene in the flat, with its resolution of the theme into the familiar nightmare of jealousy and death, can be felt only by recognition of the man's age and essential normalcy. The girl's betrayal is for him the defeat of his life. But about this book as a whole one feels a lessening of strain, especially of poetic strain, as though O'Flaherty were telling Mr. Gilhooley's story more out of duty than out of any profound desire of the imagination.

The stories in *Spring Sowing* [1926] and *The Tent* [1926] should make their appeal even to those readers who are unable to respond to the larger patterns of the novels. The trained intensity of style, the economy of detail, the exact sharpness of perception appear here with special appropriateness and combine to place these stories among the most distinguished of our time. Almost every phase of Irish life is touched on, although for the most part they deal with the land. Such stories as "Milking Time" [1925], "Three Lambs" [*Spring Sowing*] and the title-story of "Spring Sowing" are themselves like the rich exhalations of the soil; "Going into Exile" [*Spring Sowing*] is a record of its tragedy, "The Bladder" [*Spring Sowing*] and "The Old Hunter" [1927] of its robust humors. Perhaps the most perfect in achievement of all these little stories is "Birth" (published in the limited edition titled *The Fairy Goose* [1929]), which is the simple account of a group of peasants gathered together near a meadow at night to attend the birth of a calf. But the most individual are those in which O'Flaherty writes about a lost thrush, or the capture of a fish, or a seagull's first flight—unsentimental studies of animal life written with a fastidious interest usually reserved for human beings alone. From all of O'Flaherty's stories, however, one takes away a similar impression of the profound solidarity of nature, all of her manifestations being of equal importance to the artist who admits her superiority.

This conviction of the impenetrable identity of all physical nature receives its grandest expression in *The Black Soul* [1924], the second, and the most majestic, of O'Flaherty's novels. "*The Black Soul* overwhelms one like a storm," wrote Æ [George William Russell, in *The Irish Statesman* of May 3, 1924], but closer is the resemblance to a symphony, a vast prose symphony, whose most proper divisions are the four seasons of the year. The setting is Inverara, "the island of death, the island of defeated peoples, come thither through the ages over the sea pursued by their enemies"; its characters are its people, seated "on the cliffs dreaming of the past of their fathers, dreaming of the sea, the wind, the moon, the stars, the scattered remnants of an army, the remains of a feast eaten by dogs, the shattering of a maniac's ambition." Into this world comes the Stranger, bringing with him the sick body and tired soul of one who has lived too long on the mainland.

The whole tempestuous drama of the book is in full process in Fergus O'Connor's brain before it is realized in explicit action. There begins at once his long struggle to yield himself to life as life becomes crystallized for him in his love of Little Mary, the wife of the peasant [Red John] with whom he has taken lodging. Mary is a kind of island Cybele; she has no more character, in the usual sense, than nature herself; she is as hard, as wild and as beautiful. But Fergus is obliged to bore down through every layer of sentiment, culture, illusion that buries the reality of his own being. The old conflict between nature and the intellect—the single underlying theme of all O'Flaherty's novels—here is staged against the most opulent background of physical nature, elaborated with all the resources of a rich, poetic prose, and resolved finally in one of the most powerful scenes in modern fiction. During the fierce struggle with Red John in the cleft of rocks on the coast, Fergus is made to see the meaning of life through the meaning of death. Through action he is at last able to free himself. It would be much closer to a certain tradition of Romantic fiction to have Fergus, instead of Red John, meet his end in this scene. But such a solution would cause the deeper implication of the novel to be lost. The victory of Fergus is essential if the positive import of the theme is to be established: the complete reaffirmation of physical experience as the means of bringing man back into harmony with his universe.

The Black Soul is the best of O'Flaherty's novels because of the grandeur and sonority of the theme, and because of the abundance of those qualities of language and perception for which his work as a whole is distinguished. These qualities are essentially of a poetic order and, as such, difficult to define or describe by means of any available critical equivalents, although plainly manifest on every page. Moreover, they are qualities that should make a potent appeal to any modern reader. (The theme of *The Black Soul*, for example, is profoundly modern, but it is also *more* than modern.) Nature, not as the dark intoxicant of the earlier Romantics, but as something apprehended in the flesh, may come to be more and more accepted by our writers as the superstructure of our intellectual world crumbles about their feet. In the meantime, when most of our novelists seem to be frantically entrapped among the ruins, the reading of Liam O'Flaherty is like a tonic and a promise.

6. "The Story of the Little Magazines" (1930–32)

I The Revolt in the Desert

"They went forth to battle but they always fell" might be inscribed on their tombstones, for the little magazines, like the heroes of Ossian [a.k.a. James Macpherson], were not in the least discouraged by their high death-rate. In the general mind they were associated from the very start with an extravagant talent for mortality. When [in 1925 in "The Liberators"] Keith Preston wrote his malicious elegy for those of them "who died to make verse free," he was merely voicing the weary humors of a public that had assisted at too many obsequies. For at that time the little magazines seemed to be gifted with phoenix-like powers of recovery; every new victim to perish on the field could depend on two or three fresh champions to leap instantly to his place. It was difficult to imagine that the succession might not be perpetual; to realize that even the phoenix might one day rebel against mounting so regularly from his ashes. Surely no spectator of the literary scene during those ripe years had any reason to predict the holocaust that has recently come to pass.

But today we can no longer conceal the truth. Not only are fewer aspirants setting out to brave that unpastured dragon, the reading members of the public, in their den, the polite library—but even the hardier veterans—are gradually, one by one, relinquishing the ghost. Last spring, in exile, the *Little Review* brought out its final number; the *Dial* survived for a few months only; and others, with limp stride and shortened breath, hover on the brink of the grave. It would seem as if the time were at hand for the sad offices of the valedictorian, for the dusty labors of the chronicler. It would seem as if another chapter in our literary history—one of the liveliest and most colorful—is rounding to a close.

The high tide of the "little" movement in the arts parallels so closely the epoch of the Great War that it is a temptation to exaggerate the coincidence. Indeed, the movement is all too often briefly dismissed as one of the effects, one of the more regrettable effects, of the post-bellum spirit on the arts. While undoubtedly affected by the psychological tension of the time, the movement might better be interpreted as the product of forces that had made themselves felt long before the war, and of which the war itself was the ultimate product. It must be recalled that in the opening decade of the present century, the intellectual climate was as ominously overcast as the political. If the whole age in which we are now living ever comes finally to be known as the age of transition, those early years will very likely be further set apart as the period of expectancy. In philosophy, literature, and all the arts, the conviction was strong that something must happen and that something was about to happen almost at any moment.

This was the great period, in fiction, of the social novels of H. G. Wells and John Galsworthy. In the theater, George Bernard Shaw was still regarded as a very dangerous fellow; he had not yet been reduced to a benign old gentleman in bathing shorts. G. K. Chesterton, as the white knight of orthodoxy, was striving valiantly to ward off the barbarous hordes of modernism with bewildering paradoxes. Through all the arts the spirit of reform ran like liquid fire. Whenever James Gibbons Huneker returned from a trip abroad he always brought back with him a trunkful of the most startling foreign novelties. Gradually the names of Paul Verlaine, Claude Debussy, Paul Cézanne, Charles Baudelaire, and Erik Satie became part of the Anglo-Saxon consciousness. The hoary ghost of Walt Whitman was even resurrected to become guest of honor at richer dinners than he had ever enjoyed in his lifetime. Good people everywhere found themselves reviled as "bourgeois," although few of them were quite certain what the word meant. "High-brows" and "low-brows" faced each other, for the first time, on the open field. And it was to be remarked that as the "high-brows" increased in audacity, they also increased in exclusiveness: they showed a distinct preference for their own company. Indeed, by the time Maurice Browne opened his Chicago Little Theatre [in 1912], the "little" movement was already fairly on its way.

In the field of letters, the little magazine provided the appropriate medium of dissent. It differed from the established monthlies, if by no other token than by the extreme inhospitality of its tone. It made no concessions to the public taste; on the contrary, it operated on the assumption that the public was always backward and nearly always wrong. It declined to serve as an instrument for national complacency in England, or for national insouciance in America. It addressed itself, rather, to the few in both countries who felt very strongly that the twentieth century had arrived. The "littleness" of the little magazine was therefore properly an attribute of its audience. The diminutive applied neither to its size nor to its aims. It was simply a warning to the uninitiated. The *Little Review*, for example, taking further precautions, had emblazoned on its cover: "Caviar to the General." Some also reflected their independence in their choice of titles, such as *Others*, *Pagany*, *Fugitive*, and *Exile*. None neglected to let it be understood somewhere in its pages that it regarded itself as a voice crying in the wilderness.

In the United States, the first important voice to be heard was that of *Poetry: A Magazine of Verse*, which Harriet Monroe founded as long ago as 1912. The particular site in the wilderness was Chicago. If that city loomed up for a time as the literary capital of America, as the Athens of the republic, none contributed more to the hope than Monroe. In founding *Poetry*, also, she returned the nicest possible gratitude to her native city for having chosen her as laureate of the World's Fair in 1891. But the immediate occasion was furnished by the widespread interest in poetic reform throughout the English-speaking world about this time. The sources from which this movement drew its inspiration are now making themselves clear. The poets of the Celtic revival [in Ireland and Wales] had demonstrated that verse might be written which should be at once simple, clear, and direct; the *vers librists* of France, under Paul Fort, Émile Verhaeren, and Francis Jammes, had proved that even the laws of versification might be transgressed. Not less important was the rediscovery in America of Whitman, who was made to serve as a model of the truly indigenous poet.

The new movement had only just begun when Monroe realized her ambition to devote a magazine exclusively to verse; indeed, it is hard to determine which was anterior to the other, so immediate was the stimulus provided by *Poetry*. Each of its earlier volumes now reads like a select anthology of our most representative modern poets. William Butler Yeats, one of its strongest friends from birth, contributed richly at the beginning, as did also Ezra Pound, Edgar Lee Masters, Robert Frost, and Vachel Lindsay. When, a little later, the gentle art of poetry found itself borne along on the brisk winds of American publicity, *Poetry* steered a calm and dignified course. This was the epoch of poetry schools, contests, readings, and dinners; it was the epoch of Amy Lowell's black cigars. *Poetry* continued to extend hospitality to the most vital of the older poets; to grant a hearing to the wide variety of new accents that stammered at its doors. It was among the first, in some cases actually *the* first, to introduce the work of such dissimilar talents as H.D., Carl Sandburg, Wallace Stevens, Mark Turbyfill, and Maxwell Bodenheim. It accorded long, conscientious reviews to the innumerable slim volumes that tumbled hopefully from the presses; nothing bearing on the poetic art escaped its sympathetic attention. Today, it is true, some havebeen able to note a few signs of fatigue on the brow of this old veteran. But such ravages of time are easily pardoned when we recall the strenuous audacity of its youth.

The advance of the little magazine in England was not hastened by any such need for national expression as existed in the United States. But the body of dead tradition that had accumulated in the older country was even more formidable. There the older reviews basked in a tyrannous senility; Robert Bridges had just succeeded Alfred Austin as poet laureate; and the lending libraries (those sanctuaries of what Virginia Woolf has called "Mudieism" [after the name of a maid, Juliet Mudie, who frequented them]) did what they could to prolong the Victorian epoch. The more active minds seemed to be turned to politics and sociology. Nineteenth-century science threatened to squeeze the arts more and more out of the picture. Neither Wells nor Shaw, who spoke so confidently on social matters, had very much to say about the individual, that is to say, about what has been the most truly legitimate subject of literature in every age. The problem of the individual at that moment was once again the problem of individual freedom.

Around this familiar banner, then, rallied the first English martyrs of the little magazine. "Liberty is the first condition of well-being," announced *Rhythm,* a good-sized quarterly that appeared in London in 1911, for a while under the leadership of John Middleton Murry. This was a heresy instantly choked by the authorities, who suppressed a short story by the late W. L. George. Because it was so indefinite as to its ideals, *Rhythm* enjoyed little influence, but it justified its existence by providing an early vehicle for James Stephens, Lord Dunsany [a.k.a. Edward Plunkett], and, especially, Katherine Mansfield, whose stories and criticism made up much of its bulk.

Not until the *Egoist,* in 1914, does the *genus* little magazine appear in England with all its proper features. Here, at last, was "an individu-alist review" devoted to the unique aim of presenting in the making "those contemptuous literary efforts that, ultimately, will constitute twentieth-century literature." While there has not been enough time for these claims to become completely justified, the *Egoist* was certainly associated at the start with several of the more prominent post-

Georgian reputations. It published James Joyce's *Portrait of the Artist as a Young Man* [1916] in serial-form in 1914 and 1915; Wyndham Lewis's first novel, *Tarr* [1918]; and many of the poems that soon afterwards went to make up T. S. Eliot's *Prufrock and Other Observations* [1917]. For courage, perspicacity, and enterprise, the *Egoist* invited comparison with its contemporary in Chicago, for which it probably afforded the prose complement. Moreover, it was forced to hold the line in England practically single-handed until relieved for a time by the heavy artillery movements on the extreme left-flank, of a journal called *Blast*.

The début of this journal occurred on what now seems an ominous date: June 20, 1914. [The assassination of Archduke Franz Ferdinand in Sarajevo occurred on June 28, 1914, and as a result World War I commenced a month later, on July 28, 1914.] In every respect, *Blast* excelled its predecessors for sheer noise: it had a brilliant red cover; its type was the boldest ever seen in the British Isles; and its editorial voice seemed to issue thunderously from a great megaphone. Never again did Wyndham Lewis equal this early triumph of vocalization. *Blast* heralded a brand-new movement in the arts. "Vorticism" was calculated to supplant without delay such outworn dogmas as those of Imagism, Spectricism, Cubism, and plain Futurism. Somewhere in the Vortex, perhaps at the very bottom, was to be found the solution of all the problems that beset a very troubled generation of Englishmen; but what the Vortex was, or where it was situated, has not to this day been revealed, even by Lewis himself, in all his comprehensive explorations into the modern *Zeitgeist*. There remains no more definite indication of its aims than the following: "We only want the world to live, and to feel it's (*sic*) crude energy flowing through us."

The Vorticists were rather more precise about what they wished to blast or bless; the catalogue ranges, on the credit side, from castor oil to Charlotte Corday; on the debit, from cod-liver oil to Marie Corelli. None of the contributors to *Blast*, unfortunately, were able to keep up with the raucous spirit of the editorial page. Ford Madox Ford (then Hueffer) was represented by a pleasant tale that suggested the later manner of Henry James; Rebecca West discoursed rather tamely on modern marriage; and Ezra Pound presented to the public for the first time his astonishing epigram on a new cake of soap:

Lo, how it gleams and glistens in the sun
Like the cheek of a Chesterton.

It was hard to decide how much of *Blast* was to be taken seriously; how much of it was sheer burlesque, how much an overflow of the feverish energy of pre-war England. By the time its second issue went to press, most of the prime instigators were in the trenches, from which at least two of them, T. E. Hulme and the sculptor Henri Gaudier-Brzeska, never returned. The "crude energy" that the Vorticists had demanded rushed toward them with unchecked force; and for some time afterwards the voice of the little magazine in England was drowned amid louder reverberations.

But it was this same year, 1914, and once again in Chicago, that Margaret Anderson set out to produce the "creative opinion" that she had found wanting in Indianapolis, Indiana. If any little magazine must be chosen to stand as archetype of the species, none better deserves the honor than her *Little Review*. None, except *Poetry*, has drawn out to a longer history. None has had a more varied or exciting career. All those who enrolled early under its banner have won to some kind of fame. It began the serialization of Joyce's *Ulysses* in 1918, a good time before that work became part of the undeclared baggage of all Americans returning from France. It published Eliot's famous cycle of "Sweeney" poems [e.g., "Sweeney Erect" and "Sweeney among the Nightingales," 1920], and introduced the later Yeats of "The Wild Swans of Coole" [1917]. It was the first real sponsor of Sherwood Anderson, Maxwell Bodenheim, Ben Hecht, Djuna Barnes, and Hart Crane. In brief, it had the faculty for keeping its readers perpetually on tiptoe.

The restless intelligence of the *Little Review*'s editors kept it from ever lagging in the battle or the chase, from settling into a pattern, from dwindling into common sense. For that reason it was to be depended on to furnish a most reliable seismographic report of every new tremor that was being felt in the arts anywhere throughout the world. Surely on the basis of the "23 new systems of art (all now dead)" that it admits to having supported, there might be traced something like the spiritual curve of our time. From the bucolic mysticism of Sherwood Anderson to the gay insanities of the Dadaists, the register is complete. The special numbers that it arranged from time to time were milestones along one line of American cultural development: a number dedicated to the modern French poets whom Ezra Pound was reading in Paris; another to a thorough revaluation of Henry James; an "all-American" number, an International Theatre number, and one that welcomed the arrival of the Machine Age.

The migrations of the *Little Review* were also significant of the rapid shifting of center by the advance-guard of the past decade. In 1917, when the hope of a renaissance in Chicago had dimmed, it moved its offices to New York. Here the post-office authorities showed themselves such assiduous readers of its pages that they caused its suppression five or six times. The final trial of Joyce's *Ulysses* was the high dramatic moment in the journal's stormy history, if indeed not of the whole little magazine movement. Shortly after this event, Margaret Anderson retreated to Paris, and Jane Heap was left sole governess of the its destiny. The final number, brought out last May under their joint administration, bore the trademark of the Imprimerie Darantière of Dijon. [Maurice Darantière owned a publishing house in Dijon, France, and is known for having printed Joyce's *Ulysses* in 1922 for the bookseller Sylvia Beach.] This confirmed the rumor that the *Little Review*, like so many others before it, had come to Paris to die. More than fifty of its old friends and associates sent floral offerings in the shape of letters, confessions, and answers to an elaborate psychological questionnaire that demanded such intimate information as the following: "What has been the happiest moment of your life?"; "What is your world view?"; and "Why do you go on living?" Some of the results obtained by this time-honored trap for college freshmen threw a revealing light on the state of contemporary thought. And, in any case, they helped us understand Margaret Anderson when she explained that she could not go on publishing a magazine in which no one really knew what he was talking about.

Most of the little magazines in this country, notably the *Little Review*, had placed their emphasis solely on literary experimentation, without considering the nature or value of the experience available for the artist in America of the period. They uniformly resented the United States but did not bother to analyze the basis of their resentment. This was a problem for criticism that was not adequately undertaken before a group of young creative thinkers in New York inaugurated the *Seven Arts* in 1917. This energetic monthly displayed no compromise in the impersonal scrutiny with which it examined the American past, or temperance in the enthusiasm with which it hailed the American future. It was the hatching-ground of a whole school of American cultural criticism whose influence has not yet been fully appraised. In its pages Randolph Bourne and Van Wyck Brooks introduced a method for dealing with our cultural history that has come finally to be adopted in some universities. On its creative side, through the verse of James Oppenheim and the no less lyrical prose of Waldo Frank, it did much to rehabilitate the faded tradition of Walt Whitman in American letters. But on neither side was it strongly prepared against the alarms and discursions of a nation that found itself suddenly at war. Almost alone of American liberal groups in 1917, the editorial board of the *Seven Arts* refused to swallow its convictions in the presence of the event. [Bourne, for one, published such scathing anti-war pieces for the *Seven Arts* as "The War and the Intellectuals" (June 1917), "Below the Battle" (July 1917), "The Collapse of American Strategy" (August 1917), "A War Diary" (September 1917), and "Twilight of Idols" (October 1917).] And, as a consequence, it was itself promptly and summarily swallowed by the event.

When the *Dial*, newly outfitted in modern clothes, reappeared in New York in 1917, much ground had been profitably cleared by the *Seven Arts* and similar pioneer organs. It was, in a sense, their heir, the elegant flower of their many perils and disappointments. Finally, as someone remarked, the ugly ducklings of yesterday had become the swans of today; the newest generation had less to combat; even the luxurious format of the new *Dial* seemed to announce that an era of relative stability had been attained. It would be unfair to suggest that the *Dial* did not continue the good work of supporting new talent; but its distinction, in the rough annals of the little magazine, lay elsewhere. It consisted in its maintenance of a tone that was at once more detached, urbane, and cosmopolitan than any of its rude forebears had ever achieved. Toward the public, toward the whole problem of artist and public, it showed an attitude of complete indifference. It also declined to commit itself to any policy, although with a self-consciousness that almost amounted to a policy in itself.

The urbanity of the *Dial*'s point of view was most clearly evident in its table of contents, where George Santayana rubbed shoulders with Gertrude Stein, W. B. Yeats with E. E. Cummings. Here the intention was probably to make as much as possible out of the disparity between the generations. In addition, the *Dial* assembled the most imposing list of foreign contributors of any journal in the country. The leading literary figures of France, Italy, and Germany were its correspondents from those countries; it printed translations of Arthur Schnitzler, Luigi Pirandello, Ivan Bunin, Paul Valéry, Thomas Mann, and many others; it initiated English readers into the labyrinthine cerebrations of Oswald Spengler. For a time, indeed, its foreign accent became so thick that many of its admirers were impelled to object; vignettes of rural life in Czechoslovakia, symbolic lyrics by some obscure Soviet genius, all but crowded the domestic product from its pages.

Of the several native artists that the *Dial* sponsored, E. E. Cummings and Glenway Wescott are the best known. It was appreciably stronger in the critical departments, with Gilbert Seldes busily devising a rationale for the Seven Lively Arts, and young critics like Malcolm Cowley and Kenneth Burke writing what were probably the most conscientious book reviews anywhere being written. But toward the end, the special tone that the *Dial* managed to create became steadily more monotonous, and even irritating, especially to the narrow class of readers to which it might have expected to make its appeal. (Perhaps no journal in recent years succeeded in earning for itself a larger number of quietly bitter enemies.) Moreover, the apparent lack of any strong emotional conviction in the editorial chair added to the effect of sterility. It is possible that if the *Dial* never provoked the excitement of the *Little Review* and other humbler institutions, this was because it lacked the principle of growth. There were some among its enemies, in fact, who had prepared its obituary long before July 1929.

The genealogy of magazines offers one of the most confusing of studies. To pursue the different strains of heredity, to separate the tangled criss-cross of influences, when the subject is not even as dependably concrete as man himself, but only one of the more elusive and insubstantial of man's expressions, is a pretty nearly hopeless task. But for the future chronicler of the little magazines, one thing at least seems certain: the round half-dozen here selected for mention will be recognized as the founders of the line. After them, in an almost literal sense, the deluge. Amid the sound and fury of their descendants, they may be all too easily forgotten.

II Making No Compromise with Public Taste

In the bright morning of the little magazine, which broke upon the world somewhere around the year 1912, the pioneers stood out against the vermilion sky in very bold relief; they were still rare enough to be looked upon by a bewildered public as something novel, strange, and even monstrous. Wyndham Lewis's *Blast*, for example, was able to send tremors through an England that was not yet accustomed to the cannons of Flanders and Picardy [from World War I]. The *Little Review* was forced to draw out an endless *mésalliance* with a post-office department that showed itself time and again insusceptible to the Rabelaisian qualities of James Joyce's prose. And in Chicago the little green journal called *Poetry* puzzled minds incapable of thinking of that city except as "hog butcher for the world" [Carl Sandburg's poem "Chicago" (1914)]. The *Egoist*, the *Seven Arts*, and (in the beginning) the *Dial* cast their fierce red light across the tranquil waters of current journalism with a distinctness that none could mistake. But after a short time all these early beacons were obscured, or at least dimmed, by the magnitude of their own influence.

Beginning as the lonely gesture of a few discontented individuals or factions, the little magazine rapidly became the ordinary mode of communication for the revived spirit of literary reform. From every province of the literary empire, fresh recruits enlisted in the motley army that marched with such arrogant confidence against the trembling *ancien régime*. It is as hard now as then to distinguish much order or sequence in their straggling ranks, or to separate them too dependably into brigades. Individuals, every one of them, with a natural antipathy to pigeonholes, they can be met and understood only as individuals. Perhaps the sole feature they shared in common was the impulse that animated and sustained their existence.

That impulse was nothing more mysterious or unfamiliar than the perennial human need for expression, or for what is now more frequently called "self-expression." Let it be noted, however, that this impulse is one that is seldom released of its own accord, that it requires a special set of conditions to call it into full play. Self-expression, as we are so often reminded by classical writers, is a distinctly Romantic necessity, and, like everything else Romantic, thrives best when it is opposed. It is what the psychologists would describe as a negative response to a situation. In other words, we seem never more anxious to express ourselves than when our right to do so threatens to be removed. We are most eloquent when we are asked to remain silent. The little magazines felt that the pressure against certain kinds of speech was very strong in the opening years of the twentieth century; and the eloquence that they often attained was the result of this conviction. The most vital of them, certainly, were those that were most passionately conscious of oppression. This it was that supplied their courage, their gusto, and their perseverance. This it was, in fact, that constituted their *raison d'être*.

The little magazines, or at least the best of them, aimed therefore at being the expression of an individual point of view. While such a view meant usually one that was new or heterodox or in some way different from the one that obtained in the public mind, it might have been further defined according to whether it was the view of a minority, of a group, or of a single individual. All the little magazines, however enlarged their outlook seemed to become later, undoubtedly owed their origin to the faith and enterprise of single individuals. And the first class that comes naturally to mind was made up of those who were most frankly dominated by the personality of their editors or founders. As "one-man shows" were popular in the salons of new artists, so also there was a large number of what we might call "one-man" magazines. In 1913, for example, William Marion Reedy took over a weekly journal of opinion that had been known in St. Louis for some years as the *Mirror*, renamed it *Reedy's Mirror*, and made of it a vehicle for extending his formidable personal influence over the entire Midwest. In this aggressive and sympathetic figure, that region found its first great champion. Although his own interests were mainly sociological, he encouraged all the new literary men that came under his notice, including Sandburg and Edgar Lee Masters, whose sensational *Spoon River Anthology* [1915] appeared originally in his pages.

How intimately the appeal of *Reedy's Mirror* depended on its founder may be judged by the fact that it was unable to survive his death in 1920. Perhaps its influence afforded a precedent for H. L. Mencken, who was busily declaring guerrilla warfare on American democracy from the back pages of the old *Smart Set*. The readers of that anomalous monthly could have been divided into two classes: those who enjoyed the sentimental stories and epigrams in the front and those who enjoyed the unsentimental roarings that issued from Mencken in the rear. For, at that time, Mencken was still an individual; he had not yet created the larger part of the American republic after his own image. Except for the indefatigable *All's Well*, conducted by Charles J. Finger in Fayetteville, Arkansas, other single-handed attempts to corner the market of public opinion met with little success. Frank Harris, that scarred veteran of so many journalistic wars, returning to New York from England in 1917—a kind of exile in his own land—was unable to infuse enough contemporary spirit into *Pearson's* to bring it very actively back to life. *Bruno's*, which succeeded it for the length of a year, made even less impression. But *The Soil*, brought out by Robert J. Coady during 1916–1917, confining itself more strictly to the literary arts, had an influence that was no less real because it was so slow and indefinite.

For the astonishing range of novelties, hoaxes, and *bona fide* literary articles that he served his readers, Coady has never been equaled. He was among the first to proselytize in favor of Charlie Chaplin, African sculpture, prizefighting, Gertrude Stein, American slang, and dressmaking as an art. He printed a whole novel [*The Pursuit of the Lucky Clew*, in the first five issues of *The Soil*] by one of the authors of the serialized Nick Carter stories [the novel was published under the first-person pseudonym "Nicholas Carter" but was written by one of the following: John R. Coryell, Frederick van Rensselaer Dey, Thomas Harbaugh, or Eugene T. Sawyer] because he believed that for "straight and swift narration the dime-novel has not yet been surpassed." He reproduced facsimile telegram-blanks side by side with El Greco's *Sacred and Profane Love* [a.k.a. *Saint John's Vision of the Mysteries of the*

Apocalypse, 1608–14], and heralded the steel hammer as the symbol of the age. If Coady is little remembered, it is perhaps because he was too preoccupied with the future; for his future has now become our present. But he possessed to an almost exaggerated degree what is one of the prime requisites of the good editor—the ability to anticipate with certainty the next move the public mind is likely to make.

Another and different sort of editorial talent was illustrated in a tiny publication that emanated from Northampton, Massachusetts, under the curious title *S4N*. Many had tried the experiment of uniting widely divergent points of view under a single cover, but none so nearly approached success, or in a more inconspicuous fashion, than Norman Fitts. The mystic symbols *S4N* were supposed to stand for faith in "the principle of growth through disagreement." Thornton Wilder and Hart Crane, William Lyon Phelps and Gorham B. Munson—such men found themselves there, probably for the last time, in the same company. Norman Fitts offered a splendid example of the editor as bandmaster. What influence will be exerted by such other, recent specimens of "one-man" editorship as Wyndham Lewis's *Enemy* and Ezra Pound's *Exile*, it is too early to determine. In his announcement, Pound exhorted young writers to submit new work, preferably "unutterable or magnificent," but manuscripts of the second sort have apparently been slow in reaching his office. And as for *Enemy*, it is less a magazine than a rather confused bulletin of Lewis's disapproval with the world in its last quarter of a century.

Not many of the little magazines fell too clearly into the autocratic class. More often they were the products of the numerous schools, cliques, and factions that abounded at the time. The emergence of literary groups was indeed one of the novel features of the little movement; for there had never been any strong tradition of unity among young artists and writers in English-speaking countries. Something in the Anglo-Saxon temperament seemed to be opposed to the union of genius and sociability. For a time, however, there were almost as many literary "chapels" springing up in those countries as anywhere on the Continent. Few of them, it is true, were able to preserve much solidarity among their members; the definition of a literary group as a collection of people who cordially dislike each other seemed more than half true. But almost all of them managed to hold together long enough to make themselves articulate through the medium of the little magazine.

The swarm of verse magazines that followed in the wake of Harriet Monroe's *Poetry* represented about all the attitudes that it was then possible to hold regarding this particular branch of the literary art. Before 1914, Monroe had been able to take care of pretty nearly all the interesting verse being written, but after that date her slender vessel was by no means adequate to the supply. *Others*, in 1915, relieved some of the cargo and struck a few notes of its own. If it published Wallace Stevens, T. S. Eliot, and Conrad Aiken, it also introduced newer figures like Mina Loy, William Carlos Williams, and Marianne Moore to the already exhausted public. Alfred Kreymborg, author of *Mushrooms* [1916; a book of tone poems (or "mushrooms") in free verse], was the reigning spirit of the *Others* group, who stood for "a democracy of feeling rebelling against an aristocracy of form."

The very next year, Charles Wharton Stork set up *Contemporary Verse*, probably the last stronghold of the genteel verse-makers against the invading hordes of the barbarians. Unfortunately, its quiet murmur was scarcely heard above the lusty shouts with which these new champions, one after another, entered upon the field. We cannot pause to render each of them its due; their names overwhelm the imagination like the catalogue of heroes in Homer's *Iliad* [ca. 762 B.C.]: *Palms, Rhythmus, Voices, Parnassus, Muse and Mirror, Measure, Fugitive, Lariat, Star-Dust, Forge*, and *Palo Verde*. Better than in cold prose, the vanished among them (for not all have yet descended to Orcus) should be commemorated in one of those sad ballads that demand of us in their refrains, "Where are the snows of yesteryear?" ["The Ballad of Dead Ladies" (1489), by François Villon]. Each of these magazines of verse had some birthmark or other emblem of distinction that set it apart from the rest. *Measure*, for example, encouraged in such poets as Léonie Adams, Louise Bogan, and Genevieve Taggard a type of feminine talent that was at once more cerebral and more richly poetic than that which had flourished earlier in the movement. *Fugitive*, in the South, opposed a more sharply intellectual approach to the current Romanticism. And *Rhythmus*, to drop to a more mundane level, promised contributors one dollar a line for their verse.

If we have left the English contingent to one side, it is because it was smaller and had a less emphatic accent. Harold Monro was the outstanding protagonist. This excellent modern poet carried on the *Poetry Review*, which Stephen Phillips founded in 1912, and issued an interesting series of chapbooks through his Poetry Bookshop in London. For its own part, the magazine *Wheels* was the organ of an eclectic group that included Aldous Huxley and the three Sitwells [Edith, Osbert, and Sacheverell]. But *Decachord*, the London *Voices*, and a few others were so comfortably attached to the nineteenth century that they were scarcely to be considered contemporary. At no moment, then, were the verse magazines in England so serious a menace to national tranquility as in the United States.

Even more numerous, as was natural, were the literary reviews consecrated to experimentation in other forms than verse. The more enterprising of these marked a reaction against the largely sociological preoccupations of the generation then in the spotlight. There came a time finally when Mencken, Theodore Dreiser, and Sherwood Anderson were so much in the spotlight, so wholeheartedly adopted by the great reading public, that they could no longer expect to hold their prestige with the younger literati. Not only had the alternately somber and hilarious view of American life that these writers promulgated become quite monotonous, it had also proved itself wholly non-creative. It was non-creative because it lacked both the imagination to envisage the future possibilities of experience in America and the ability to convey its own sense of limitations in any very potent or beautiful form.

Among the first to sound the reaction was *Secession*, which began in Vienna in 1922 but later moved to Brooklyn. It was an earnest attempt on the part of a few highly charged young writers to come to some working terms with their time. *Secession*, in its literary sense, was defined by its principal spokesman, Gorham B. Munson, as "a calm, intelligent, resolute swerving-aside, an unemotional sloughing-off of irrelevant drains upon our energies and a prompt deviation into purely aesthetic concerns." The Secessionists, in other words, preferred to regard their native land more as a rich field for artistic exploitation than as a subject for satire. In certain of his apocalyptic poems for this magazine, Hart Crane strove to merge his own intense personal vision with the confused panorama of modern industrial civilization. Matthew Josephson and Malcolm Cowley [each of whom co-founded *Secession* along with Munson] wrote sometimes in a style that was intended to resemble advertising.

Shortly after *Secession* went the way of all similar endeavors, Edwin Seaver provided shelter for some of its members in *1924*, which dispensed with any set policy. "*1924* has no policy," it explained, "we are not investing in a mausoleum." *Folio*, with a distinctly Jewish bias, belongs to this same period. And three years later, *The Figure in the Carpet*, whose baffling title out of Henry James [from an 1896 story of the same title] was alone sufficient to discourage most readers, defended the practice of writing as a serious craft throughout its brief and almost clandestine existence. Devoted solely to prose, it offered a retort courteous to the verse magazines. It was superseded the next season by *Salient*, which, like *The Figure in the Carpet*, has owed its support to the New School for Social Research in New York City.

There were also a number of journals whose aesthetic programs were supplemented by local or regional ambitions. The sluggish cultural consciousness of what New York always called "the provinces" was finally aroused by the arrogant domination of that city, and something like a renaissance threatened in certain sections of the country. In Philadelphia, for example, the *Guardian* was quite frank in admitting that it was "an attempt to be no longer suburban to Cosmopolis [i.e., New York]." Boston, former capital of letters, emerged more slowly with *Hound & Horn* and the recent *Pagany*. *The Modern Review* emanated from Winchester, Massachusetts, and *Phantasmus* from Pittsburgh. As for Chicago, it had challenged Eastern despotism from the beginning, and to its long list of entries it now added *Youth* and *The Wave*. From the Midwest also came *Midland* and the *Golden Galleon*. The Bohemian colony in New Mexico relieved itself through several ventures, of which the *Laughing Horse* has been the most determined. The Pacific coast was almost inarticulate until Janet Lewis and Yvor Winters commenced to send out mimeographed sheets of the *Gyroscope* from Palo Alto, California.

But in the South, where literary independence is rooted in social and political tradition, the movement toward regional expression had been notably strong. Several publications rose up instantaneously to give the lie to Mencken's assertion that Southern literature had expired with the mint julep. The most deliberate in its aims was *Fugitive*, of Nashville, Tennessee, which protested at the same time that it fled from nothing faster than "the high-caste Brahmins of the old South." Asheville, North Carolina, responded with the *Southern Review*, and Richmond with the *Reviewer*, for which Emily Clark enlisted several of the more obvious local reputations. In the *Double Dealer*, whose scope was national, New Orleans recalled the high position she once occupied in American culture. And, at the moment, the strongest friend of the new tendencies anywhere in the provinces is *Blues*, whose offices are in Columbus, Mississippi.

There is no parallel for this fever of regionalism in England during the same period. Apparently the literary hegemony of London was not regarded as a cause for protest by the successors of *Blast* and the *Egoist*. Indeed, the protests of any sort that were heard after the war were few and subdued. *The Calendar of Modern Letters* was a substantial, well-mannered review that published D. H. Lawrence, Stephen Hudson, E. M. Forster, and Siegfried Sassoon. None of these writers, however, was in urgent need of left-wing support by the year of grace 1925. *The New Coterie* was even less explicit as to its aims and squandered rather too much of its space on translations.

It is possible that the progress of the little magazine in England was impeded by the tenacity of the older generations. *The Golden Hind*, the *Apple*, the *Owl*, and *Life and Letters* were all unexciting studies in anachronism. Probably the best example of the species was the *Gypsy*, with its sonnet by Theodore Watts-Dunton, its essay by Edmund Gosse, its aquarelle of Paris by Arthur Symons. It was like a final sigh from the yellow 'nineties—a last sweep of their ghostly garments upon the macadam pavements of the twentieth century. Not exactly that, to be sure, may be said of either the *London Aphrodite* or *Experiment*, which have been desperately contemporary in accent. Both have taken occasion to vent their undergraduate spleen against the melancholy diagnoses of Wyndham Lewis. And the *Criterion* (which happens to be edited by a former American [T. S. Eliot]) is so very modern that its sympathy at the moment vacillates between the thirteenth and the seventeenth centuries.

But English along with American writers figured in what may be considered the most recent stage in the evolution of the little magazine. Any résumé at present must conclude with that volatile group of expatriate journals, those internationals of letters, which have found better reasons for being born on European soil than on their own. We cannot allow ourselves to go too deeply into these reasons; they would take us too soon into matters that are better treated in the stories of Ernest Hemingway and the poetry of Archibald MacLeish. But we may suggest what was probably a strong stimulus in many cases: the cheaper costs of printing on the Continent, an advantage that made possible larger and more frequent risks than might be taken at home.

It is extremely doubtful, for instance, whether *Broom* would have been able to make such an elegant entrance in New York or Chicago as it did in Rome. Founded in 1921 by Alfred Kreymborg, who will be remembered for earlier escapades on his native soil, *Broom* was a perfect cosmopolite, migrating from one capital to another, appropriating for its uses whatever current novelties it encountered on the way. The result of so much globetrotting was sometimes confusing and bizarre, but nearly always interesting for the contrasts and comparisons shown between the younger generations of the New and the Old World. Less cosmopolitan in scope was Ford Madox Ford's *Transatlantic Review*, whose territory did not often extend beyond Paris's Left Bank. Ford was more specially interested in opening a medium for his own work and for that of the several talented young English and American writers who happened to be living in his adopted neighborhood around the year 1924. Of those who were encouraged into later achievement by having their first work appear in the *Transatlantic*, Hemingway is easily the most celebrated.

Ford set the model for the various other exile publications that followed his retirement: *Contact, Close Up, Tambour, This Quarter*, and *transition*. None of these set up its long-range guns more effectively than *transition*. In fact, since the heyday of the *Little Review* in 1918, no little magazine has adhered so closely to definition or excited such general consternation. When Max Eastman undertook last year to prosecute what he called "the cult of unintelligibility" in contemporary letters, he revealed the principal offenders as the two most eminent of *transition*'s contributors: James Joyce and Gertrude Stein. The charge that Eastman and many others have raised against this journal has to do with its obscurity. It is maintained that in *transition*'s pages the breach between the modern writer and the modern reader has become so widened that the effort toward understanding is no longer worth the trouble.

The argument has reduced itself to the question of vocabulary, of how words are to be considered—whether as counters in a game, where values are mutually agreed upon in advance by reader and writer, or as highly personalized *signs*, whose meanings the reader must not expect to grasp in their entirety. The editors of *transition*, supported by the examples given by Stein and Joyce, hold to the latter interpretation, and advocate an immediate and drastic "Revolution of the Word." While *transition*'s editors have never undertaken their defense in exactly this way, they might cause some temporary embarrassment to their opponents by reminding them that every advance movement in the arts has been similarly taxed with its want of clearness. They might even establish that the slowness of the general comprehension is the most reassuring thing in their favor. But, at the end, the objection would no doubt still remain valid that for the greater number of readers, *transition* reads like an almost totally inscrutable scroll.

With this literary review, whose credit rests so largely with the future, the little magazine passes into its current phase. The desire for self-expression, which we have seen manifested in such a lush variety of forms, appears finally to have developed into something that little resembles expression at all. The lid that held down writers' minds has been at last completely removed, but the things that leap out before our startled readers' eyes no longer bear any correspondence to our experience. And the result of this orgy of freedom, as far as modern writers are concerned, has been a serious questioning of how far they may legitimately carry their ideals. "Self-expression is not enough; experiment is not enough," remarks Margaret Anderson, the editor of the *Little Review*, reading herself out of the party. A little later this former champion of ultra-modern tendencies concludes that literature, in its origin and function, has broken faith with the other arts.

If what Margaret Anderson says is true, it would seem that the little magazines should declare a truce. That this has actually come about, and is not merely a logical necessity, has been seen in the recent decline of their birth rate and the wholesale decimation of their older members. Of all those that were founded before the year 1920, *Poetry* alone lingers on—a somewhat chastened survivor of that gay, irreverent, and diverting age. All that remains to consider is a few of the more definite effects these publications have had on the even flow of contemporary letters.

If the little magazines have lost much of their thunder these later days, it may be because they forced their enemies to compromise. The older English and American monthlies are no longer blindly opposed to the advancement of the newer modes in writing; they have discovered, in some cases, that these pay even from a commercial viewpoint. Those that have not already deepened a shade or two in their contents have at least changed the color of their covers. The heresies, the *bizarreries*, "the insults to common sense" of yesterday have become the platitudes of today, accepted casually in the most polite reading circles. To offer but one example, the recent suppression in Boston of a well-known monthly [*The Atlantic*] for printing fiction by Ernest Hemingway ["Fifty Grand," in 1927] was held remarkable not because it reflected the altered taste of that monthly but because it reflected the unaltered taste of Boston.

At the same time, by pressing the opposite attitude as far as it seems likely to go, the little magazines have very probably hastened the advent of a more lucid, tranquil, and responsible attitude toward literary art. By spending their own energies so lavishly, they may have taught others valuable lessons in economy. The generation to which most of them were pledged was a Romantic generation whose Romanticism, with all its excesses and all its waste, may not be wholly without fruit. It cleared ground, opened new paths, made discoveries. But, more than anything else, it prepared the way for a strong reaction against itself, which in the end may be more important. Already we have numerous signs of this reaction against so much creative libertarianism, toward a recovery of that equilibrium which Eastman and others have found wanting in modern literature. Several of the very recent publications are marked by their extreme sobriety; a few of them have even proceeded so far as to revive the once dreaded word "classicism." In other ways, also, it is apparent that the little magazines have come full circle.

But as soon as that is quite accomplished, as soon as the present movement toward classicism in the good sense relaxes into something that resembles classicism in the old, bad sense, the cycle will recommence. The function of the little magazine will be once again to stir the lifeless forms from their contented slumbers. For the respite that they are granting us at the moment cannot be other than temporary.

III *transition* and the Apocalypse of the Word

Perhaps not until quite recently has it been possible to distinguish with adequate sharpness between what promises to be the principal directions of literary criticism in our time. But however confused that criticism may still remain to the cursory reader of reviews and articles, particularly in the little magazines, it is now almost certain that there are not more than three or at the most four clearly defined points of view open to the critic of today who would be both consistent and positive in his approach to literature. The time has come when the critic who refuses to identify himself with one or another of these points of view must seem either too superficial or too confused to be very much worth the trouble of reading. As for the critic who devotes himself to examining and dismissing the views of others without venturing to advance one of his own, the only position he can claim is the anomalous one of having no position at all, and his work suffers correspondingly in vigor and direction.

Without pausing to consider the peculiar merits attached to such an Olympian attitude at the moment, one turns to the more boldly articulate groups who have aligned themselves under the more or less recognizable banners of classicism, romanticism, and communism. Of these groups certainly the most articulate so far has been the first; for the followers of T. S. Eliot in the *Criterion* in England and the *Hound & Horn* [founded by Lincoln Kirstein in 1927, with R. P. Blackmur as its first managing editor] in America have had the very distinct advantage of working with a lucidly intellectual, indeed classical, vocabulary. More recently we have also had, in the pages of the *Modern Quarterly,* the spirited correspondence between Henry Hazlitt and V. F. Calverton on the relationship between communism and literature. But not until the publication a few months ago in the Netherlands of the new, enlarged *transition* have we had anything like so definite a statement of principles from what we may call the "Romantic survival" in contemporary letters.

"The crisis through which we are passing is not only politico-economic in character, but encompasses all the manifestations of the [human] spirit" ["The Language of Night" (1932)], announces Eugene Jolas [the editor of *transition*] in the course of his counterattack on what he believes to be the "intellectual hypnosis" of communism in the offing. The logic of the *transition* group [which includes, in addition to Jolas, Elliot Paul, Robert Sage, Kay Boyle, Hart Crane, and Maria McDonald] may be summed up in somewhat the following manner: the world, as pretty well everyone agrees, is in a bad state of spiritual and intellectual disintegration. Everything has been affected, including our literature, which still persists in being written around the same ideas and in the same language as when the world and society were in a better way. The problem for literature in our time, therefore—at least according to this journal—is fundamentally a problem of words. Writes Jolas: "The vast political, philosophical, and psychological revolutions in recent history have shifted the significations of many terms to such an extent that the original ideas have become obscured, necessitating wearisome redefinitions to avoid the misunderstandings produced by the difference between the primary image and the superimposed one" ["Wanted: A New Communicative Language!" (1932)].

So far one may recognize much that is justified in *transition*'s platform. But almost immediately Jolas is led to an apotheosis of the individual poet, to whom he would restore something very much like the vatic role the latter occupied in primitive society. Jolas places his faith in the poet, in the "orphic" vision of the poet, because he alone can give back to language its pre-logical functions and thus make a spiritual revolt, "the only revolt worth making today" ["Wanted: A New Symbolical Language!" (1932)]. It is the business of the poet to undermine all rationalistic dogmas and ideas that stultify current literary expression by discovering in his own subconscious the elements of a new language. For this reason *transition* announces itself the champion of all hallucinative, mantic, and "mediumistic" experiments in writing. The current issue [March 1932] of the magazine has an ample representation of such experiments under the title "anamyths, psychographs, and other prose texts." An "anamyth," we are informed, is "a fantastic narrative that reflects preconscious relationships"; a "psychograph" expresses hallucinations and phantoms.

It is unfortunate that the editorial plea of *transition* for a new and living language should be expressed in such a pretentiously vague and ultra-intellectual vocabulary. It is the more unfortunate because the effect will be to discourage the few people who might be willing to admit the truth of some of the magazine's assumptions. Certainly no reader of contemporary writing can help agreeing, for example, that all but the best of it is written in a style that is rapidly losing whatever direct associations with the senses the English language once possessed. Triteness, abstractness, weary journalese—almost any page by the late Lytton Strachey might serve as an example for study. Moreover, the cleansing process begun by Gertrude Stein as long ago as 1904, and carried on by Sherwood Anderson and Ernest Hemingway, has had but one result to date: it has set up a new euphuism as artificial as the old. The parodies of English prose styles in James Joyce's *Ulysses* [1922] have turned out to be only a prelude to the international dream language [that is, as if it were translating a dream, where words are not the words of a language understood but of an unconscious language] of *Work in Progress* [a.k.a. *Finnegans Wake* (1939), various sections of which initially were published serially—in *transition*—under the title *Work in Progress*].

But even admitting all this to be true, one is left with grave doubts as to the feasibility of any program that attempts to bring about reform by deliberate and self-conscious means. Without reviewing the whole overworked question of "intelligibility" suggested by those few who have put the theories of *transition* into practice, one can question to what extent a language can be systematically created or reformed by any individual or group of individuals. There is certainly no precedent for any such effort in the history of the world's languages. New life is usually infused into a language by the necessity of a younger race to communicate new energies and a new response to experience, which was what happened in Europe after the collapse of Rome, and which is what may be happening in the United States today. The process is slow and extremely complicated (there is, after all, the whole science of philology); and a language is not fully revived as an instrument until it has been taken up by a first-rate literary genius. A first-rate literary genius, in turn, is not born in every generation; he is the product of a culture that has settled itself into a complete social and intellectual unity. Language, in the last analysis, is not personal but social, whatever variations the individual may play on it.

To say this, of course, is at the same time to object to the Romantic assumption that a "Revolution of the Word" would entail a corresponding revolution in metaphysics, art, and religion. It is very much like believing that all the problems in the world would be solved by a new dictionary of Esperanto. We have seen in our time poetic imagery, extremely vivid and picturesque in itself, itself devoid of significance because it was insufficiently related to any cohesive background of ideas behind it. The narrowing of all our problems down to a problem of the individual word, therefore—as *transition* advocates—rather than leading to that integration which we would all welcome, leads on the contrary to an infinite process of fragmentation. In fact, the course of Romanticism in the past few hundred years has been leading in exactly that direction.

For the truth is that the group associated with *transition*, whatever else we may make of it, does represent the most complete expression of Romantic individualism, philosophical as well as literary, to be found in our time. If we consider Romanticism to consist essentially in a process of reduction—from society to the individual, from the individual as a whole to the separate emotion, impression, and sensation—no other group has brought the process to a further point of culmination. With it, we are reduced at length to the lowest integer of conscious or subconscious communication. We are offered the *Apocalypse* of the Word. And in this ultimate simplification of the Romantic gesture lies perhaps the real importance of *transition*, among all the little magazines, in the scheme of contemporary letters: it does force us to make up our minds decisively whether or not we believe that gesture, as well as the organ of its transmission, to be the appropriate one for our time.

7. "Proof Positive" (1930)
The Proof, by Yvor Winters

Between the boards of this thin volume, titled *The Proof*, is represented something like the transition of American poetry in our generation: from a successful concentration upon the single image to an extension of the poetic province over the whole of human experience. Yvor Winters has already been known to us as one of the last and most authentic of the Imagists. In certain poems earlier in the present collection—"Bisons," "Goatherds," "November"— he is still content to render sense-impressions with a hardness, economy, and certitude that give to their expression a value almost absolute in itself. So triumphant, in fact, is his achievement within the purely literary discipline that it would be impossible for him to develop further if he did not happen to be an extremely ambitious poet.

But both by temperament and by the pressure of his time, Winters is compelled to go out in search of much bigger game than the single circumscribed image that occupied his immediate predecessors. His maturity as a poet coincides too closely with the moment when poets everywhere are discovering that the very life of their art depends on a more complete and ordered mastery of their universe. For the modern poet the task entailed is a creative reconstruction of the harmony between intellect and perception; and for a poet as acutely sensitized as Winters, the task is more than ordinarily difficult.

It would be inaccurate, however, to claim that he has succeeded where so many others before him have escaped mysticism only to be trapped into one or another type of sterile dogmatism. At times his verse also disintegrates into a somewhat febrile mysticism; at times his habit of vatic utterance borders on the dogmatic. Intellect too often enters in the guise of a pompous, abstract diction that merely serves to obfuscate the experience; intellect is too often the murex that discolors the original clear perception. A conviction that classicism of form means emulation of models from the past is probably responsible for the misalliance of influences in Winters' poetry.

Yet Yvor Winters is important despite his failure to express an intelligible personal synthesis. The proper view of him would be as a poet who creates on the level where the fusion between intellect and perception is in the process of being accomplished. The desperate tenacity with which he pursues his object lends the passion to his verse; the passion is responsible for the rare vitality of its style. "The mind alone is mind, and it must wait" ("The Fable"), Winters reminds us, in a statement that seems less cryptic if read as an apology for all that remains unachieved in his work to date. And again, in a ringing last line to the whole volume, "Nor is the mind in vain" ("Simplex Munditiis").

8. "Nathan's Testament" (1931)
Testament of a Critic, by George Jean Nathan

Now that George Jean Nathan *nel mezzo del cammin* has offered us his testament with portrait bust in bronze reproduced on the dust cover; now that there exist scholarly exegeses of his work by Vladimir Kozlenko and Isaac Goldberg, Ph.D. [respectively, *The Quintessence of Nathanism* (1930) and *The Theatre of George Jean Nathan* (1926)]; now that the complete roster of that work ominously approaches the proportions of a Collected Edition, one is impelled to halt and inquire, ever so reverently, just what it is all about.

At first blush the table of contents of the present book promises much toward an answer: "Revelation," "Proverbs," "Chronicles," "Lamentations." The naïve hope is that the author is going to break down and confess everything. But before many paragraphs one is made aware that here again is the old familiar Nathan style, distilled down a bit to an almost Baconian sententiousness, aphorized out of all pity to make a Phelpsian holiday [a reference to Yale English professor William Lyon Phelps, a garrulous author and speaker]. Before ever we enter upon the threshold of that Drama which Nathan guards with his formidable adjectives, we are set right on such matters as happiness, egotism, marriage, money, and the nature of truth. Nathan does them up in neat little bundles that have all the compressed inevitability of a two-line joke from a trial judge.

The method adopted is any process of dissociation that allows the writer to arrive atsome conclusion to an idea in any respect different from the one commonly held. "There is not an idea which does not include its own possible refutation, nor a word, the contrary word," remarked Marcel Proust in *Albertine disparue* [*Albertine Gone* is the title of the sixth volume of Proust's seven-part novel, *Remembrance of Things Past* (1913–27)]—with a weariness that did not permit him to go on. Nathan does go on, for the rest of his book, making dissociations that seldom have any more validity than their effectiveness as a wisecrack disguised as an epigram. Is the subject the New Humanists? [New Humanism was a literary-critical movement in the United States (between 1910 and 1930) that sought to recapture the moral quality of past civilizations in an age of industrialization, materialism, and relativism.] Their motives were really quite transparent. Down-at-the-heels young men, chiefly college instructors, they glared enviously at the fat plenty of men like Theodore Dreiser, James Branch Cabell, and Ludwig Lewisohn. The whole movement becomes clear when we picture Gorham B. Munson looking in at the window of the room in Baltimore where H. L. Mencken plays his Viennese waltzes and sips his magnum of Niersteiner wine.

But this happens to be the testament of a dramatic critic, and accordingly references to the titles of plays and their authors are not infrequent. One whole section is given over to a rapid-motion drill parade of all the dramatists of any note who have appeared in this country in the lasttwenty years. All these dramatists with the exception of Eugene O'Neill are so many pins that Nathan bowls over with his long, strong arm. They are rather so many names rattled off with brief reprimand by some hurried and irate sergeant major. For the New Playwrights group, which included such dissimilar talents as Michael Gold and John Dos Passos, the command is brief and unconditional: Dismissed. If one knows nothing of this group, such a criticism is too arbitrary to be really helpful; if one does know something about it, the absence of discrimination is annoying.

Now and then one is rewarded by a remark that implies a solid knowledge of dramaturgy and an ability to weigh the ideological assumptions of a drama. But on the whole the survey reveals no more than this critic's almost total reliance on cataloguing for emphasis, his fondness for declamation, and his habit of unsubstantiated generalization. All these traits derive from the theory, stated early in the book, that the only worthwhile criticism is destructive criticism. Here is room for inquiry. By destructive criticism Nathan means destruction clearly enough, but does he mean criticism? When a household has smallpox the doctor does truly tack a card on the door reading "Smallpox." But is the critic's function not a little different from that of the doctor? And does not the proper exercise of that function call for the use of some more revelatory expletives than junk, tripe, claptrap, rubbish, and hocus-pocus?

The difficulty is that the sole alternative recognized by Nathan is an excess of praise that is equally as far from criticism as his own special brand of annihilation. The difficulty is that he has mistaken "favorable" criticism for constructive criticism. The function of the critic, of the authentic critic, has never been to pass arbitrary judgments of good or bad. On what ultimately would such judgments be founded? Either on a set body of canons, which Nathan would himself be the first to deny, or on the vacillations of personal taste, which have no better authority than the particular sensibility of the writer at a particular moment. Of the two possible views, Nathan's is apparently nearer the first; his writing consists of the adventures of his soul among masterpieces, or at least nightmares; his allegiance is with the sage of the Cyrenaic academy [a reference to the hedonistic school of philosophy founded ca. 400 B.C. by Aristippus the Elder of Cyrene, which holds that pleasure is the highest good and that virtue is to be equated with the ability to enjoy]. As in philosophical outlook he is a professed hedonist, so in criticism he is concerned only with the partly emotional, partly intellectual satisfactions of his ego. The question now is whether hedonism is the proper state of mind for a critic.

Everything does in the end rest on the sensibility; but sensibility can express itself, as it has first refined itself, only through the analytical powers of the intelligence. The real function of the critic, his true "constructive" merit, consists in the revelation in intelligible terms of what he has experienced—in the theater, of all that he has seen and heard. There can be no relaxation of his intelligence as a critic any more than there can be any lessening of his response as a spectator. It is only in this way that the critic has his role, that he justifies himself to those who turn to him for illumination, guidance, or simple information.

Because richness of sensibility and fine intelligence are so seldom allied, there are perhaps not more than two or three dramatic critics in America who even partially fulfill the role—and George Jean Nathan is notably not one of them.

In the absence of intelligible analysis, Nathan has given us erudition (nomenclature) and a style that is compounded largely of a cataloguing of the latter and of the names of certain Central European beverages in the original. There is also his undoubted political vigor, an attribute more pertinent to the journalist than to the critic, who is necessarily too occupied with his object to be distracted by such outside matters as censorship, prohibition, and happiness.

9. "Symbolism as a Generating Force in Contemporary Literature" (1931)

Axel's Castle, by Edmund Wilson

When the introductory chapter of this work first appeared in the *New Republic* [March 20, 1929], it was titled "A Preface to Modern Literature," and both from its title and content it was apparent that Edmund Wilson's purpose was to lay the groundwork for a more extended critical survey of contemporary letters. The general title he has now chosen for the collection of his essays as a whole is less transparent, but it has the distinct virtue of creating at once the special atmosphere of the French literary movement that he considers the proper starting point for any approach to modern literature. For *Axel's Castle* calls to mind the ancient and mysterious habitation of Count Axel of Auersberg, the hero of Villiers de l'Isle Adam's *Axel* [1890]— the fantastic prose poem, in dramatic form, that gave expression not only to the aesthetic idealism of the French symbolist poets of the last century, but also to the attitude behind each of the six contemporary writers whom Wilson discusses in the present study.

The symbolist movement in France, beginning as early as the 1870s, was a partly deliberate, partly unconscious reaction against the scientific temper of the mid-nineteenth century mind as reflected in such literary groups as the naturalists in fiction and the Parnassians in poetry. It corresponded very closely to the Romantic movement that had swept over European literature at the beginning of the century—a movement that had in its way registered protest against the scientific rationalism of the seventeenth and eighteenth centuries. As the Romantics had rebelled against the ideas brought into fashion by the rise of physics and mathematics, so now the symbolists sought to break through the distorted patterns of experience built up by the mechanistic philosophy that had grown out of biological experimentation in the nineteenth century.

The term symbolism itself is probably incapable of exact definition, and in the course of Wilson's study it is used to include so many things that it seems almost to depart from its original meaning. As a technique symbolism represents the effort to communicate, by means of a unique personal language, ideas, feelings, and sensations more faithfully than they are rendered through the conventional and universal language of ordinary literature. The function of this language is "to intimate things rather than state them plainly"; it depends on suggestion rather than statement. The archetype of the symbolist poet is Stéphane Mallarmé, the superb technician of French verse whose imagery was so personal that few people in his lifetime were able to understand his work any better than the later writing of James Joyce is understood in our own day.

From Mallarmé (who was influenced by Edgar Allan Poe) was derived the method behind the early Celtic symbolism of William Butler Yeats; and Paul Valéry may be considered as a disciple of Mallarmé who has, in the perfection of his verse, refined on the master. T. S. Eliot has openly acknowledged his debt to two other earlier symbolists—Tristan Corbière and Jules Laforgue. It is when Wilson attempts to fit writers like Marcel Proust and Joyce into his scheme, prose writers depending less directly on imagery for their communication, that he is forced to extend the application of his term. Here, symbols, with their "multiplied associations," are also supposed to include characters, situations, places, motifs, patterns of behavior. In other words, the term is applied no longer only to a particular way of using words, but to a particular attitude toward experience as a whole.

In his chapter on Gertrude Stein, Wilson seems to contradict the assumption that symbolism, as a distinct and self-conscious literary movement, owed its primary character to its use of words for their suggestive power. By quoting extracts from expository prose by Yeats, George Bernard Shaw, and finally Stein, he illustrates convincingly that all words, even those in the most rational prose of a Courts-Martial Guide—those directed solely toward "sense"—owe their effectiveness to the same power of suggestiveness. The difference between Stein and Shaw therefore becomes basically a technical one: a difference of syntax and of the order of selected images.

If this is as true as it seems, if all words actually "intimate rather than state," how can one place symbolism in a separate aesthetic category?

The real identity of symbolism would then seem to consist less in its verbal technique than in certain other features of its program—most notably, as Wilson so clearly shows in its over-development of the individualistic conception of the writer's role, its detachment of literature not only from social values alone, but from human action itself. This would have the advantage of distinguishing it as surely from Romanticism as from the more opposite tendencies of classicism and naturalism.

Wilson's method of treating the separate subjects of his essays is not one of unqualified appreciation: his judgments are attained after a careful exposition of their works and an analysis that is rigorous and often profound. His effort to differentiate sharply between different work by a single man, as in the case of Valéry, even leads him at times to an excessive severity. In general, Wilson brings to his problems an intelligence that is alert, informed, and catholic to a degree rarely found in contemporary criticism. He writes in a style whose ideal of absolute lucidity has undoubtedly entailed many sacrifices in a writer who is also a poet and a novelist. His manner of dealing with reputations and ideas that still invite hostility in certain quarters is gracefully disarming.

It is of course natural that in a work of this scope one should not be in complete accord with all the judgments stated nor even with the approach followed in several instances. Although Wilson is excellent in his résumé of T. S. Eliot's poetic and critical development up to *The Waste Land* [1922], he is less dependable in his interpretation of the later phases of the poetry and thought. The sections on Eliot's *Ash Wednesday* [1930] and the chapter on Gertrude Stein are the least successful in the book. Despite the remarks on Stein's humor, the author of *Tender Buttons* [1914] remains at the end "the great pyramidal Buddha of Jo Davidson's statue [of Stein, 1923]." The failure to relate Stein's aesthetic to the system of Bergsonian metaphysics on which it rests makes the discussion as superficial as it is indefinite.

The structural analysis of Proust's great epic [*Remembrance of Things Past* (1913–27)] is unquestionably the best yet available in English; but the centering of the critical problem in Proust's individual psychology is too facile to be useful and compares unfavorably with the metaphysical approach of continental critics like Ramon Fernandez and Ernst Robert Curtius. Quite the most satisfactory and original essay in the volume is the one on Yeats, in which Wilson has not only successfully identified this poet with the direct tradition of French symbolism but also, for the first time, provided an orderly account of his development up to his position as one of the few truly universal poets of our time.

In the last chapter, there is something like a stocktaking of contemporary literature, with a consideration of its possible directions in the near future. There are, according to Wilson, two alternative courses to follow—Axel's or Rimbaud's. The hero of Villiers's *Axel* stands for all that increasing individualism, that cultivation of one's private fantasies in the face of contemporary realities, that incarceration in one's own dark tower which has characterized all the successors of symbolism. Both in his writing and in his career Arthur Rimbaud suggests the second alternative—the escape from twentieth-century industrialism and democracy, the cult of the primitive and the childlike. It is Wilson's conviction that neither of these directions is possible or desirable and that we must look for some combination of the symbolist vision with the naturalistic sense of fact.

But to those writers whom he has discussed he believes we owe a tremendous debt, for "they have yet succeeded in effecting in literature a revolution analogous to that which has taken place in science and philosophy, and they have revealed to the imagination a new flexibility and freedom." Edmund Wilson does not, however, undertake to prescribe what we should do with this new freedom; he does not offer any cohesive program; his final faith is in the "untried, unsuspected possibilities of human thought and art."

10. "Henry James and Young Writers" (1931)

I

It is perhaps another evidence of his genius that Henry James, like certain other great writers of the past, has come to mean something different to each of the successive literary generations that have taken up his work. What James meant to the readers of and the *Atlantic* in the 1880s and 1890s, what he meant to the generation of H. G. Wells, or to the generation of T. S. Eliot and Ezra Pound, was probably not any of the things that he means, or may come to mean, to the generation in which we are naturally much interested—the present one. So abundant are the implications of his work that he is capable of being read—or misread—to suit the needs of widely different classes of readers, of distinct periods of literary taste; capable also of being "used," in a very real sense, as Shakespeare was used by the German Romantics of the eighteenth century, or as Charles Baudelaire is now being used by a whole wing of contemporary French and American poets. Of what possible "use" in this sense may James prove to be to the present generation of novelists? What lesson may this formidable and often-disputed master offer to the inheritors of his craft in our time? If his example includes anything of value special to them, if his strength corresponds to any of their numerous weaknesses, he should be appropriated at once, reinstated in the direct current of our letters.

It happens, moreover, that James is in immediate need of some sort of reinstatement at the moment. He remains suspended in that vague limbo of disrepute to which the last generation of Freudian critics so often consigned their victims. He is easily the most tolerated author of his size in modern literature. The elaborate exception that Van Wyck Brooks performed in *The Pilgrimage of Henry James* [1925] was simply the final blow in the long catastrophe of his reputation. For more than forty years James had been chiefly read by people who admired him for hardly any more palpable reason than the vague penumbra of gentility that surrounded his pages. The close of his life was rendered positively unhappy (as we know from his letters) by the ribald humors of a new order that dismissed him as nothing short of a pompous old fool. Wells's brutal parody in *Boon* [1915] served to lay the ghost for pre-war England. All that remained for Brooks in 1925 was to dispose of James in a more comprehensive fashion and in terms that should be more effective for the period. What Brooks did to James's reputation, however, is important, for the semi-ridiculous, semi-tragic figure that he created is the most popular conception of the novelist at the moment.

For Brooks, it will be recalled, James offered nothing more nor less than a case history. Here was an example of an American who had sacrificed not only his promise as an artist but also his identity as an individual in the fruitless effort to adjust himself to an alien culture. All the habits of James's mind—"the caution, the ceremoniousness, the baffled curiosity, the nervousness and constant self-communion, the fear of committing himself"—are traceable to the long years he spent in England, where he had never been anything but "an enchanted exile in a museum-world." A self-conscious guest in a house where he had never been at home, James reflected even in his style "the evasiveness, the hesitancy, the scrupulosity of an habitually embarrassed man." The diagnosis becomes steadily more emphatic toward the end. In James's later writings, Brooks can discern no more than "the confused reveries of an invalid child." It is as if the author of *Roderick Hudson* [1875] and *The Portrait of a Lady* [1881] had developed at the last into a kind of "impassioned geometer—or, shall we say, some vast arachnid of art, pouncing upon the tiny air-blown particle and wrapping it round and round." What stands out most remarkably today in this analysis is a single statement that throws ever so much more light on Brooks than it does on Henry James: "What interested him (in his novels) was not the figures but their relations, the relations that alone make pawns significant."

To Brooks and his generation, as such a remark implies, an interest in relations was almost certain evidence of sterility in a writer. To concentrate on relations was to be faced immediately with the problems of value on which they hinged, and to betray an interest in any such problems was to be rendered more than a little suspect at the time. It was genuinely difficult for Brooks to conceive how a writer of James's manifest intelligence could have considered the relations of his "figures" more important than the movements of pawns in a game. It was difficult because it was almost impossible for his generation to recognize the existence of values or the part they usually play in vital literary creation. Even a game, it was forgotten, must have its rules; and for a game to be properly absorbing, for either player or spectator, the values assigned the rules must be accepted temporarily at least, with something like seriousness. For James himself the rules did exist, and he accepted them with a passionate seriousness. Before ever they were apprehended by the mind, they were *felt*, and with enough intensity of feeling to provide the center, the very foundation of his artistic task. The "pawns" of his game, however inanimate they may sometimes seem in other respects, are always alive, even violently alive, in that portion of their being which James chose to explore and represent, because he believed it to be the richest and "most finely contributive" [*Notes on Novelists* (1914)] of all—the conscience.

By such a term as conscience one need not understand anything more definite than James himself ever intended by the term—that region of the mind, that area of our habitual mental activity, which is reserved for the recognition and solution of moral conflicts. At least to the extent that his "figures" do, every one of them, function in this region are they worthy of being called *characters*—or the label is without meaning. Often, it is true, the relations, situations, or patterns in which the somewhat special experience of their creator involves them are so unique or complex, so extremely tenuous, as to make them seem to respire a little outside the usual zone of verisimilitude. But the comparison with a geometer is inaccurate if it refers to anything but the hard and luminous detachment with which a given intellectual terrain is surveyed. For Henry James the conscience that controlled the actions of his personages was something real and concrete; the values that determined for Fleda Vetch [*The Spoils of Poynton* (1896)] and

Lambert Strether [*The Ambassadors* (1903)] and Milly Theale [*The Wings of the Dove* (1902)] the solution of their delicately attenuated problems were for him *true* values. For James's reader, however, who is primarily concerned with the interest that these problems afford, with their possible aesthetic result, there is no such obligation to accept these particular values as true. For him it is simply necessary to accept their reality in the minds of the characters, to imagine, if only for the time being, that they *might* be considered true, for the sake of the satisfaction that their representation provides in an orderly executed work of art.

For various reasons, this was an effort of the imagination that few in the last generation showed themselves able or willing to make. Perhaps the chief reason was the particular psychological absolutism of the time, which submerged personality beneath that plane of conscious judgment that for James and others before him had constituted the real domain of character. The belief in character that had sustained him was not recognized because it was not understood; and his fervid explorations could only be explained as the mystifying vagaries of someone who had ventured too far outside the normal bounds of experience. He could be accounted for only as a kind of exquisite monster, as the victim of some fundamental lesion of personality or— as the critics would have it—as a psychological "case." The formula was ready at hand and it was rich in possibilities of embroidery. Everything in James's mind and work—his characters, his themes, his form and style even—became immediately clear when it was once remembered that he was an American who had spent most of his adult years in Europe.

Whatever truth there may be in this formula as applied to other native American writers who have forsworn their country for the warm securities of European culture, one may question its validity as a total explanation of all that characterized Henry James as a man and an artist. Some of the more superficial biases of his mind, some of the minor idiosyncrasies of his style, can doubtless be traced to the influence of his prolonged residence in England. But one might show the equivalent consequences on his contemporary William Dean Howells, of a migration from Ohio to Boston at about the same period. Unquestionably also, in his choice of backgrounds, characters, and the situations in which he placed them, James was affected for better or worse by the particular foreign milieu in which he happened to pass the greater part of his life. If certain subjects, like that of American "innocence" caught in the toils of European duplicity, recur constantly throughout his work, it is merely because these subjects repeated themselves so often in the course of his experience, and therefore became the most familiar patterns of reality available to him. To complain of these subjects, however, on the grounds that they are too narrow, or too special, or too refined, is illegitimate. It is to decline to play what James himself called "the fair critical game with an author," which is to grant him his postulates. "His subject is what is given him—given him by influences, by a process, with which we have nothing to do; since what art, what revelation, can ever really make such a mystery, such a passage as the private life of the intellect, adequately traceable for us? His treatment of it, on the other hand, is what he actively gives; and it is with what he gives that we are critically concerned" [*Notes on Novelists*].

Behind and above everything else was Henry James's mind, with its special quality, endowment, and direction. What is all too seldom realized, for it would alone discredit Van Wyck Brooks's thesis, is that the main set and direction of that mind were already well established long before James ever made his decision to settle in England. Already he had formulated, in a review of Walt Whitman written in 1865, what was to be the principle of his artistic creed for the whole of his career: "To be positive, one must have something to say; to be positive requires reason, labor, and art; and art requires above all things a suppression of one's self to an idea" [*Views and Reviews* (1908)]. The real problem before him in those early wander-years was not the quest of some place that might change or modify the native bent of his mind, but one that should offer to his mind greater opportunities for play, a richer field in which to grow and expand, a more *plausible* background for the working-out of his particular "idea." It was a problem of nutrition. And it was only after a trial-and-error process—for there was the important experiment of his year in Paris—that he hit upon the country that seemed most suitable to his purpose.

It might quite as easily be shown that the truth is the exact opposite of what Brooks and others have contended: that for James residence in England, rather than being a source of sterility and corruption, was an indispensable condition of fulfillment. Since these critics had made up their minds not to occupy themselves with his work, with what as an artist he had "given," they might equally well have considered the reverse-side of the coin: What would have happened to James if he had turned to the society that awaited him in the Boston or New York of the late nineteenth century? Would he, with his peculiarly refined sensibility, have escaped an ordeal less intense than that which Brooks has elsewhere traced in the career of Mark Twain? Indeed, there was hardly any means of salvation for the artist in Brooks's scheme of nineteenth-century America. Upon further reflection Brooks might well have concluded that in one sense there is never any salvation for the artist—

at any time or in any place. His only chance of fulfillment is to be as good an artist as he can under the conditions of his time and the limitations of his own temperament. But such a view would lead instantly to an entirely different kind of criticism. One would have to concentrate more directly on the study and evaluation of a writer's work.

II

The specific question that I set out to examine was in what sense and to what extent may Henry James's example have any special meaning for the novelists of our generation. How, we may inquire, may he show them the way to make their work more deeply and broadly *interesting*?

For the sole obligation of the novel, its one excuse for being, as James insisted, is that it be interesting. The question that such a demand leaves in the mind is, of course, what, properly speaking, constitutes the interest of a novel? Fortunately, in his essays, prefaces, and letters James has provided us with a complete and lucid exposition of his own view of the problem. There is life obviously, which is the novel-writer's material, and there is art, which consists of the special use that he makes of his material. Life is common, inexhaustible, chaotic—a "splendid waste," to use James's fine phrase [preface to *The Spoils of Poynton*]. It is art alone that gives it beauty and meaning, through the form and expression with which the creative mind endows it, for "expression is creation and makes the reality" [*Notes on Novelists*]. To be interesting, therefore, a novel must give or lend something to the "splendid waste" that is life. That something is "composition," the design that the artist makes out of the scattered and unchecked flow of his impressions and responses. Without such design the novel would have no identity as an art form, no value as a projection of reality, and hence no meaning to the mind or the imagination. "I hold that interest may be, *must be*, exquisitely made and created, and that if we don't make it, we who undertake to, nobody and nothing will make it for us," James wrote to H. G. Wells [in 1915] at the close of his life. And in the same letter he makes an even more complete avowal of his belief in the unique and absolute value of the artistic process: "It is art that *makes* life, makes importance, for our consideration and application of these things, and I know of no substitute whatever for the force and beauty of its process."

The various alternatives to this view of the novelist's special role and function are necessarily vague and contradictory. There are, for example, the exponents of "life"—of life *tout court*, of life at any cost.

What precisely, however, do these people mean? If the novel is to be classified at all, it is as an art form, and if art means anything it means the process by which the materials of life are arranged and fused into a unity. It is only through its unity that the meaning and value of a given work of art are to be discovered. A novel with insufficient evidence of unity represents mere arbitrariness, or ineptitude, or the surrender of the mind to the rich disorder of nature. It is possible, James admitted, to reproduce life—its substance and even its quality, its imponderable multiplicity—but without art ("composition") the result would be devoid of meaning. As he put the matter, "There may in its absence be life, incontestably, as *The Newcomes* [1855, William Thackeray] has life, as *The Three Musketeers* [1844, Alexandre Dumas] and *War and Peace* [1867, Leo Tolstoy] have it; but what do such large loose baggy monsters, with their queer elements of the accidental and the arbitrary, artistically *mean*. . . . There is life and life, and as waste is only life sacrificed and thereby prevented from 'counting,' I delight in a deep-breathing economy and an organic form" [preface to *The Tragic Muse* (1890)].

Yet it would be wholly wrong to interpret such a statement as merely another expression of the "art for art's sake" doctrine that was so loudly articulate in Henry James's own lifetime and to which he objected from the beginning. While James was firm in his recognition of aesthetic values, he was definitely not an aesthete—that is to say, one for whom the means is also the end. For James even the patterns of art owe their initial suggestion to reality. Even composition depends on the existence of elements already present in life, elements capable of being drawn together with greater tightness, concentration, and beauty through the artistic process. Form is not therefore something distinct from life, but the arrangement of something already there, or at least there for the artist's specially trained observation. Unlike the real aesthete, James distrusted all constructions of the mind that did not derive their parallel somewhere in experience. "Never can a composition of this sort," he writes of *The Ambassadors*, "have sprung straighter from a dropped grain of suggestion, and never can that grain, developed, overgrown, and smothered, have yet lurked more in the mass as an independent particle" [from this novel's preface]. And surely *The Ambassadors* is a good enough example of his later, more complex and "geometrical" style! Whatever were the limitations of his experience, his brain was never, like Stéphane Mallarmé's, haunted by the memory of azure skies shut out, never drained of content *comme le pot de fard gisant au pied d'un mur* ["like the pot of paint at the foot of a wall," from the 1864 poem by Mallarmé titled "The Azure"].

But what, since I have only mentioned them, are the elements of those patterns that life is made to assume in the imagination of the artist? Since they can be observed, they must be objective; and objective patterns of human life can be built on one thing only, action. Action, to James, is therefore the soul of the novel. All else is subordinate—description, "local color," incidental ideas, everything in fact not strictly related to the progressive explication of the central narrative core. At the same time the highest interest cannot be created by action alone, that is, action considered for its own sake. If incident is the illustration of character, character itself is the determination of incident. What is always really interesting is character, and that can only be fully understood through an imaginative reconstruction of the motives that precede action in the mind. The external patterns of life—and this is commonplace enough—have significance only insofar as we are made acquainted with the complex, and never to be wholly apprehended, background of motives behind them.

The moment we speak of motives we are headed straight into the whole field of difficulties whose attempted solution afforded the passion of Henry James's task as an imaginative artist. These are, in a word, all those difficulties that are set up by the necessity of the individual to adjust himself to some moral order. The most interesting patterns of art are in fact just those that the novelist is able to construct out of the often wasted, unrealized possibilities thrown up by these predicaments in life. Motives exist in all their confused and multiple variety; sometimes, but rarely, they fall into design of their own accord; it is the novelist's special business to see that what is thus accidental is always achieved. His business is with the motives behind conduct because they are what make fiction, as they make life, difficult—and, so, interesting. For that reason, James exclaimed at "the moral timidity of the usual English novelist, with his (or with her) aversion to face the difficulties with which on every side the treatment of reality bristles" ["The Art of Fiction" (1884)]. To shun these difficulties was in fact to miss the peculiar excitement on which, in the last analysis, everything depended.

To imply solution of any absolute sort is of course to assume a standard, a criterion to which in the end all problems may be referred. Here it will have to be enough to say that by a moral order, James understood some body of felt values existing through one or another process of absorption in the individual's mind. For the individual's adjustment to be imperative these values must not only exist, but exist in a strong and potent way. Without this assumption of values as something felt, one cannot make the assumption of art; for one cannot otherwise account for the extreme intensity of those conflicts around which the fiction artist erects his constructions. Nor can one explain the quite real importance that these imagined conflicts take on in the reader's interest. Against some background of felt values, therefore, every individual conflict must be set; and on some such individual conflict the scheme of every novel must rest.

In these terms, plot, for instance, becomes more easily definable: it is the abstract curve of the moral drama being enacted in the mind or conscience of a character. It is quantitatively all that development, growth, and expansion of "the dropped grain of suggestion" which has excited in the first place the novelist's passion for difficulties. In the same way, it may be seen how aesthetic values are necessarily subordinated to other values anterior to them in reality. Subordinated is perhaps hardly the word—for the two kinds of values are really so identified as to be altogether indistinguishable. The aesthetic pattern *is* the moral pattern—or the beginning, middle, and end of all that has taken place in the active conscience of the individual.

III

Unlike almost all of his fellow novelists in English, Henry James served a deliberate apprenticeship during which he learned everything he could about the nature and function of his craft. Before writing as he did write (for, once established, his style and method progressed only in refinement), he had surveyed the field, measured the hazards, and envisaged all the possible alternatives. In his own lifetime he had the opportunity to study all the later mutations of the novel-form—the English Victorians (with their "fluid puddings" [from a 1912 letter to Hugh Walpole]) and the Russians, French realism and naturalism, and two whole epochs of pure aestheticism. During his memorable year in France, he learned so much about what the novel as novel might be that a contemporary French critic like André Gide finds his work too much in the native tradition to captivate his taste. But he also learned, from Gustave Flaubert especially, the ultimate emptiness of even the most perfect work of art that pretended to an absolute moral indifference. From the Goncourts [Edmond and Jules] he learned that mere *décor*, no matter how sumptuous, was a poor substitute indeed for motivated human action. (Thus, years afterwards, writing *The Spoils of Poynton*, he avoids offering any detailed description of the furniture and other objects that are actually the source of the drama.) Most of all, from Émile Zola he learned that art and science were two different quantities, and that art at least was a quantity that was not to be amassed through perspiration alone. Of the group as a whole his indictment is significant: "The conviction that held them together was the conviction that art and morality are two perfectly different things and that the former has no more to do with the latter than it has with astronomy or embryology" ["Ivan Turgenev" (1884)].

Because he had eliminated all these alternatives, James may be said to have escaped all the blunders and excesses to which the novel after him was condemned. He himself could hardly have foreseen that so long after his pointed remark about Zola—"if he had as much light as energy, his results would be of the highest value" ["The Art of Fiction"]—the same process of burrowing in the dark would be resumed by Theodore Dreiser. Hardly less could he have guessed that aestheticism would one day fade away into the pallid *fabliaux* of James Branch Cabell and the variegated pastiche of Thornton Wilder. But James must certainly have realized that naturalism carried far enough was bound to result in a subjectivism that should be opposed by its very nature to the traditions of an ordered art. He was certainly aware that to desert the living world of action was to descend to a region where anything resembling order was impossible. Did he not refer to impressionism like that of Gabriele D'Annunzio as "the open door to the trivial" [*Notes on Novelists*]? Impressionism in our day is called by a different name but the Jamesian objection is still valid. Psychoanalysis in fiction is simply impressionism supported by a method; and impressionism in the novel has meant the same abandonment of character at the level where its possibilities for the artist are most interesting. For James as an artist, order, the assumption of order, was essential; and to submerge beneath the plane where order was possible was merely to renounce one's aspirations to the primordial chaos, to become lost in the "splendid waste."

The real difficulty in our time has of course been values. The old ones are no longer capable of generating enough conviction in actual living to justify their continued representation in fiction, and the new have been found uniformly insufficient. Here, it must be granted, James can hardly be expected to offer any more immediate succor than has been thus far offered by contemporary life. But as he has already revealed the necessity and the exact function of values in narrative art, he can now do much to prevent a certain confusion in regard to the novelist's proper relation to them.

Nothing in James's own example or declaration, let it be said, allows us to understand that it is ever the business of the novelist to establish values. As he assumed them from the society of the period in which he lived, so must those who follow after him in the path of the novel assume them from the moral consciousness of their own time. The contemporary writer can only hope to discover in the complex welter of our time those standards of judgment that emerge with sufficient strength and frequency to stand the test of being submitted to the artistic process. He must search, observe, experiment, and then make his test with the almost certain prospect of defeat for a considerable time to come. It may be that for some years he will have to be content to operate without nearly so cohesive a body of felt values as obtained in the past. He may be compelled to devote himself to the rapid atrophy and decline of those values in the present; to the issues caused by their dramatic refusal to be displaced; or to the equally dramatic effort of those new values that shall gradually assert themselves in the future. Any one of these courses would be more truly creative, according to the Jamesian point of view, than the blind appropriation of values that are no longer felt because they are no longer sufficiently alive.

IV

What the writers of our time can learn from Henry James is not anything distinctly represented in his achievement; nothing implicit in his style or method, which are both too personal ever to be duplicated; not his "philosophy," not even the assumptions about human character that were for him the source of so much eloquence. What they can learn from him is the deepest meaning of the phrase "the integrity of the artist." He can show them to what an essential degree the artist is dependent on something anterior to himself in life; how the truest values of art are never to be dissociated from the most potent values of the world about him; and how, although the particular values of the one are always in one sense relative to those of the other, the single constant in the whole relationship is the fact of the artistic impulse. And as a last check on the possible interpretation that all this implies a certain dangerous relativity of values for art, James has written [in "The Art of Fiction"]: "There is one point at which the moral sense and the artistic sense lie very close together; that is in the light of the very obvious truth that the deepest quality of a work of art will always be the quality of the mind of the producer . . . that seems to me an axiom which, for the artist in fiction, will cover all needful moral ground."

11. "Rimbaud, 'The Literaturicide'" (1931)
A Season in Hell: The Life of Arthur Rimbaud,
by Jean-Marie Carré

If there has ever been any question as to whether it is Arthur Rimbaud's work or his life that supplies the clue to his increasing hold on the modern imagination, the appearance of this first complete biography in English should remove all doubt. At the moment no full and satisfactory translation of Rimbaud's work is available in English. Moreover, his poetry is not very well known to those able to read French literature in the original, and there is good reason to believe that it is not well enough known even to those who use his name as a rallying cry for one or another disturbance in contemporary letters. If this biography will find a ready audience in the United States, therefore, it will be because of his life—his life, which was written in characters so bold and terrible that it is comprehensible in every tongue.

The truth is that Rimbaud's career provides one of the great modern stories—perhaps the great modern story, if one takes into account the number and range of conflicts involved, the completeness of its pattern, the arresting implications of its theme. Rimbaud realized within his thirty-seven years of violent existence all the possibilities of the modern imagination. Not only poet, seer, and prophet, but also scientist, explorer, and man of affairs, he comes nearest to the ideal of the "universal man" than anyone since the Renaissance. In the past sixty years many have adventured into the world of ideas, and as many others into the actual world, but in this period no single individual has penetrated as far into both worlds as Rimbaud. For this reason he has become a figure of myth, supplying in the outline of his life an illustration and a warning.

Perhaps Rimbaud is most often remembered as the boy prodigy who completed his poetic career at the age of nineteen. By that age this tall, unkempt, ill-mannered youth from the provinces (to quote his biographer) "had passed through the entire literary evolution of modern times." Having outgrown the Romantic social and political ideologies of his epoch almost in childhood, he soon relinquished ideas for pure sensations, and through "a long, immense, and systematic derangement of all the senses" sought to make himself a "seer." What he wrote he preferred to call, not poems, but "illuminations," brief and hieratic notations of that unknown whose secrets he pierced by a kind of organized technique of hallucination:

I accustomed myself to plain hallucination: quite frankly I used to see a mosque in place of a factory, a school of drums made by angels, carriages on the road of heaven, a salon at the bottom of a lake; monsters, mysteries; a ballad title raised up horrors before me. Then I explained my magical sophistries with the hallucination of words. I ended by finding the disorder of my mind sacred. [*A Season in Hell* (1873)]

Either before or after his unfortunate encounter with Paul Verlaine in Brussels, which ended in prison and disgrace for the elder poet, Rimbaud wrote his farewell to literature in *A Season in Hell*. This astonishing document is usually referred to as a work of literature like any other; but in the sense of an ordered, self-conscious composition it scarcely belongs in the field of literature at all. It is rather, as Stéphane Mallarmé said, a unique adventure in the history of the mind. It is better considered either as the molten stuff of literature not yet crystalized into form, as the innovation of a form that transcends literature. Certainly, in the course of this work Rimbaud renounces literature along with all the other "chimeras" of Western civilization; he is a declared literaturicide. "No more words!" he cries; and elsewhere:

I have created all festivals, all triumphs, all dramas. I have tried to invent new flowers, new stars, new flesh, new tongues. I have hoped to acquire supernatural powers. Very well, then. I must bury my imagination and my memories. [*A Season in Hell*]

A Season in Hell is also Rimbaud's definitive farewell to Europe and everything for which it stood in his mind. The disorder of mind he had come to find sacred ended in this youth of nineteen in a crisis of nerves that could only be resolved through some tremendous effort of will. *A Season* is itself the first-hand record of the struggle. Neither Jean-Marie Carré nor anyone else has been perfectly clear as to what was the exact nature of the redemption Rimbaud held out for himself. Paul Claudel has read into certain lines a savage mysticism, implying a return to Christian dogma. For Carré the work ends with a "rejection of God." There have been some interesting variations in the printed texts that may one day assist in clearing up the difficulty.

Carré's biography surpasses all others in its information on the later period of Rimbaud's life. It recounts in great detail his wanderings over Europe before quitting it forever, his labors as foreman of a quarry in Cyprus, as trader and merchant in Abyssinia, his discoveries as an explorer of new trade routes across the desert. We are grateful for the documented accounts of his dealings with King Menelik [of Ethiopia], of his expeditions into Somaliland and Ogaden, and of his establishment of the route across the desert now followed by the Ethiopian railway. While it is not possible to relate even the baldest summary of Rimbaud's life without evoking some degree of interest, Carré has written an admirable book. His is an unusually impartial and well-informed presentation of the central facts in the story. If one has an objection it is to the almost unrelieved heightening of the material, which is the more offensive in that it is unnecessary. The result is a frequent aroma of the spurious, as, for example, in the treatment of the legend that a girl accompanied Rimbaud on his first flight to Paris. Carré makes too much of an incident that is apocryphal at best. Similarly, one regrets an excess of sentimental commentary in the description of Rimbaud's last illness and death. The perfect Rimbaud biography remains to be written: one that shall present the facts with the same absence of facile emotional bias, the same brutal concern for realities, which we associate with the subject.

In the book's preface Carré's translators, Hannah and Matthew Josephson, refer to a "Rimbaud revival" in a way that impels one to inquire whether there has ever been a decline in this poet's influence since his adoption by the symbolists in the 1880s. As a patron saint of this school, his presence is felt in the technique employed by later followers of the tradition as unlike as Claudel and Paul Valéry. The surrealists , although their apotheosis has been the most vocal, can hardly be said to have "revived" Rimbaud. As Valéry's is said to have remarked, "We have all been feeding upon Rimbaud, these forty years." At the same time there is a tendency to exaggerate this influence, especially on contemporary writing in English. An acute critic like Hansell Baugh [who wrote for the *New Republic* and the journal *The Bookman*] may suggest that the "interior monologue" used by James Joyce and other contemporaries, although borrowed from Édouard Dujardin, really derives from the style of Rimbaud's *Illuminations* [1874]. But the direct influence of Rimbaud on modern English and American poetry has been slight. The pattern of style set for one whole department of modern verse by T. S. Eliot derives not from Rimbaud but from his contemporary, Jules Laforgue. If Eliot, as a young student of poetic form in Paris, had read Rimbaud instead of Laforgue, it is possible that one whole tradition of modern poetry would be different.

Unfortunately, the translations offered in the appendix are not enough to give an adequate impression of Arthur Rimbaud's literary stature. Like Charles Baudelaire, he must be read in his entirety if his real significance, which is that of a total spiritual development and progress, is to be appreciated. Rimbaud cannot be understood through a few isolated fragments. Perhaps one of the chief consequences of this biography will be a recognition of the immediate need of a complete version of his work in English.

12. "The New Intellectual" (1932)

I

For more than ten years the American intellectual has been gazing apathetically into his soul; now he seems ready to act. Indeed, for some time now one has been aware of a gradual shift of tactics along the intellectual front. That the intelligentsia have become weary, that their shibboleths must seem a little frayed even to themselves, we have long suspected, but we have been no more certain than they as to the direction in which the intellectual weathervane of the next few years would finally choose to point. Of one thing only we have felt reasonably sure and that is that weariness, being a static state, will hardly be allowed to endure in such an energetic nation as our own—for it is of America in particular that we are speaking. Apathy is not a part of our national character. If the intellectuals have fallen into an apathetic state, all the habits and traditions of our country are in favor of their doing something about it without delay. The question of what precisely they are going to do about it, or at least one large section of them, has quite recently approached closer to an answer.

The 1920s perished amid a carnage of dead enthusiasms, mutilated ideals, and exploded loyalties; the twenties are being buried with little pomp and slight evidence of respect by the still younger generation that has arrived soberly on the scene. Disappointment, satiety, and chaos— these are the heritage with which the new generation has been left. One is reminded of John Dryden's fine lines on a similar occasion:

All, all of a piece throughout!
Thy chase had a beast in view;
Thy wars brought nothing about;
Thy lovers were all untrue.
'Tis well an old age is out,
And time to begin a new. ["The Secular Masque" (1700)]

Bohemianism as a cult is at present so dead that it has become a theme for those poets and writers who are peculiarly affected by the nostalgia of the past. Greenwich Village in the spring is little more than a memory in the minds of middle-aged poets (and poetesses) now teaching Milton to reluctant sophomores at the state universities, or running for Congress in their home district, or tilling the soil in Tennessee. Romany Marie's in the Village is but a pallid replica of its old self [Marie Marchand, known as Romany Marie, was a Greenwich Village restaurateur who played a key role in Bohemianism from the early 1900s through the late 1950s in Manhattan]; Chicago's Dill Pickle may soon shut its doors after being in business for fifteen years [the Dill Pickle Club was once a popular Bohemian club in Chicago, Illinois, between 1917 and 1935; the Dill Pickle was known as a speakeasy, cabaret, and theater and was influential during the "Chicago Renaissance" as it allowed a forum for free thinkers]; and one hears less and less of that earnest attempt to resuscitate the vanished Bohemian glory of old New Orleans.

For a whole season recently, moreover, there was a "To Let" sign outside the old Provincetown Theater in New York, once the Aeolian cave of the many brisk winds that enlivened the American theater in the early days of George Cram ("Doc") Cook, Eugene O'Neill, and Susan Glaspell. The Provincetown has now taken on an interest almost entirely historical, as have also the ideals for which it stood and most of the people for whom it was once a sanctuary. The huge rusty padlock, so often clamped over its door these days, is a grim symbol of what has happened to one whole generation of cultural endeavor in America.

For the deeper reasons behind this fairly early demise of a movement that promised so much, one would have to examine the whole complex background of ideas to which it sought to give expression. But it is perhaps sufficient to recall to mind what was its single and most abiding characteristic, its total and almost unparalleled addiction to intellectual *and* emotional self-analysis. While the very nature of analysis calls for a distinction to be made between the two, the distinction was actually seldom observed. The intellectual and the emotional were all too rarely separated, and the intellectual result was more often than not a product of the emotional desire. Certainly in their own scheme of values the members of this generation left no doubt as to which of the two processes they considered the more important. The emotions, so to speak, had only just been discovered; they offered something of the risk and fascination of a new cause; and by a quite natural progression they came in time to be glorified for their own sake. Perhaps it would be simplest to say of this generation that it was inclined to endow its emotions with an importance that caused it to ignore pretty much everything else besides them. Beginning as an age of emotional stocktaking, developing into one of emotional advertisement and glorification, the period ended in what for a time appeared to be an almost complete paralysis of intellectual and emotional powers alike.

II

Undoubtedly, the spread of what used to be called the New Psychology was most responsible for the orgy of introspection in which the period culminated. To Sigmund Freud more than anyone else belongs the honor for having ushered in the nightmarish era of phobias, manias, neuroses, and unimpeded "self-expression." Psychoanalysis owed its advantage to being a technique so elastic that it could be applied to almost everything in sight—from one's preference for certain kinds of scenery to one's neighbor's bad boy. It was a kind of handy tool around the intellectual house, a tool with which one could pry open the most curious old doors, lift off the lids of the most fabulous treasure chests of the mental interior. As long as it was able to provide a constantly new series of shocks, discoveries, and odd sensations along the spine, it was an unsurpassed instrument of enlightenment. Only gradually did it come to be recognized that psychoanalysis was perhaps after all no more than a tool, a method or a technique, and not an adequate system of values on which to erect a workable scheme of individual or social living. While it had a great deal to do with life, it seemed to have little or nothing to do with living, or with those problems that are called forth by the daily necessities of human conduct.

Not only psychoanalysis but other influences, as well, gave the last generation its special passion for introspection. Although the doctrines of Henri Bergson were familiar only to the more professional students of philosophy, their part in determining the mental direction of our time was considerable. Here was a philosophy that frankly discarded the claims of the scientific intellect, that placed intuition above all other modes of perception, and that tended to undermine human action at its very source in the will. If the Bergsonian conception of time as the flux of consciousness came largely through fiction and other fields, its effect was only the more insidious and profound. It came, for example, in an only slightly disguised form, in the cyclical theory of history expounded by the German philosopher-historian Oswald Spengler. History, for this writer, was an essentially irrational sequence of events, swung along in the flux of time and wholly unaffected in its course by individual will or effort. This was a view that was thoroughly absorbed in the minds of a great many people who had never seen or even heard of Herr Spengler's two fat volumes [*The Decline of the West* (1918–22)]. Today we can realize that these volumes found such an eager world audience because the passive view of history they embodied was especially welcome to a civilization that was tending to lose all desire for action, along with a belief in its validity.

Add to all of this the tremendous impact on an already disorbited intellectual world of such gargantuan explorations of the unconscious mind as are offered in the two great literary monuments of Marcel Proust and James Joyce [*Remembrance of Things Past* (1913–27) and *Ulysses* (1922)]. Literature has thus joined hands with psychology and philosophy to escort modern man into those abysses of his nature where the motion is so rapid that it can only be imagined as a kind of rest, apprehended only through a more or less complete surrender of the conscious mind and will. (Nirvana is only just around the corner.) Passivity, as a matter of fact, is the only logical result of self-contemplation carried beyond the point where the immediate demands of living cease to have any more interest or importance. Self-contemplation is the natural enemy of action. To retreat indefinitely into the unconscious world of instincts, sensations, and impressions is to renounce everything that is usually included under the name of action. The effect of such a retreat is a gradual forgetfulness not only of the necessity but also of the capacity for action.

Here, however, the retreat to nirvana is seriously impeded by certain fundamental needs of the human organism as a whole, which refuses to subordinate itself to the mind's intense preoccupation with its own difficulties. Human nature rebels against the state to which so much modern thought has reduced it. Because men are so constructed that they cannot do without some exercise of their faculties for overt behavior, because their physical well-being alone depends on some such exercise, the passive state is one that cannot be tolerated for long without an oppressive sense of sterility and confusion. Men's instincts, as well as their thoughts, demand expression; their muscular, visceral, and glandular systems cannot be ignored; and their nerves, too long denied, shrilly insist on the release that comes through action alone. Perhaps it is the last-named, the human nervous system, that is most surely responsible for the current protest against nirvana.

III

"Self-yeast of spirit a dull dough sours," wrote Gerard Manley Hopkins [in the poem "I wake and feel the fell of dark, not day" (1885)], and thirty-odd years of introspection have only succeeded in making the intellectuals of our time more uncertain of themselves, less satisfied with their condition, and more anxious about their future. The diet of self in which they indulged with such gusto and so much hope of nourishment has ended by surfeiting them.

It is only natural that one of the commonest remedies proposed should be in the nature of a pretty violent antidote. The opposite of groping around among the shapeless monsters of the intellectual underworld is a more open espousal of everyday actualities. The proper reaction to sterility is a renewed thirst for living and a desire for concrete experience. To confusion of any sort the only possible reaction is a reorientation of the will along a single line of directed activity. It is in action, as a matter of fact, in one or another of the various forms of action, that the decade already begun promises to seek its salvation.

If action promises to become the key word of the next few years, it is at the same time a word capable of an extremely wide range of meaning. Any decent religious system, for example, inasmuch as it includes ethics, requires a certain amount of action, as do also to a certain degree such efforts at religious substitutes as Humanism, Gurdjieffism [after George Gurdjieff (1866–1949), influential spiritual teacher of the early to mid-twentieth century who taught that most humans live their lives in a state of hypnotic "waking sleep," but that it is possible to transcend to a higher state of consciousness and achieve full human potential], and other present-day cults. Here the word may be taken to refer to one specific kind of action—moral conduct; yet it is action in a quite genuine sense, and the tendency toward a return to traditional standards in religion and philosophy is but further evidence of a fundamental change in direction. It is evidence of the increasing desire to relate the individual's random impulses to a consistent and meaningful pattern of behavior.

But it is action in a cruder, more obvious, and rather more detached sense than we can see in the current movement away from intense introspection toward an absorption in various objective realities outside the individual. It is impossible, for example, not to have remarked the increasing popularity of reading matter distinctly removed from the reader's set of intimate emotional interests. The detective story has never been so flourishing; books of travel and adventure were never so abundant. In poetry, the long narrative has had an unexpected return to favor. The mystery play and the social comedy or farce have all but displaced the depressing naturalistic tragedy that darkened our theater in the years right after the Great War. On a distinctly lower level of recreation, game-books of various sorts—anagrams, crossword puzzles, questionnaires—have afforded relief to a public a little weary of being so often reminded of its psyche.

In intellectual circles, the whole current of speculation has undergone a remarkable change of tone. Whether or not the current financial depression is responsible, the intelligentsia have lately manifested an unprecedented interest in political and economic questions. Critics of art and literature who were yesterday concerned with the advancement of "significant form" in painting or the exposition of Proustian aesthetics, are now writing articles on Detroit Motors or the Plight of the Proletariat. Now at last it is possible to become absorbed by these matters without losing caste with the intellectual elite. It is no longer considered unintelligent to apply one's intelligence to the problems of practical existence.

Not only in theory but in practice, as well, our intellectuals are turning to politics as a means of expression. Probably the most spectacular recent example was the columnist Heywood Broun [1888–1939], who ran for Congress in a New York district last fall. The fact that he was defeated does not in the least diminish the importance of his gesture. Many different signs point to a renewed interest in public affairs in our colleges and universities, and therefore to the possibility that the educated class in this country will play some such part in government, as did the corresponding class in England and other European countries. The challenge offered by Russia to American capitalism has had considerable influence in focusing attention on the groundwork of our political and social systems. The necessity for some point of view in the matter, defensive or otherwise, has been followed by direct action in a number of instances.

Indeed, it has been a cause of anxiety in some quarters that communism has appealed to some of the best minds at such institutions as Harvard, Columbia, and the University of Pittsburgh. Undoubtedly the strict communistic discipline attracts these undergraduates as a way out of the perplexing moral and social confusion that attends them upon graduation, as an available course of action with sufficient risk and promise of adventure to match their youthful energies. Almost all of them have betrayed some curiosity about the Russian experiment, several have considered applying for membership in the Party in America, and a few have actually booked third-class passage to Leningrad. It is much too early to measure the real importance of this active participation in politics on the part of a large section of the intellectual class; but of one thing we may be quite certain: there has been nothing to compare with it in this country for the last fifty years.

Another symptom is the growth of what may be described as a self-conscious agrarian movement. That Greenwich Village, with its palettes, chisels, and fountain pens, has been slowly migrating to the hills of Connecticut and New Jersey, to the mesas of New Mexico and the tobacco fields of Tennessee, is a phenomenon that has already received due attention. There is a difference to be noticed, however, in the motives that determine these reformed children of Nature in our day. It is much too simple to overemphasize the artist's traditional insistence on solitude; many artists, especially writers, require the tempo and gregarious warmth of city life to keep their perceptions properly awake for their work. Chances are that artists will not abandon the benefits of society until social conditions become positively detrimental to their welfare as human beings as well as artists. The present revolt against the city may not be so much a protest against communal living as against the uncertainties of modern life, which happen to be peculiarly accentuated in our modern cities. If some of our most distinguished lyrical poets have turned their talents to the cultivation of Martha Washington asparagus or super-vitalized strawberries, the reason is more than likely that they have been suddenly overcome by the necessity of getting their fingers into something as real and uncorrupted as the soil, or re-establishing themselves with old verities of growth and recurrence that have been all but forgotten in our contemporary world. Or it may be nothing more mystical than the quite comprehensible desire of the nervous system to relieve itself by engaging in a very agreeable form of activity.

I have spoken of the great current popularity of travel and adventure books. It would seem at first as if the public were merely taking its usual vicarious pleasure in setting off for remote lands and places that only a few are ever able to visit in the flesh. But the emphasis today is not so much on the interest or strangeness of the places described in these books as on the prodigies of human energy recorded by their authors. Once we were curious to know everything that wanderers had seen and heard on their voyages; now we are chiefly concerned with what they have *done*. Adventure is a very large term indeed and it includes not only the exploits of aviators, polar explorers, and deep-sea divers but also the life histories of persons who have been specially favored or buffeted by circumstances—tramps, generals, journalists, and lost princesses. In an age when the human will is so rarely allowed to assert itself over destiny or environment, these testaments of will triumphant respond to a deep inner necessity.

But what is also implied by all this is that there has been a distinct renaissance of adventure. One of the consequences of modern invention has been an opening-up of new fields and methods of exploration that is comparable only to the heyday of the Elizabethans. And those who have availed themselves most of these opportunities have been as a rule a more intellectual class of individuals than had ever turned to exploration in the past. The modern adventurer is probably most often a scientist who is using his knowledge for the gratification of his impulses. The scientifically trained are more fortunate than others, for their labor is their passion. Inasmuch as one type of modern intellectual has turned with zest to the fields of scientific discovery and exploration, we may say that adventure, the most absorbing of all forms of action, is an eminently contemporary mode of expression.

Another not unrelated tendency is the very recent abandonment of Europe by a large number of those who once resorted to it for that spiritual nourishment which was supposedly not to be had at home. The writers and artists of the postwar generation have closed up their French chateaux, said good-bye to the cafés of Paris and Vienna, and reconciled themselves to the crudities of our Western continent. In fact, it seems to be such very crudities that have suddenly become so attractive to these former exiles. Europe had been peaceful, charming, and comfortable. It had permitted no end of leisure for contemplating one's ego. But after ten years the contemplation of one's ego, as we have seen, has yielded nothing better than a dull sense of confusion and sterility. During the last few years Mexico, with its promise of raw, unformed, and highly colorful life, has threatened to rival even France in the favor of the intellectuals. If not Mexico, the West Indies, or South America, there are the still beckoning plains and mountains of our own Far West. In one or another of these yet unspoiled regions the newest breed of intellectuals have situated their hope that "out of this nettle, danger, we pluck this flower, safety" [Shakespeare's *Henry IV, Part I* (1597)].

IV

Action is the invariable reaction to a period of sustained inaction. Action is the readiest available antidote for the pernicious autotoxin that introspection has become for a great many people in our time. But like certain other kinds of antidote, its effectiveness may possibly be too temporary to be altogether satisfactory as a remedy.

The special feature of the cult of action as it emerges in our day is its desperation—the fact indeed that it is a cult, a more or less conscious protest against a situation that has become intolerable. In this respect the present is fundamentally different from those periods of the past that we think of as being notably active in the sense in which I have been using the term—the thirteenth century in Italy and France, the Elizabethan era, or the pioneer epoch in America. The difference lies in the hardly deniable truth that in every one of these ages men's actions were an expression of their ideas, sometimes of a whole closely interwoven system of ideas, which in turn usually rested on firm religious foundations. Action was an expression of the mind, not a revolt against the mind or a way of escaping from the mind. It was the reflection of a solid inner health that was potent enough to generate and control the energies of the body. It was, to use the language of the Catholic Church, the outward sign of an inward grace.

It seems hardly possible that any concerted movement toward action can endure for long without some unified system of convictions at its base. Action as a cathartic, or as a kind of spiritual intoxication and release, is understandable only as a form of immediate and temporary relief. It is really valuable only as an absolute symptom that the malady exists, and as a means of alleviation until such time as a more permanent remedy can be effected. To achieve consistency, direction, and permanence, action must derive its origin from a secure and harmonious faith.

This is not to suggest that the present movement, although obviously motivated by an intense desire for escape, may lead to results wholly devoid of value and benefit to those most concerned. If the modern personality is in urgent need of being reconstructed, that end is to be accomplished not by an indefinite contemplation of its present disorder but by a constant and vigorous pursuit of the perennial realities of experience. Before new values of life can be discovered and integrated into a generative system of ideas, life itself must be lived, the enterprise of living must be undertaken with all the zest that can possibly be mustered. For all those whose variously elected careers of action are worthy of consideration, salvation—or partial salvation at least—may be found to consist largely in the exhilaration of the quest. The modern intellectual, so troubled about the state and even the existence of his soul, may come to rediscover that soul in his strenuous endeavor to forget it.

13. "Cummings' Non-Land of Un-" (1933)
Eimi, by E. E. Cummings

E. E. Cummings has written a very big book. It is almost as big a book as *Ulysses* [1922], but the comparison—which is suggested by a reference to "Comrade" Joyce—must not be carried any further. *Eimi* may be superficially described as the diary of an American poet's thirty-six-day sojourn in that "uncircus of noncreatures, calling itself 'Russia.'" In addition to its complete lack of statistics, it is distinguishable from other works about the same country by its author's fairly candid admission of unfair-mindedness from the moment he crosses the border. Cummings is no capitalist, to be sure, but he is a poet, and it is as a poet that he announces his prejudice against the Soviet Republic. As a poet he is opposed to all dogma but his own, "Dogma—the destroyer of happens, the killer of occurs, the ugliness of premeditately."

For Cummings, Russia is not a country but a ghost land of non-men, skeletons, theories made visible but not quite substantial. The Russian Revolution resembles "a running-amok street sprinkler, a normally benevolent mechanism that attains—thanks (possibly) to some defect in its construction or (possibly) to the ignorance or (probably) playfulness of its operator—distinct if spurious loss of unimportance." And the spectacle has value for him only because it prompts a violent reassertion of the creed perhaps best summed up in the single word of the title—*eimi*, the Greek first-person singular, active indicative of the verb "to be." For nothing in this "kingdomless of specters" can imitate the "indescribably everything and suddenly which is ourselves, which self is and whatever only creatively annihilates hatred with laughing."

But better than in any of these eloquent affirmations, Cummings' fierce individualism is to be seen reflected in the style and manner of his book. The style is of course the same highly personal, ultra-mannered style with which we have been made familiar in Cummings' poetry. There hardly seems any need, therefore, to review or defend its peculiarities at this late date. Here again the general intention is to communicate concrete sensations and perceptions in all the immediacy with which they are experienced. Because conventional syntax is historical, that is, based on an arrangement of thoughts, feelings, and sensations *already* completed, Cummings annihilates conventional syntax and with it conventional punctuation as well. The instantaneous alone is his concern; "suddenly," for example, is among his favorite words.

Typography also is made to perform a dynamic function by approximating visually the actual thought, object, sensation being rendered. To facilitate directness, the imagery is either telescoped ("sunlitness high-ceilinged") or simultaneous ("breathing Spring twi (after rain) light"). And of course Cummings takes his customary liberties with word forms, manifesting a special fondness for the prefix "un-." The placing of this little prefix before any noun deprives the thing for which it stands of its very essence. Thus in these pages we move in an unworld of unmen lying in unsleep on an unbed of preternatural nullity.

In general, such prodigies of language and syntax do succeed in creating the effect intended; certain pages throughout are as good as all but the best of Cummings' poems. The only question is how well adapted these devices are to a work of this purpose and these dimensions. We cannot raise the usual objections to the use of a lyrical style in a narrative form. Cummings would certainly protest that what he was writing was not a narrative but a "book." The objection, then, is simply that the reader's powers of instantaneous response become exhausted before he gets through very many of the 432 pages of this particular "book." There is no progression of action to beguile him on his way. There is no design or pattern to give unity (cf. "Comrade" Joyce) to this jumble of crisply developed *instantanés*. Cummings might just as well have dashed off a dozen or so lyrics in his Metropol Hotel room [in Moscow] and brought them together, properly spaced, in a volume. Not a book, the reader feels, but an unbook.

Yet *Eimi* has passages and individual lines ("I have eaten, however, of sunset") that admirers of E. E. Cummings' delicate, if still not yet fully realized, talent will return to.

14. "Fragmentary Ends" (1933)
Death in the Woods, by Sherwood Anderson

With two important exceptions, the stories in *Death in the Woods* represent a very definite retrogression on the part of an American writer from whose work one has become accustomed to receive an impression of constant growth and development. Neither the sentimental phallicism of "Perhaps Women" [1931] nor the timorous overtones of social consciousness of the more recent "Beyond Desire" [1932] are present in this book. The crystallization of one or the other of these attitudes that one had half expected does not take place. Nor is it possible to discover any still newer attitude that is offered in their stead. It is as if Sherwood Anderson has at last given up the search for some principle of meaning in life that might give order and scale to his writing. Like one of his characters, the professor who is trying to write a book on values, he seems to have decided, "There are only floods, one flood following another."

In a word, Anderson has relaxed into his old and well-known habit of "groping." Such stories as "The Return" and "The Lost Novel"

mark a return to the thinness of characterization and detail, the diffuse
lyricism, that we associate with his very earliest work. There is the same
monotonous insistence on the inarticulateness of life, the mysterious
complexity of even the most ordinary human existences. "There you
are. That is all. Life is more like that than people suppose. Little odd
fragmentary ends of things. That is about all we get" ["In a Strange
Town"]. If we cannot respond to this philosophy with the same
sympathy that we did fifteen or even ten years ago, Anderson himself
is to blame. He has played too long on such a fragile theme. And he has
at times played on it so well that nothing but his best will satisfy us.
Only two of the stories in this collection can compare with the best in
Winesburg, Ohio [1919] and *The Triumph of the Egg* [1921].

The title story is marred by the usual self-consciousness of Anderson
when he feels himself in the presence of a character who is somehow
exceptional or "significant." We are reminded just a little too often that
the recollection of the old woman in the tale is to the author like "music
heard from far off." The objective circumstances of her life are what
make her come alive; and the reader's only regret is that these are not
"rendered," to use Henry James's favorite word, with sufficient directness and completeness. Especially is this true for the scene in which the
woman's dead body is set upon by the hungry dogs in the woods. But
despite this failure to make the most of its possibilities, the story is effectively moving. "The woman who died was one destined to feed animal
life" is the formula that Anderson works out for his character; and
because he is able to discover so definite a formula, the story has more
significance than any other in the volume.

"Brother Death," which is interesting for a number of different
reasons, itself succeeds chiefly by virtue of the tree symbol, which binds
it together with a greater artistic unity than is common in Anderson's
work. The distinct superiority of these two tales over the others in the
collection merely serves to confirm the feeling that Sherwood Anderson
is a writer whose triumphs are accidental, whose command over
his material is most precarious, and whose greatest need is for some
established point of view that will enable him to develop his medium
with more certainty.

15. "Newer Novelist" (1933)
Miss Lonelyhearts, by Nathanael West

Perhaps the most salient characteristic of *Miss Lonelyhearts* is the quite
negative one of being without that proletarian self-consciousness which

has become the keynote of recent American fiction. It is true that the people in Nathanael West's second novel [after *The Dream Life of Balso Snell* (1931)] can be found during any rush hour in the Bronx or Brooklyn subway. But there is nowhere in this novel any effort to relate the vicissitudes of the characters to any particular economic system. There is no evidence that for this writer the hardships of the body have yet replaced in interest or importance the more traditional and possibly more complicated hardships of the soul.

In this work, therefore, still "issues from the hand of God, the simple soul" [T. S. Eliot's poem "Animula" (1929), by way of Dante's *Purgatorio* (1320, second part of *The Divine Comedy*)]. Newspapermen, artists, college boys, fishermen, seminarians—these characters are less affected by the universal rumblings of the class struggle than by the more private shocks of the flesh and the spirit. The spirit has gone suddenly very flat and dry, to be sure, and the flesh is in some instances twisted out of all recognition. But the conflict here is psychological, not social or economic, and on this conflict of the individual with himself and with others the interest is sharply focused.

The hero of *Miss Lonelyhearts* is a young man who earns his living devising replies to "Desperate," Brokenhearted," "Sick-of-it-all," and others of the lovelorn who write to him for advice. But it must not be gathered that West's book is the sort of rollicking, whimsical *Arabian Nights* adventure into modern Baghdad that Christopher Morley, let us say, might write. There is no color in the bazaars of this Baghdad, as the creatures who inhabit it have the shaggy contours of a James Thurber drawing. The hero himself suffers from what he calls a "Christ-complex"; he keeps primed for his task on a heavy mixture of Dostoevsky and gin. When in a half-hearted gesture of compassion he attempts to help one of the frustrated people who have appealed to him, he is rewarded with death.

It is all very sad, bitter, and hopeless. If it were not for West's prose, which leans too much to the baroque, and for a certain ambiguity of genre ("the actual and the fanciful" are here too often confounded), *Miss Lonelyhearts* would be a better book. As it stands, however, it is one of the most readable and one of the most exceptional books of the season.

16. "Bundles of Fragments" (1933)
The Best Short Stories of 1933, edited by Edward J. O'Brien

Twentieth-Century Short Stories, edited by Sylvia Chatfield Bates

In the prefatory remarks that always precede the stories in his annual anthology, Edward J. O'Brien is this year even more hopeful than usual about the prospects for the American short story. He finds as much difference between the better short stories published in 1913 and those published in 1932 as between the poetry of Alexander Pope and the poetry of John Keats. After the long period during which the short story in this country suffered from a complication of ailments arising out of our too great devotion to the past, our writers, following the examples of Sherwood Anderson and Ernest Hemingway, are hard at work trying to establish a "usable present." This "usable present," as defined by O'Brien, means something much more than a body of contemporary materials or experience. "It is the sum of all the ordered living we achieve ourselves from day to day." It includes the idea of under-standing, adaptation to society, and knowledge of what it is possible for us to become. It is presumably everything that O'Brien understands by good art, and since he refers to the current short story in such lyrical terms, we take it that he considers the better recent short stories typical of art of this kind. The magazine *Story*, for example, is described as "the most important milestone in American letters since *The Education of Henry Adams* [1907]."

After such an astonishing statement as this, one naturally turns with avidity to the pages that follow in *The Best Short Stories of 1933*. What one finds is a group of stories, taken from such different sources as the *Saturday Evening Post* and *Prairie Schooner*, of an average level of quality that is neither very far above nor below that of any of O'Brien's anthologies of the past five or six years. It is especially disappointing to discover that the selections from *Story* are among the least distin-guished in the volume. Only two of the stories, those by Erskine Caldwell and Katherine Anne Porter, are likely to impress the reader as being able to survive the twofold "test of substance and of form" that O'Brien lays down for his five-star group.

Caldwell's "The First Autumn" is so unlike his novels, both in substance and manner, that one does not easily identify it as being by his hand. It is the most objectively constructed story in the book and will therefore be liked or disliked for the same reason. The moment that its point is grasped the reader is divided between a feeling of irritation at the author's reluctance to state his meaning explicitly and a feeling of admiration at the skill with which he lets the action relate his meaning. It is Katherine Anne Porter's "The Cracked Looking-Glass," however, which most nearly realizes O'Brien's contention that the past year was an exceptional one. Building on an epigram in the first episode of Joyce's *Ulysses* [1922], Porter has written a study in the vicissitudes of an Irish Madame Bovary stranded in the Connecticut hills that is at once a fully developed portrait of an individual, a type, and a race. So expert is Porter in her knowledge of the Celtic sensibility, so subtly attuned to the rhythms and idioms of Irish speech, that it is hard to believe she is not by right of birth an Irish writer, although she must hereafter be counted as one by right of sympathy and comprehension.

Of the twenty-nine stories in O'Brien's collection, thirteen are written either directly or indirectly from the point of view of a character whose intellectual level is obviously below that of the writer. It may be that of a small-town Rotarian, a trolley-line employee, or a Tacoma mine-worker. In no fewer than seven stories the point of view is that of a child. It is possible that this may be put down to coincidence or simply that more of our fiction writers are learning the advantages of a specially selected point of view. The playing on a child's half-conscious grasp of facts and events may only be a vogue. But one is compelled to seek some better explanation for this wholesale abandonment of the traditional authorial point of view in recent fiction.

The growing tendency among certain writers to set down, in narrative form, the exact speech of Rotarians, trolley-line employees, mine-workers, and children instead of addressing us in a vocabulary and style more closely resembling their own, is undoubtedly a consequence of the so-called "documentary" impulse in current literature. But the documentary impulse itself is open to a closer examination. It will usually be found that those writers who lavish on us a great many facts (sometimes referred to as "life") do so because they do not know what else to do with them. The curious contradiction is that while these facts do not have any meaning for the authors themselves, they are expected to seem very important to their readers. And it is somehow made to follow that if the facts are presented from the point of view of someone not the author, they are even more important. Besides, the author has the advantage of playing it safe; he is relieved from the responsibility and increasing difficulty of making something out of the facts. Because such themes as love, death, and sorrow have become too complex for the mature intelligence, they can be saved only by being relegated to the stupid, abnormal, or infantile mind. The short story is thus able to move on to new heights, if one believes O'Brien, by devoting itself to a kind of stenography of bewilderment.

This bewilderment and the profounder reasons behind it are more frankly revealed in such a story as Thomas Mann's "Disorder and Early Sorrow" [1925], which Sylvia Chatfield Bates has the good taste to include in her collection of thirty-one stories from six different countries titled, simply, *Twentieth-Century Short Stories*. So perfectly does Mann communicate the *sentiment* of transition in this story that we are left with little wonder as to why the modern short story is the uncertain, evasive, fragmentary thing it is. Bates's selection from the field is marked by thoroughness, intelligence, and more good taste than has been shown in a long time. One regrets, of course, the inclusion of certain entries at the expense of certain favorites of one's own—James Joyce's "Araby" [1914], for instance. But these changes would not alter the impression left by the collection as a whole, that of a "bundle of fragments," to use William Butler Yeats's phrase [from the auto-biographical *Four Years* (1921)], or contribute in the least toward any effect of unity in this volume's reflection of the contemporary world.

17. "Literary Trapezist" (1933)
Orphée, by Jean Cocteau

"Tell Jean Cocteau that I adore him," wrote Rainer Maria Rilke in a 1926 telegram to a friend, "the only person for whom the Myth opens its gates and from which he returns bronzed as from the seaside." Here it is the myth of Orpheus and Eurydice whose gates are thrown open for Cocteau: an Orpheus, it is true, who turns out to bear a striking resemblance to the dramatist himself, and a Eurydice who belongs to a period when Dada was the rage of the boulevards and postcard photographs were supposed to possess "a harmony, a harsh simplicity" that made them preferable to the major works of Rubens and Velásquez.

There is also a character here called Heurtebise, who belongs to "the race of the horse": this means that when the chair on which he is standing is withdrawn, he is capable of remaining suspended in mid-air. One gathers (Cocteau himself played Heurtebise when Georges Pitoëff produced the playlet in 1926) that with this ingratiating fakir one may also identify, if not with the author, then at least what is the wish-fulfillment of the author of this charming, ingenious, and delicately mad little offering.

It seems rather foolish, however, to designate *Orphée* as Cocteau's masterpiece, as the translator [Carl Wildman] does in his preface, since the 1929 novel *Les Enfants terrible* [*The Holy Terrors*] is an infinitely more serious and substantial work, and, what is more to the point, Cocteau would consider producing anything so pretentious as a masterpiece as constituting something of a breach of faith. Of Cocteau one may say what Arthur Symons said long ago of Oscar Wilde—that he is "an artist in attitudes." In this work the attitude is that of the trapezist, "playing at a great height, and without a safety net." As always Cocteau manages to get through the performance without a fall, although one is not sure from beginning to end whether it may not all be an optical illusion. But that is the essence of the pleasure that everything Jean Cocteau does is able to provide.

It must be added that the book is exquisitely produced, with typography by John Johnson and a Chiricoesque frontispiece by Pablo Picasso.

18. "Hemingway's Opium" (1933)
Winner Take Nothing, by Ernest Hemingway

It is among Ernest Hemingway's admirers that the suspicion is being most strongly created that the champion is losing, if he has not already lost, his hold. In the current *Contempo* [*A Review of Books and Personalities*], for example, Henry Hart administers a sharp castigation to those ungrateful people who were the first to applaud him when he was in his prime. Briefly stated, Hart's thesis is that the generation into whose veins Hemingway poured such badly needed flow of rich red blood should be the last to revile him now that his task is done. Despite his eloquent recapitulation of the champion's past glories, however, Hart only succeeds in delivering what is really a politely modulated funeral oration.

Similarly, in a review of the newest Hemingway volume, Horace Gregory lauds the author of *In Our Time* [1924, Hemingway's first collection of short stories] and *The Sun Also Rises* [1926] for his services to his generation, of which he is still represented as the principal spokesman, without anywhere making clear whether those services ever did, or do now, include an intellectually satisfactory statement of the position they represent. The reason, in the cases of Gregory and Hart, for this manifest attempt to let the champion down as easily as possible is not very hard to discover. Whatever have been Hemingway's limitations of mind and sensibility, he has stood out for his generation in America as preeminently the type of pure artist, concentrated on experience and on its disciplined expression in literature. His very limitations have seemed at times to be his greatest virtues. At any rate they have saved him from saga-making, from vatic exuberances, and from the mechanical illustration of politico-economic ideologies. To turn against this writer, therefore, seems almost tantamount to turning against art itself or against the artist's role in culture or society. It is to take sides with the Philistines—by whatever name they may now call themselves.

Now some such reservations must be understood when one reports that Hemingway's latest collection of stories includes what is actually the poorest and least interesting writing he has ever placed on public view. One cannot but regret, for instance, that a specimen like "One Reader Writes" should ever have been exposed to that view. As for most of the stories in the volume, their dullness may be traced either to a lack of growth or to growth along what is for Hemingway a new and unfortunate direction. There is, first of all, a recurrence of all the old nostalgias—the nostalgia for Europe ("Wine of Wyoming"), for the church ("The Gambler, the Nun, and the Radio"), for adolescence ("Fathers and Sons"), and for death ("A Clean, Well-Lighted Place").There is also the monotonous repetition of the subjects attached to these themes—eating and drinking, travel, sport, coition. In one story the café waiter sums it all up in the now celebrated prayer: "Our nada who art in nada, nada be thy name thy kingdom nada thy will be nada in nada as it is in nada. . . ."

The new direction mentioned is an increasing fondness for subjects and characters that are usually distinguished by the label "special." Ignoring the preoccupation with death, which in the reprinted "A Natural History of the Dead" almost amounts to an enthusiastic *delectatio morbosa*, there are enough other indications that Hemingway is in danger of becoming as *fin de siècle* as his contemporary William Faulkner. At its worst this tendency results in such delicacies as "The Mother of a Queen," which deals with a homosexual bullfighter who permits his mother's bones to be thrown onto a dump heap, and "God Rest You Merry, Gentlemen," which deals with a sex-crazed adolescent who commits self-mutilation. As it happens, the real objection to this kind of subject matter has quite recently been expressed once and for all by Hemingway's own literary godmother: "She [Gertrude Stein] says she dislikes the abnormal, it is so obvious."

"The Gambler" story is from every point of view the most successful in the book: Sister Cecilia and the Mexican Cayetano are both admirably realized characterizations, the narrative is dense, and there is one remarkable passage of serious reflection. Examining the statement that religion is the opium of the people, the convalescent Frazer decides that economics, patriotism, sexual intercourse, the radio, gambling, and ambition, each in its own way, are also opiums of the people. The real, the actual opium of the people, he concludes, is bread. "Revolution, Frazer thought, is no opium. Revolution is a catharsis; an ecstasy which can only be prolonged by tyranny. The opiums are before and after. He was thinking well, a little too well."

Too well? One wonders whether Hemingway can produce any more interesting volumes so long as he stops off as abruptly as this, turning to play the radio so loud that it can no longer be heard. Fiction is an opium as long as it contents itself with playing over the surface of things. Action, too, is an opium if it is thought of simply as a catharsis and not as an expression. Unless Ernest Hemingway realizes within the next few years that fiction based on action-as-catharsis is becoming less and less potent as an opium, he will not be able to hold the championship much longer.

19. "Sean O'Faolain" (1934)
A Nest of Simple Folk, by Sean O'Faolain

Sean O'Faolian is not a new writer, although this is the impression that one might get from a reading of the many enraptured reviews with which his first novel, *A Nest of Simple Folk*, has been greeted. Although he is still quite young [1900–91], O'Faolain has been writing, and writing extremely well, for at least six or seven years. His "The Bomb Shop," published in the *Dial* in 1927, remains, in the opinion of this reviewer, his single best piece of writing to date, and several of the stories in the collection *Midsummer Night Madness* [1932], particularly "Fugue" and "The Small Lady," surpass in intensity both of style and characterization anything that may be found in his new work.

Nor is O'Faolain so isolated a figure in recent Irish writing as the almost certain popularity of this new book is likely to make him appear. He belongs, as a matter of fact, to that generation of Irish writers whose common conscience was forged, some fifteen or more years ago, out of the smithy of Stephen Dedalus's soul. O'Faolain could not write of Ireland as he does, could not make political passion a subject rather than a motive, if James Joyce had not written his *Portrait of the Artist as a Young Man* [1916]. This is of particular relevance in any study of O'Faolain's style—a style that reflects a sensibility which has absorbed, with exquisite tact and certainty, all that is best in modern Irish writing.

From Joyce this writer has learned much about the use of homely words and images for unsuspected values of imaginative association:

> Leo stirred the splinter-end with his toe, and it leaped into flame and then died out. A fir tree grew in his mind, tall and snow-clotted, waving in the flame. Then, sliver of a root, levered from its womb in the bog, it fell like all its ancient branches into a little dust.

O'Faolain has learned also—what few of Joyce's imitators have ever learned—that in projecting a subjective state, a feeling for the precise rhythms of the mind or consciousness is at least as important as the choice of words:

> But he soon forgot him and all of them, his eyes big with Limerick and the evening that was coloring the tall red houses and the muddy streets wide as a sea.

But neither O'Faolian's use of images nor his handling of rhythms allows us to class him among the many crude imitators of the author of *Ulysses* [1922]. What has been learned has been assimilated into a personality that is in most respects fundamentally different. It would be better to say that what O'Faolain, like so many of his contemporaries, owes to Joyce is an enrichment and reorientation of the sensibility that make it possible for him to treat familiar Irish materials with a new freshness and beauty. Of Joyce himself it may be said that he has changed the whole landscape of a country—no longer does Ireland even *look* the same as the Ireland of Thomas Moore, Charles Lever, and Dion Boucicault. Of this new landscape O'Faolain is an accomplished painter—on the whole, the most accomplished of the several who have recently appeared.

A proper comparison, therefore, would be between O'Faolain's novel and the earlier novels and stories of Liam O'Flaherty, who gives a more violent reading of the Irish temperament, since he is writing of Aran and the west rather than the "soft" south of Kerry and Cork. Or between O'Faolain and Peadar O'Donnell, whose tenderly etched studies of the poorest class of Irish peasantry have won him the disfavor of the Church and the admiration of the extreme left in Irish politics. And it is impossible, in reading O'Faolain's evocation of Cork on a sunny morning, to forget the fine descriptions of that city in Frank O'Connor's *The Saint and Mary Kate* [1932]. This comparison alone, if properly undertaken, would reveal how much all these younger Irish writers share in common. If O'Faolain's novel seems like a miracle among recent works of fiction, then, it is a miracle that does not come as too great a surprise to those who have been following the current development of Irish letters.

A Nest of Simple Folk covers a longer span of time than any other Irish novelist, except Joyce in *Work in Progress* [a.k.a. *Finnegans Wake* (1939), various sections of which were initially published serially under the title *Work in Progress*]: the narrative begins in 1854, with the boy Leo O'Donnell standing before his aunts' house in Kerry, and ends with the same character fighting in Dublin in the rebellion of 1916. [The Easter Rebellion or Rising was an armed insurrection in Ireland during Easter Week, April 1916; it was launched by Irish republicans to end British rule in Ireland and establish an independent Irish Republic while the United Kingdom was heavily engaged in fighting during the First World War.] Between these two events is crowded enough material to make the substance of at least a half-dozen novels of the average sort. In form it represents a fusion of the biographical with the chronicle or "panel" type of novel: Leo Foxe-Donnell, the son of Judith Foxe and "Long John" O'Donnell, sums up in his psychology and in the contradictions of his career the old conflict between the Anglo-Irish gentry—Protestant in religion, English in manners and loyalties—and the native Catholic peasantry. Any discussion of the work as a whole, its form or its theme, gets down, therefore, to the question of how skillfully O'Faolain has rendered the fundamental ambiguities of his hero's character.

Without going into this question in detail, one must point out that the transition from the sensitive, Romantic boy of Book I to the rollicking and incredibly callous landlord of Book II is much too abruptly indicated. The sympathetic treatment of the first part, written in a thoroughly poetic subjective style, prepares us for a very different sort of development. The trouble is that O'Faolain has fallen into that quite common error nowadays which consists in an author's confusing his own sensibility with that of his character; the boy of Book I could not grow up to be the man of Book II, for the boy of Book I is too much like O'Faolain himself, or like his own image of himself in childhood. In the final section Leo takes on a new and much more credible identity as an old man, surrounded by his wife, Julie Keenew, whom he had seduced in the old days; his nephew, Johnny Hussey, who had got him sentenced to jail for ten years; and his son, Johno, in whom he finds a fellow conspirator against the forces that have wrecked his life.

It is impossible to enumerate all the brilliant character creations that O'Faolain has fitted into this pattern, all the way from Judith Foxe, who betrays every instinct of her class in a single dramatic scene, to young Denis Hussey, whose disgust with his father's treachery brings the book to its thematic conclusion. The pattern has been so richly filled in that there is little that bears even remotely on the theme that has been left out. If there is rather less political material than one might expect, it is because O'Faolain wishes to allow politics to enter no more than it actually does into the everyday lives of these simple folk. But by the same argument one is forced to object that he has allowed religion much too small a place in his scheme. It is true that the hero denounces the priests in several passages; but there is an eloquent suspension of any sort of attitude on the part of the author, who probably wishes to profit by the examples of other Irish writers in recent years.

Despite this important blank space, *A Nest of Simple Folk* is a truly comprehensive picture of the social, economic, and political forces in Irish life during the last century that were to lead to the fateful bonfire of 1916. But what is truly admirable in it, what gives it its special significance in this country at the present moment, is the manner in which these forces are represented, not explicitly like so many abstractions, but as actively operative in recognizable human experience. This is to say, finally, that Sean O'Faolain is something rarer and more necessary to us at the moment than the critic, the social historian, the orator. He is, first and last, the artist.

20. "Studs Lonigan's World" (1934)
The Young Manhood of Studs Lonigan,
by James T. Farrell

In his new novel, James T. Farrell is more directly occupied with the theme of Catholicism in the modern world than in either of the other two books [the novel *Gas-House McGinty* (1933) and the collection of stories titled *Calico Shoes* (1934)] that he has published in the last three years. Young Lonigan, whose unbeautiful adolescence in the streets of Chicago's South Side formed the subject of the first volume of the trilogy [*Young Lonigan* (1932), followed by *The Young Manhood of Studs Lonigan* (1934) and *Judgment Day* (1935)] that Farrell is devoting to this character, is shown grown to manhood, and unquestionably the greatest of his problems is the attempt to reconcile the moral and religious teachings inculcated in him at St. Patrick's parochial school with the standards of conduct admired and put into action by the gang at the corner poolroom.

The great difference between Studs Lonigan and most other hard guys in recent fiction, then, lies in his possession of a still very active moral and religious sensibility. None of the characters in *The Young Manhood of Studs Lonigan* is as completely dehumanized, for example, as the characters of William Faulkner and Erskine Caldwell. They are not so tough that they cannot indulge in occasional moments of remorse and self-disgust. They do not retire to the neighborhood brothel before listening to a thoroughgoing excoriation of modern youth by the visiting retreat orator, whose sermon, reproduced in full, is one of the many *tours de force* in the book. Studs Lonigan and his friends are not without the sense of sin, and that perhaps is what gives the special quality of horror to the picture of them that Farrell draws for us.

A concentration of this horror is managed in the next-to-last chapter, in which Studs and friends are all brought together at a New Year's party, and which has much the same effect as the famous Walpurgis Night episode in James Joyce's *Ulysses* [1922] and that last gruesome reunion in *Time Regained*, the final volume of Marcel Proust's seven-volume *Remembrance of Things Past* [1913–27]. It is a terrible chapter, one of the most terrible that has ever been written, and one that no other novelist of Farrell's generation could possibly have written. By means of a device that makes for the greatest economy of presentation, here and in the other chapters—the fragmenting of the narrative into thirty-two numbered episodes—the author emphasizes the almost insane disintegration of values that has occurred in the particular corner of the modern world on which he has chosen to concentrate.

Also, it may be said that in this brilliantly managed penultimate chapter Farrell avoids most of the defects that have so far stood in the way of his being the most mature, as he is already the most compelling, of the several young American writers who have emerged in the last few years. His faults, from the beginning, have been the consequences of an excessive enthusiasm, of an insufficient discipline. This is most easily to be seen in his habit of using the extraordinarily violent and picturesque language of abuse current among his South Side "punks" and "goofs" almost for its own sake. Moreover, in his Celtic fondness for the racier forms of expression, Farrell frequently fails to distinguish properly between the vocabulary of his characters and the vocabulary of his own style: "It was Saturday night. Husk Lonigan had the dough from the first pay he had earned since starting to work for the old man." The effect of this confusion is particularly disturbing in the more subjective passages.

It might further be objected that a good deal of the narrative in *The Young Manhood of Studs Lonigan*, although interesting enough in itself, is too loosely connected with the theme; the novel is certainly too long. But so successfully has Farrell brought together the many characters and disparate elements of the story in his amazing penultimate chapter that one is left with an impression of extraordinary unity. "Some day," Danny O'Neill tells himself, in one of the obviously autobiographical passages of the book, "he would drive this neighborhood and all his memories of it out of his consciousness with a book." This is that book, and James T. Farrell has succeeded so well in driving his South Side neighborhood out of his mind that we are not likely to forget it for a long time to come.

21. "T. S. Eliot, Grand Inquisitor" (1934)
After Strange Gods: A Primer of Modern Heresy, by T. S. Eliot

In a curious preface to *After Strange Gods* in which he seems to apologize for putting these three lectures into print at all, T. S. Eliot announces that he has no desire to preach (this is the word that he uses) to those whose views are fundamentally opposed to his own. Controversy, in our time at least, he believes to be entirely futile: there are not enough common assumptions, and the most important assumptions are, in any case, those that are felt rather than those that can be formulated. This should be properly discouraging to most readers—to all, in fact, except those whom Eliot designates in his preface as the "possibly convertible." It should probably serve as a sufficient warning to all others to absent themselves from his services, to leave him at peace among his candlesticks and prayer books.

But there is a certain note of challenging arrogance in this reasoning. It consists not so much in the implication that the assumptions Eliot is going to make are the only right ones as in the implication that these assumptions are necessarily peculiar to the particular point of view that he has expressed in all his recent criticism. The most fundamental of these assumptions is of course the importance for criticism, the primacy over all other kinds of problems, of the moral problem—the conflict between Good and Evil. And in his preface to the present collection, Eliot warns us quite fairly that it is once again in the role of moralist that he ascends the platform; the subtitle of his book is "A Primer of Modern Heresy." He is perfectly right, therefore, in insisting that all those not interested in his subject should withdraw from the congregation. But it does not follow that anyone interested in morality in general, or in the particular question of the relations between morality and modern literature, should pay him the same courtesy. Morality is one of the broadest of the many broad terms that we are in the habit of using in criticism; and it is the right, indeed the duty, of anyone genuinely concerned about modern literature to examine a little into the application of the term that Eliot makes in this collection.

Tradition is again his principal subject in these lectures—that view of tradition which is the fruit of the grotesque misalliance in France at the beginning of the present century between American pragmatism and ultramontane Catholicism. As a view of society and culture requiring a fundamental religious emotion at its base to give it any true validity for this or any other time, tradition like this reveals its weakness through the inappropriate ardor with which it is usually expressed—an ardor that is much more distinctly of the mind than of the heart. Like his masters, Charles Maurras and Jacques Maritain, Eliot makes the mistake of protesting quite a little too much; his logic is much too fluent; and in such a passage as the following what we hear are the accents of a man trying hard to convince himself of something rather than those of man who is completely—that is, emotionally as well intellectually—persuaded of what he is taking about:

> What we can do is to use our minds, remembering that a tradition without intelligence is not worth having, to discover what is the best life for us not as a political abstraction, but as a particular people in a particular place; what in the past is worth preserving and what should be rejected; and what conditions, within our power to bring about, would foster the society that we desired. [Lecture I of *After Strange Gods*]

Obviously in such a statement, Eliot is more concerned with expressing a desire than with recognizing a reality. His confusion is a result of failing to distinguish between what is, at the present stage in the development of Western European culture, possible and what his sensibility sets up as desirable. Eliot is a poet, and since poets not infrequently fall into such confusions, he may be understood—if not altogether pardoned. For the danger of such confusion becomes apparent a little later on the same page when the corollary that homogeneity is necessary for tradition leads him to conclude that "reasons of race and religion combine to make any large number of free-thinking Jews undesirable" [Lecture I of *After Strange Gods*]. Using such a remark as a basis, we need not stumble over ourselves in the effort to prove that Eliot is a fascist. Theoretically, he is for royalism rather than for fascism, which are not the same thing in theory, although in actuality they may be the same thing today. What the remark illustrates is the kind of inhuman and unrealistic conclusion to which Eliot's confused and sentimental view of tradition inevitably leads the moment that he touches a particular contemporary reality.

And this brings us back to the fundamental question of morality as it enters into his inquisition of modern letters. For it is possible to discover in the confusion just pointed out, in Eliot's persistent refusal to see the modern world as it is, a willfulness that is at least as morally reprehensible as any of the sins of the several heretic modern writers whom he singles out for rebuke. D. H. Lawrence undoubtedly suffered from being cut off from a settled religious and social tradition; his work is tainted to a marked degree with the modern vices of "sincerity" and "personality." It is even possible to agree that in many cases his influence has been more harmful than good. But what still gives to his work a moral justification, what cancels whatever incidental unmoral or "diabolic" elements may be found in it, is his effort, the essentially *moral* effort, to include all of the truth as he perceived it in the vision of the modern world that he left at his death. There was in him no sacrifice of honest perception for the sake of an intellectual structure that, however appealing it may be to the dialectic faculties, no longer has sufficient feasibility for our time.

A distinction that may be made, therefore, is between the morality of the writer conceived as effort—the unrelenting effort to integrate his perceptions with his beliefs, to reconcile the actual with the ideal—and the morality of the artist conceived as conformity to a systematized body of beliefs deriving from the conditions of an earlier period of religion and culture. Of these two views of morality Eliot has chosen the second; and the unfortunate consequences of his choice are revealed not only in his verse, in the progressive weakness of everything that he has written since *The Waste Land* [1922], but also in his prose, in such a frank admission as this of the separation in the same personality between the artist and the critic: "I should say that in one's prose reflections, one may be legitimately occupied with ideals, whereas in the writing of verse one can only deal with actuality" [Lecture I of *After Strange Gods*].

In psychological terms, such a formulation amounts to nothing less than a "schizoid" state of the personality; and since one of the objects of morality is the unification of the personality, one can only conclude that there is something profoundly wrong with Eliot's view of morality. For the poet nothing could be more useless or infertile than a system of beliefs that cannot stand up under the pressure of the actuality with which he has to deal. And in the critic who, like T. S. Eliot, is also a poet, nothing could be more indefensible than this blithe acceptance of the divorce between "ideals" and "actuality." Do we not have here an example of that *unregenerate* self-deception which, as everyone knows, is one of the ways in which Eliot's favorite antagonist, the devil, works in the modern world?

22. "The Worm i' the Bud" (1934)
Tender Is the Night, by F. Scott Fitzgerald

To label F. Scott Fitzgerald's new novel, *Tender Is the Night*, a study in psychological degeneration is not strictly accurate, for such degeneration presupposes an anterior dignity or perfection of character, and none of the characters in this book is made sufficiently measurable at the beginning to give to his later downhill course anything more than a mildly pathetic interest. None of them is even what one might call, in the loosest sense, mature. Richard Diver, young American war veteran turned psychiatrist, is too perfect a specimen of the Yale man of his generation to seem quite plausible as a surgeon of souls. Nicole recovers from her schizophrenia, the effect of an incestuous assault in childhood, only to acquire the neuroses of the frivolous, luxurious, and empty-pated society to which she is restored. And Rosemary Hoyt, that incredible flower of the Hollywood studios, begins, and ends, as hardly more than a glamorous moron.

Yet the effect of the novel as a whole is quite as depressing as that of any authentic study in moral and psychological degeneration. The vague depression that hovers over the opening chapters increases in intensity as the book moves on to its sordid termination. It increases, as a matter of fact, in an exact ratio to the growth of our confusion as to the precise reason for the hero's disintegration. Is it that once Nicole is cured of her disease she no longer has need of Dick's kind of love— the old story of the physician unable to heal himself? Is it that her money has acted like a virus to destroy his personality and with it his life-work? Or is it simply that he is a man of weak character, unable to resist temptation and concealing the fact from himself through immersion in alcohol? All these causes are indicated, and any one of them might be made sufficient, but the author's own unwillingness to choose among them, his own uncertainty communicated to the reader, continues to the last. And the result is depressing in the way that confusion in a work of literature is always depressing.

Glamor is here, as elsewhere, one of the most frequently used words in Fitzgerald's vocabulary; and because this very abstract word so obviously sums up much important feeling, constituting perhaps a key to such a novelist's sensibility, it may be worthwhile to submit it to that process of "dissociation" which Remy de Gourmont recommended [in *Dissociations* (1925] for cases of this kind. Now the word glamor, in Fitzgerald's writing, is usually applied to people or things or ways of living represented as being, in some total and general sense, attractive. It stands for a whole imponderable compound of desirable qualities—youth, beauty, gaiety, romantic charm. Daisy Buchanan in *The Great Gatsby* [1925] possessed glamor, and so do the two heroines in the present book, Nicole and Rosemary. But it should be noted that in the case of each of these exquisite creatures, to the possession of glamor is added another and more palpably attractive possession—money.

In *The Great Gatsby*, the narrator, fumbling for an exact description of Daisy, is told by Gatsby himself, "Her voice is full of money":

> That was it. . . . It was full of money—that was the inexhaustible charm that rose and fell in it, the jingle of it, the cymbals' song of it. . . . High in a white palace the king's daughter, the golden girl. . . .

And now again, in this new book, we find Nicole's lover [Tommy Barban] reminding her, "You've got too much money. That's the crux of the matter." In other words, for Fitzgerald's heroes youth and wealth, romance and luxury, love and money become somehow identified in the imagination. "Glamor" becomes a compound of glittering opposites. And because it consists for them in a confusion of essentially irreconcilable elements, their surrender to it leads, in the end, either to inglorious death in Long Island swimming pools or to slow deterioration on foreign sands.

This conflict, since that is what it really amounts to, is probably the thing that makes Fitzgerald an artist, the very distinguished artist that he revealed himself to be in *The Great Gatsby*. But the time has come when we must demand a more clean-cut recognition of its elements and a more single-minded effort toward its resolution. The biographer of Gatsby [the narrator Nick Carraway], weary of his riotous excursions into the human heart, returned to the Midwest wanting the whole world to be "in uniform and at a sort of moral attention forever." But Dick Diver turns out to be Jay Gatsby all over again, another poor boy with a "heightened sensitivity to the promises of life" betrayed by his own inability to make the right distinctions. And the repetition of the pattern turns out to be merely depressing. It is time now for F. Scott Fitzgerald, with his remarkable technical mastery of his craft, to give us a character who is not the victim of adolescent confusion, who is strong enough to turn deaf ears to the jingling cymbals of the golden girl.

23. "Flower of Manhattan" (1934)
A Backward Glance, by Edith Wharton

Among the many crisp utterances on her craft that Edith Wharton sprinkles throughout *A Backward Glance* is the following: "There could be no greater critical ineptitude than to judge a novel according to *what it ought to have been about.*" For the reader of these reminiscences desirous of extracting their very special quality of charm and interest, this remark is an excellent one to keep in mind. Nothing could be more foolish than to throw down this book with the objection that its backgrounds, its people, and its events seem lacking in vital significance to the harried and very much preoccupied reader of today. It is beside the point to make uncomplimentary comparisons between the author of *The House of Mirth* [1905] and the man with the dinner pail—that latter-nineteenth-century specter whom Wharton quaintly invokes in one passage.

The point is rather that Edith Wharton was the flower, the exquisite and certainly altogether undeserved flower, of a social group in America whose always tenuous existence has for some time now shaded off into oblivion. Possessing an English heritage with a slight mixture of Dutch and French [among her relations were the Roosevelts and the Astors], debutante of the Age of Innocence [also the title of a 1920 novel by Wharton], intimate of those frail and neurasthenic lovers of culture who flitted back and forth between Europe and America in the 1880s, Wharton was unquestionably affected by the moral and social values of the period and milieu into which she happened to be born. She would have been something of a monster not to have been so affected—up to a certain point. For like every authentic novelist, Wharton was at once the product of a very particular set of conditions and the observer and critic of those conditions. What made her a novelist rather than just another occupant of a box at the Metropolitan Opera was of course a very early perception of what she herself calls the "flatness and futility" of the society of her time.

But what was in the first place responsible for this perception on the part of a young woman who had every reason to be admirably conditioned, as one says nowadays, remains something of a mystery. Heredity, in her case, offers no clue: her mother seems to have been a perfect model of her class; and her father, except for a slightly adventurous taste for Spanish travel, was apparently undistinguished by any special sensibility or intelligence. Yet sensibility and intelligence were both gifts that Edith Wharton possessed and that set her apart automatically from her family and her class. The weaknesses of her writing—the thinness of her most characteristic material, the increasing fragility of her point of view, and the still insuperable aura of gentility—can all be laid to her time and her class. But her strength is her own—the strength that enabled her, in her very best work, to pass so far beyond that conditioning process which is regarded as so inevitable today. This is the mystery that will not be found revealed in either the handbooks of American cultural history or in the gospel according to Karl Marx.

If there is any continuous dramatic interest in these pages, it consists in the unbroken persistency of Edith Wharton's effort at emancipation—the old battle of the artist with the world. Contrary to what might have been expected, reconstruction of old New York, its manners and its people, occupies rather little of the book. Most of it is concerned with Wharton's personal friendships with people who, like Walter Berry [an American lawyer, diplomat, Francophile, and friend of several great writers, among them Wharton, James, and Proust] and Henry James, had made the same renunciations as she or who, like the novelist Paul Bourget and the salonnière Comtesse de Fitz-James [a.k.a. Rosalie von Gutmann], belonged by right of birth to the "richer soil" of Europe. For Wharton's life, once she had decided to commit herself to perspective rather than participation, was necessarily cast on the more intensely personal plane of friends, books, gardening, and travel. But even these compensations were not tolerated when they encroached too much on the practice of her craft. Unlike Gertrude Stein, she found in war-work less a romance than a distraction. And there is something half-apologetic in her account of the brilliant salons in Paris attended during the pre-war epoch. What emerges throughout is an insistence on the priority for the novelist of the claims of his craft over all other claims that might be made.

The question will occur, of course, how well this attitude is sustained by the evidence of so much of Wharton's actual practice of her craft—especially in recent years. It is not an exaggeration to say that it is almost impossible to believe that *Ethan Frome* [1911] and *Twilight Sleep* [1927] could have been written by the same hand. Speaking of Honoré de Balzac and William Thackeray and Marcel Proust, all novelists of manners like her, Wharton remarks on the tendency of such novelists "to be dazzled by contact with the very society they satirize." But she goes on to justify them with the suggestion that *pour comprendre il faut aimer*, and perhaps this is the best justification that can be offered for

Edith Wharton herself. Because in all her later fiction love takes precedence over understanding, the ambiguity that has always marked her writing is less productive of those qualities that we look for in the true satirist. But there is in the present work a kind of recrudescence of that old ambiguity that gives it a much more interesting quality than will be found in many works by authors who have definitely made up their minds about things.

24. "The Conversion of André Gide" (1934)

In 1925 André Gide, at the age of fifty-five, set out to realize a lifelong ambition to explore the region of the French Congo. Accompanied by a young disciple and an equipage of more than a hundred bearers, he began his journey, as he tells us in his journal [*The Journals of André Gide*, vol. II, 1914–27], with the fullest expectation of "voluptuous delight, forgetfulness," enjoyment of blue skies and virgin forests.

But almost on landing Gide met with certain things that produced on him a quite different effect. In the Ubangi country he saw "fifteen men and two women attached by the neck to a single rope . . . scarcely able to walk . . . escorted by two guards armed with five-pronged whips." He learned very soon that the colonial administration rules the blacks with an iron hand and that the French business concessions rule the administration. The sole function of the administration appears to be to keep 120,000 blacks in virtual slavery by means of terror, bloodshed, and coercion. The inhabitants of the villages are "mobilized," as they were in the war, and the lives of some 17,000 of them are calmly sacrificed to build a railway.

If a black does not wish to work, he may starve, although the pay for gathering rubber in the forest is only ten francs a month. Sometimes the concessionaires themselves do not hesitate to use force; and in one of the villages through which Gide passed, twenty natives had recently been tortured by agents of the great Forestière company [Begium's Societé Internationale Forestière et Minière du Congo]. What added to Gide's shock and indignation was the simplicity, honesty, and friendliness of those members of the exploited population with whom he had any personal dealings. "So much devotion . . . so much good will . . . and capability of affection, meeting almost always nothing but rebuffs . . . I feel here a whole suffering humanity, a poor, oppressed race."

On his return to Paris, Gide allowed himself, for perhaps the first time in his career, to become engaged in the life of action. He brought all the pressure of his reputation, and what political influence he had, to bear on the big colonial companies, managing after much contro-versy to secure some vague promises of reform. His two Congo journals [*Travels in the Congo*, 1927; *Return from Chad*, 1928] were found more indiscreet by the authorities than the most scandalously intimate pages of his autobiography [*If It Die*, 1924]. But the most important consequence of his holiday expedition, from the standpoint both of his own career and of the present direction of literature, did not manifest itself until a few years later when, in various magazine articles, he announced a complete and passionate conversion to communism and with it an unqualified sympathy with the present regime in Russia. "I should like to cry, to cry aloud my sympathy for the U.S.S.R., and have my voice heard; and that it should be of importance. I should like to live long enough to see the success of this tremendous effort, a success I long for with my whole soul, and for which I should like to be able to work. . . ."

To most readers in England and America, this declaration is undoubtedly less startling than to the French public, for whom André Gide has been the symbol of moral and philosophical individualism for more than thirty years. Gide has never been popular in the Protestant Anglo-Saxon countries for the simple reason that the central principle of his thought, the acceptance of individual authority in morals and reli-gion, is so commonplace as to be hardly interesting. It is not to be expected, therefore, that this new development in his career should have anything like the significance in those countries that it has in France, where he has owed his distinction from the beginning to the fact that he is a Protestant writer in a Catholic country. But such a development will be found to have significance enough if we discover in his career another parable of the bankruptcy of Romantic, Protestant individualism as an attitude in modern literature.

To the French the writings of Gide have represented the ultimate application of the principle that the individual can be depended on to work out his own salvation without the assistance of any outside authority. Supplementing a Calvinist upbringing and education with a youthful immersion in Friedrich Nietzsche, he very early managed to effect a curious reconciliation between an over-scrupulous moral conscience and the Dionysian ideal set up by his sensibility. Unlike Gustave Flaubert and Marcel Proust, André Gide has always been principally concerned with morality and the moral aspects of every problem of life with which he has had to deal. It is to be recalled that where Proust, treating the phenomenon of homosexuality, is content to treat it as a malady, Gide is compelled, in *Corydon* [1924, four Socratic dialogues on the subject of homosexuality] and elsewhere, to offer a defense of it in terms that are distinctly moral and ethical. His special modification of Nietzsche consisted in the addition of the notion that the "transvaluation of values" was not only desirable but necessary—a kind of moral duty imposed on the individual by his conscience.

Similarly, the public confession in his autobiography, *If It Die*, was dictated, as Gide assured the poet and critic Edmund Gosse, by the dread of hypocrisy, the inveterate habit of honesty. In his assaults on traditional ideas and institutions, it was always in the name of morality, his superior personal morality, that he addressed a scandalized bourgeois congregation. And the result was all the more disconcerting because he brought to the expression of his *immoralisme* a method and style that were reminiscent of the classical French moralists of the seventeenth and eighteenth centuries. His persuasiveness was that of a Protestant divine using the language of Buffon [a.k.a. Georges-Louis Leclerc, Comte de Buffon] and Blaise Pascal to lead the youth of France to a complete emancipation from everything that might be understood by conventional moral conduct.

As for the Dionysian ideal that is proposed in the expansive pages of Gide's *Notebooks of André Walter* [1891, semi-autobiographical novel] and *The Fruits of the Earth* [1897, prose-poem], it is less and less clearly defined in his later works. The vision of the Promethean hero, triumphantly released from all bonds and purely spontaneous in his movements and behavior, condenses into the cruel and perverse figures of Lafcadio in *The Vatican Cellars* [1914, novel] and Bernardin in *The Counterfeiters* [1925, novel]. What had been, in the loose nineteenth-century sense, *positive* in his work becomes a purely negative indulgence in moral and social irresponsibility. The Satanism with which Henri Massis and others charged Gide was thus more than the resentment of outraged orthodoxy. The transition from the intellectual justification of pleasure as a necessary condition of individual fulfilment to a predilection for that special form of pleasure that consists in doing injury to others is one that few nineteenth-century romantics themselves avoided, as Mario Praz has recently demonstrated in *The Romantic Agony* [1933]. In fact, it would seem that in Gide, only through the so-called "gratuitous act" is the individual able to become aware of himself at all. Lafcadio must push the harmless, long-suffering little provincial through the train window in order to assure himself of his own complete freedom from hampering conventional restraints. In the end, then, the individualism of Gide, with its unhappy misalliance between Protestant theology and nineteenth-century Romanticism, leads to a dehumanization rather than a heroic realization of the individual.

Yet in a recent full-length study, *André Gide: His Life and His Work* [1934], which attempts to do for Gide what its author has already done so successfully for Proust, Léon Pierre-Quint calls attention to the presence in Gide's work of a quality that is much less often recognized than his perversity. The quality is in many respects an opposite, and it might be referred to as tenderness. If Gide is at times capable of the most brutal indifference toward his characters, he is also at times capable of an almost caressing sympathy in his treatment of certain problems of human love and suffering. The character of Emmanuèle in the autobiography, the pathetic idyll of the pastor and the blind girl in *The Pastoral Symphony* [1919, novel], the relationship between Olivier and Édouard in *The Counterfeiters,* are all rendered with a directness of emotional sympathy that one does not ordinarily associate with the name of André Gide. The novelist in *The Counterfeiters* (Édouard [Gide's alter ego in this novel-within-a-novel] or Gide himself) who has traced out the terrible story of little Boris's persecution and suicide, decides in his journal not to use the incident in his book because there is "something peremptory, irrefutable, brutal, outrageously real" about it. The reason that he gives for its *indecency* is that he was not expecting it. But all the same there is an implied moral revulsion.

The purpose of recalling this occasional emergence of what might be called the human point of view in the most "satanic" of contemporary writers is to reduce a little the surprise that accompanies the news of his recent conversion. For the first thing that must strike us about this conversion is that it is a conversion in the strictest sense, that is to say, that it has occurred on the plane of the emotions rather than on that of the reason. It is based on intuition—on such an intuition, for example, as he has of the whole existence of the native boatman, Kara, who dies on the journey up river, and of whom he writes: "He leaves life without hope, and during his whole life he never had any certain hope of being able to earn more than one franc fifty per day." It is the intuition of misery and injustice on a scale such as he has never been able to imagine—"a whole suffering humanity"—that leads to that crystallization of thought and feeling which constitutes faith.

That what Gide has arrived at is closer to faith than to logical conviction is admitted in one of the *Autumn Leaves* [1949, reflective essays], first published in journal-form, in the *Nouvelle Revue française*, in the early 1940s: "'Fifty per cent illusion,' they say, when it is a question of the confidence accorded to the U.S.S.R. As if that were not equally true for every love, for every *faith!*" Ramon Fernandez is quite right in making the distinction that what attracts Gide is not Marxism but communism, not the doctrine but the ideal. In communism his capacity for sympathy and devotion, which had been able to express itself only rarely and through the most disparate personal objects, becomes attached to a general intellectual belief. The movements of his sensibility become one and the same with the movements of his mind. This is perhaps the deepest significance of Gide's conversion, and the process by which it has been achieved is the surest guarantee of its authenticity. (It may be compared in this respect with such another recent conversion as that of T. S. Eliot, which inspires just about as much conviction as a blackboard demonstration in logic.) In his conversion, André Gide has given a lesson to the present generation in the only *method* of conversion that is possible and justifiable for the artist.

At the same time it would be wrong to leave a picture of Gide, a repentant bourgeois individualist, throwing himself at the foot of the Lenin mausoleum in a gesture of pure emotional abandonment. He has made the effort to reconcile his old principle with his new faith, his individualism with the conception of the collectivist state. The intellectual dilemma is embraced in two statements that he has made, the one in 1923 (quoted by Pierre-Quint in *André Gide*), the other in 1930:

> Political questions seem to me less important than social questions; social questions less . . . important than moral questions. It is fitting to blame institutions less than men, and . . . it is they, first and foremost, whose reform is of importance.

> For the economic system, what is important to reform is man himself; and one will not reform the one without the other.

Between these two statements lies the decision that everyone attempting to understand contemporary reality must make. If the decision that André Gide has made takes on a momentous importance, it is because no writer in our time has stood so long and so desperately for the method of reforming man through lifting him by his own bootstraps. His rejection of this method, represented by his conversion, marks the dramatic collapse of one whole movement in modern European literature. But the alternative to the attitude of sterile, negative, backbiting individualism is not, according to Gide, a complete submergence of the individual in the state. And the final formula with which he leaves us is the following: "Individualism, properly understood, should be *at the service of the community.* . . ."

25. "Romains's Progress" (1934)
The Proud and the Meek, by Jules Romains

Toward the close of *The Proud and the Meek*, which is the third in the long series of novels [*Men of Good Will*: thirteen novels in two parts and a last novel in one part, 1932–46] in which Jules Romains is attempting to reconstruct the whole of French civilization of his time, the young and tender-hearted Abbé Jeanne arrives at a formulation of his private or "unofficial" philosophy. His conclusion is that human society, when all is said and done, can be reduced to a very simple dichotomy. There are, on the one side, the humble and the meek; on the other, the proud—those who are haughty and overweening "in the imagination of their hearts." According to the Abbé, this division has nothing to do with any effort to split up society into different social classes. The humble are sometimes to be found among the rich and the proud among the poor. "Social condition was not the origin of the difference. . . . It might simply be the sign of that difference, or mark where it had momentarily come to a head." The Abbé is aware that his view amounts to a kind of Manichaeism—but of the feelings only, not of the intellect.

On this very simple schematization of mankind, Romains has chosen to base the scheme of this third volume of his work, which, like the earlier volumes, is made up of two distinct parts. The first part deals exclusively with those characters in the work who illustrate most conspicuously the traits that the Abbé ascribes to the proud—"an appetite for power, or manifestations of power; a craving for conquest and possession."

Part I ["The Proud"] traces out, that is to say, the progress of the liaison between the arrogant and unscrupulous Sammécaud and the morally invertebrate Madame de Champcenais. A great many chapters are devoted to the detailed explanation of Havercamp's business operations, and it becomes more certain that the role of this unknown but energetic opportunist in the field of Paris real estate is to be that of pre-war "big businessman," American-style. Gurau, whose self-intoxication is of a different order, goes farther along the path of political compromise when he hires a young secretary to keep his conscience for him. The worldly young Abbé Mionnet attracts the interest of the right people and is on his way to becoming something more important than just another parish priest. And Quinette enjoys a little more of his peculiar kind of power when he toys with the idea of love in the company of a young musical composer, who will probably be his next victim. It is clear that in placing such people as Havercamp and Quinette in this first half of the volume, Romains is illustrating the Abbé Jeanne's contention that the proud are not always the rich. Of all the characters in this part, Havercamp alone is motivated by any material object, and even for him money is not so much the source as the symbol of power.

In Part II, "The Meek," we cross the bridge into the world of the pensive, the lovely, the compassionate—the kingdom of Christ. Little Louis Bastide is bought a new pair of tan shoes, which only serve to make him feel very guilty, especially since his father, a little later on, loses his job in the factory. A walk down one of the more squalid streets in the city suddenly turns the gentle Jerphanion into a revolutionist, and he begins to communicate with a kindred spirit, the schoolmaster Clanricard. The Abbé Jeanne visits an abandoned mother in a hovel outside the city's fortifications, and it is then that he has his clairvoyant vision of the double structure of society.

A few new characters are introduced in this second part: Madame Camille, the vendor of contraceptive preparations, to whom Madame de Champcenais is forced to have recourse; Stephen Bartlett, an English newspaperman, who is presented entirely through the travel diary in which he records his first impression of Paris; and Madame Yvoy, the wife of the employer of Bastide, Sr., who rebuffs little Louis brutally when he makes a plea for his father's reinstatement. And again it is to be noted—in his treatment of Bastide, Sr., who is too proud to accept a job that looks too much like charity, and of Madame Yvoy, who is afraid to allow her feelings to take precedence over her rights—that Romains is stressing the lack of correspondence between the two methods of dividing up society, the proud and the meek, on the one hand, and the economic and the spiritual or emotional, on the other.

Whether the dichotomy that the author follows in this particular volume represents any final and definitive social philosophy of his own is, of course, very much in question. The philosophy is, after all, expressed through the mind of one character or another and does not necessarily possess any more auctorial authority than the belief of Jerphanion, toward the close of the book, in the immediate necessity of a social revolution. The notion of the proud and the meek may be, therefore, only a notion—one of the many incidental ideas or conceits possible in a work of this length—which Romains here uses as a kind of structural device. Or it may simply be a rather homely and specific expression of some broader and more general philosophical attitude that will emerge more clearly in the later volumes of the series. Certainly it seems unlikely that a writer like Romains, who is capable of the most

117

abstract statement of his ideas, will be content in the end to allow such an emotive and even sentimental set of terms to speak for themselves.

As for the problem of Jules Romains's political identification, which has occupied certain of his American critics, there is nothing in the present volume, any more than in the earlier ones, to justify the somewhat hysterical cry of "fascist." The truth is that it is much too early to point with certitude to any one of the several political attitudes represented in the work as being unmistakably that of Romains himself. It has been one of the triumphs of *Men of Good Will* so far that it has presented the different social levels with their corresponding points of view so exclusively in terms of individual character that no explicit point of view on the part of the author has been necessary. Between Gurau's kind of radicalism and Jerphanion's, between Sammécaud's values and those of Clanricard, there can be no question of choice; and in his characterization of these people, Romains has thus relieved himself of the necessity of any judgment.

In view of the extravagant praise that the opening volumes of this series have received in the United States, however, it may not be too early to venture some very general estimate of Romains's powers as a novelist, some opinion concerning the more strictly literary qualities of his work. Unquestionably, the scale of his project is impressive; and its scale has perhaps been most responsible for the extraordinary claims that have been made, in advance, for his work. But scale in itself is not a sufficient guarantee of the excellence of a work of fiction. We need only recall the Rougon-Macquart cycle of Émile Zola [twenty novels, 1871–93] and the more recent prodigies of John Dos Passos [*The 42nd Parallel* (1930) and *1919* (1932), from the *U.S.A. Trilogy*, 1930–36]. It is well, therefore, to keep in mind Gertrude Stein's observation that a masterpiece does not always look like a masterpiece. And masterpiece on the same plane with the major works of Marcel Proust, James Joyce, or Thomas Mann, *Men of Good Will* has so far not given evidence of becoming.

Despite his technical virtuosity, his familiarity with the most diverse social backgrounds, and the maturity of his point of view, Romains has a mind that, for want of a better description, can only be called commonplace. As an analyst of the sentiment of love (in Wazemmes, Havercamp, Sammécaud), he is neither as subtle nor as profound as Proust; he belongs, as a matter of fact, somewhere between Proust and the latest popular writer in the French yellow-back tradition. The whole treatment of Quinette's psychology and criminality, moreover, is on a level somewhere between Fyodor Dostoevsky and Edgar Wallace. A close inspection of Romains's style itself would perhaps best reveal the quality of relaxed intellectual tension that marks his writing and that keeps him from becoming a master of the first order.

At the same time, *Men of Good Will* continues to be the most absorbing experiment in the field of fiction being made anywhere in the world at present. The pervasive weakness just pointed out does not in actuality prevent the series from supplying a solider and more continuous kind of interest than any number of works that reveal a greater depth, intensity, and brilliance. If it were not too much of a paradox, one might say that the very lack of intensity in these volumes becomes a virtue for a novel-reading public that has been provided with too rich a psychological fare for at least a generation. Jules Romains's *Men of Good Will* thus marks a new period for the novel, a period of recovered composure, in which the novelist can roll up his sleeves and quietly embark on mighty projects.

26. "Priapus in Georgia" (1935)
Journeyman, by Erskine Caldwell

Whatever else may be said of this new novel by Erskine Caldwell, it should dispel the notion that he is to be considered a realistic interpreter of conditions in the South—or anywhere else for that matter. For those persons who felt that the references to the tenant-farmer system in *Tobacco Road* [1932] and the description of the factory strike in *God's Little Acre* [1933] were really irrelevant distractions from the principal interest in those two books, *Journeyman* will prove a complete justification. It is now quite evident that Caldwell is interested in only one thing, and that whatever does not bear on that one thing is altogether beside the point. What both he and his admirers are most genuinely interested in, of course, is what T. S. Eliot, in one of the more somber poems of his later period ["Marina," 1930], describes as "the ecstasy of the animals."

To insure proper concentration on such a theme, Caldwell has necessarily to select a background and characters as little encumbered by traditional moral and intellectual impedimenta as possible. In this sense alone does his choice of the backwash region of rural Georgia have any particular significance. The essential need is for a background in which so few strictly human characteristics persist that the process of abstraction may be carried on with a minimum of difficulty. For the personages in Caldwell's idylls are not subhuman, as some critics maintain; they are so divested of everything that we understand by the human that there is scarcely any point in trying to establish a kinship

119

at all. What each of them is reduced to finally is a kind of abstraction—from the human to the animal, and even farther, as in *Journeyman*, from the complete animal organism to the single instinct. The world of Caldwell's three novels does not exist in heaven or on the earth, nor do the monomaniac creatures with which it is populated. It can be accepted only as a world of pure fantasy, a world of potentialities rather than actualities, in which man, that paragon of animals, is reduced to the lowest common denominator of his animal nature.

In outline this new book possesses the bald simplicity of the very earliest stories of the race. In particular, it recalls the old tales of gods mingling with men, the legends of Dionysus, Priapus, and Pan—in which the effect of the divine visitation was a considerable upsetting of the regular human order. So mischievous were these deities on their rare terrestrial holidays that mankind was thrown for the duration of their stay into what the Greeks were forced to call a "panic." The disturbing god was usually associated, it will also be recalled, with the cult of fertility or generation; and Semon Dye, the hero of *Journeyman*, is quite distinctly a divinity of this kind. As in most of the myths, it is never certain whether the name that this wandering preacher gives himself is really his own; his origins are left obscure; he arrives and departs like a will-o'-the-wisp. But in the course of his brief stay he swindles the dull-witted Georgia landowner out of his farm, his automobile, and his wife. He shoots down a Negro who protests against Semon's seduction of one of the girls on the farm, and he ensnares the whole neighborhood into the village schoolhouse to hear him preach against sin.

Toward this great event everything in the story is made to move; and it must be admitted that Semon Dye's efforts to instill "religion" into the sluggish congregation provide some of the most astonishing chapters in recent fiction. While neither the use of the Southern revivalist meeting nor the identification of sex with religion is exactly new in the contemporary American novel, these closing sections exceed in graphic concreteness anything that even Caldwell has so far offered to the public. And it is during this orgy that the resemblance between Semon Dye and the early gods of the phallic cults is most likely to strike the reader. He will seem to be less a man, even a caricature of an itinerant Southern preacher, than some incarnation out of time and space. When he is gone, the man called Clay remarks, "God help the people at the next place Semon picks out to stop and preach. . . . But I reckon they'll be just as tickled to have him around as I was."

In itself such a statement need not be given too much importance, but coming as it does at the close of this strange fable and paralleling so exactly the Dionysian resolutions of Caldwell's other two novels, we are probably justified in believing that we have finally come to rest in another rather homely reassertion of the religion of the flesh. In other words, Erskine Caldwell belongs to the tradition of modern writers who seek to discover an escape from the uncomfortable situation of being a man in the more limited satisfactions of the animal. Without reviving any of the familiar intellectual arguments against such a point of view, one may inquire whether Caldwell, in so limiting his own interest in his characters, does not also limit the possibility of very much future interest in his writing. In the last analysis, his reduction of man to animal, of experience to sensation, involves eliminations that the novelist who addresses himself to men, and not to animals, can hardly afford to make through very many successive works.

27. "New Country" (1935)
Collected Poems, 1929–1933, by C. Day-Lewis
Vienna: A Poem, by Stephen Spender
Cry of Time, by Hazel Hall

As the poems in C. Day-Lewis's volume are dated from 1929 to 1933, these four years presumably contain the full period of his practice as a poet. It is not often that a poet has the good fortune to have a "collected" edition so early in his career; but so generous have the fates already been to the group of young English writers of which he is a member that one is not too much surprised by the pretentiousness of the present occasion. Or, rather, it adds nothing to the astonishment with which one has followed the breathlessly hasty distribution of laurels that the arrival of these poets has stimulated in certain circles. From being something like the next step in a logical argument about modern verse (as Lewis demonstrates in his very self-complacent way), their poetry soon became a fashion; and from being a fashion, apparently, it has now become an institution.

C. Day-Lewis is, in one sense, the most articulate member of the group. Where W. H. Auden communicates his dissatisfaction with the present order through satire, concrete allegory, and technical indirections of every sort, Lewis comes straight to the point: his harangues have the blunt lucidity of a school coach warming up his team against a rival. Indeed, he is so intent on being articulate at all costs that he does not permit himself to have any of the feelings that usually confuse and retard the poet. Among these rejected feelings must be included the

121

distrust of rhetoric, the fear of repetition, and the sense of difficulty of the craft in which he is working.

In the long essay printed at the end of the volume and titled "A Hope for Poetry," Lewis selects Gerard Manley Hopkins, Wilfred Owen, and T. S. Eliot as his "ancestors." But all these poets differ from him in at least one important respect: none of them was quite so prolific. And from a reading of Hopkins' letters, Lewis might well have learned the meaning of what is understood by the humility of the artist.

In the recent uprising of the Vienna Socialists [the February Uprising, also known as the Austrian Civil War, is a term sometimes used for skirmishes between Fascist and Socialist forces in Austria between February 12 & 16, 1934], Stephen Spender has struck upon a subject in every sense appropriate for the theme that he has been attempting, in a diffuse and uncrystallized form, to express in his lyrics. If he has failed to write a magnificent poem, therefore, it is not because of the subject, which is a tremendous one from almost any point of view, but because of a still insufficient fusion between his theme and his emotions. The theme is there, and the emotions are there, but the two do not coalesce in a way that would give an ordered intensity to the whole. The theme and the emotions seem to exist on different planes, to be expressed in separate sections of the work.

It is not an accident that the subject comes through most successfully when the personal feeling about it is temporarily withheld; as, for example, on page twenty-three, where Spender drops into a few lines of straight prose reporting. The difficulty would seem to be that the imagery employed to render the feeling is not suitable for the proper rendering of the subject. And the jarring discordances between the somewhat hysterical modern feeling and the very simple realities of the situation confirm the suspicion that the complex type of imagery that Spender and his friends have taken over from Hopkins and Eliot may not be appropriate for charting the "new country" whose discovery they are announcing in their verse. For this may be required a revolution in the imagery and rhythm of poetry as drastic as the revolution in society. At the same time, Stephen Spender's ambitious sortie into the narrative form, if it is not a success, includes some of the finest and most brilliant single passages that he has yet written.

Speaking of fineness and brilliance, the publication of the posthumous volume *Cry of Time*, by Hazel Hall [1886–1924], suggests the immediate need of a total revaluation of her work. Her poems, read separately or as a whole, constitute one of the clearest, deepest, and most individual testaments presented by any modern poet. Although Hall was an invalid, she did not write a sick poetry. Her work, on the contrary, possesses a solid and wholly unsentimental health that might put to shame the most robust of her contemporaries:

> I am better for what is mine
> And for love of what I lack,
> Better for the tremulous design
> Of a leaf the moon made black.

In such poems as "Hand in Sunlight," "For a Broken Needle," and the group "Protest," Hall unites the clairvoyance of the invalid with the fastidious impatience of the true artist. The impatience is directed partly against the too facile abandonment to sorrow that her condition always threatened, partly against the dim looseness of words. Desiring to match the darkness of her mind "With syllables so taut they wind / Their meaning in a living death," she shows herself closer to Emily Dickinson than to any of the woman poets of her generation. Hall arrived, shortly before her death, at an even more harmonious vision than did Dickinson, and her verse attained a smoother texture without losing compression. In her "Audience to Poet," she expresses belief in a kind of salutary virtue to be derived from perfect verse:

> That we may live enough to feel
> Living, with something more than heart,
> Lay on our eye your tonic smart,
> Clang in our ear your uttered steel.

Hazel Hall's anxiety to cultivate the "something more than heart," besides relieving itself in the practice of a fine and aristocratic art, led also to her scorn of conventional variations on the themes of pain, melancholy, and despair. Her ultimate triumph was the unmystical process by which she was able to lose her own emotional identity in the impersonal realities of nature. To understand how this was accomplished, it is necessary to read Hall's "Tract on Living," one of her last poems, whose mood of quiet ecstasy may prove to be the right one for the apocalypse—if not the "new country"—that this generation is awaiting. These lines of recapitulation are broad enough to account for all the Jehovahs, all the lost sails and cities, stars and gods, for which the poets of today are mourning:

> Almost it seems that you,
> The seeker, are the something sought,
> Yourself the bell that called you through

The dawn, the noon, the dusk, the dew.
Almost it seems the tiger beat
Of your own pulses is the all,
The only answer is the call.

28. "And Tomorrow" (1935)
Pylon, by William Faulkner

For his central observer or "reverberator" in his new novel, *Pylon*, William Faulkner has chosen a character that is like a grotesque caricature of the typical hero of the postwar generation of poets and novelists. From one of the chapter headings, "Lovesong of J. A. Prufrock," it is apparent that Faulkner himself would have us make some such ironic connection. The unnamed reporter in the story is the bedraggled heir of the pallid Laforgian celibate of early T. S. Eliot, the masochistic intellectuals of Aldous Huxley, and the sterile *aficionados* of Ernest Hemingway. The outward and visible sign of his impotence is his almost ghostly physical fragility: "a scarecrow in a winter field," "a paper sack of empty beer bottles in the street," "a dandelion burr moving where there is no wind." From such comparisons it should also be plain that he is being made to serve as the whipping boy for Faulkner's whole generation. He is, or has been, the image which that generation has found staring back at itself every morning in the mirror. And the mirror must somehow and in some way be broken.

Although the image is not once and for all shattered in Faulkner's novel, it is at least temporarily dissolved in the blinding light of a rather new and certainly stirring expression of human indifference to the discomforts of living and the menace of death. On an aviation field outside New Orleans, while Mardi Gras is at its height in that city, the half-crazy reporter, "patron saint of all waifs," picks up with a group of barnstorming aerial performers consisting of the pilot Schumann, his wife, a parachute jumper, and a small child of undetermined parentage. There is also Jiggs, the mechanic, whose eyes are like electric bulbs and whose legs are like a polo pony's.

For the reporter, these people "ain't human like us . . . crash one and it ain't even blood when you haul him out: it's cylinder oil the same as in the crankcase." They are in every sense the inhabitants of another element: the bright emissaries of a vacuum "beyond flesh and time." Yet the enchanted reporter shelters them, lets them rob him, and in his inchoate fashion falls in love with the woman. It is through his efforts also that Schumann secures the ramshackle plane with which this flier hopes to win a two-thousand-dollar prize, but in which he is doomed to mark his last pylon. Disaster and savage disillusion are not to be escaped; and the reporter's story ends with a scattering of discarded purple patches on a city-room floor.

Of course, it is a familiar Romanticism that causes Faulkner to turn to what is for our time the most spectacular expression of the perennial instinct of flight. These reckless nomads of the air are not essentially different from the graceful toreadors that court death so beautifully in the pages of Hemingway. (And it may be remarked that they are presented with the same remoteness and opaqueness: none of them is quite so real as the sensibility for which they exist with such charm and fascination.) Admiration of their careless intrepidity does not drown the burden: "Tomorrow and tomorrow and tomorrow; not only not to hope, not even to wait: just to endure."

If *Pylon* still manages to be much the best that William Faulkner has yet written, therefore, it is not because this writer has at last discovered a permanent balm for his generation. It is not because one can point to any growth in a philosophical sense, any modification or enlargement of his theme. It is rather that in this novel he has found an almost ideal subject for the presentation of his theme. By writing about fliers and flying machines, Faulkner has indeed made his subject indistinguishable from the theme of flight into the life of action, which has been one of the three or four dominating themes in contemporary fiction. And he has given to the treatment of such a theme an interest and power which one had believed that it was no longer capable of sustaining.

29. "Portrait of an Age" (1935)
Judgment Day, by James T. Farrell

As James T. Farrell has revealed throughout the trilogy of which *Judgment Day* is the concluding volume, he is the most terrifying novelist now writing in America. The typical characters of the slightly older generation of fiction writers can usually be comfortably dismissed as being in one way or another very special cases. Studs Lonigan, on the other hand, is, or is intended to be, a representative product of one whole region of contemporary American culture. He is Farrell's version of *l'homme moyen sensual* [man of average appetites] of our time. He is the man in the subway, the man who fixes the plumbing, the man who walks into a thousand cinema palaces throughout the land. His obsessions—health, religion, financial security—are those inculcated by his environment. He is, according to most of the standards of that environment, a thoroughly *normal* specimen. This is what makes Farrell's portrait of him so terrifying.

There is nothing in this final volume comparable for sheer terror with that penultimate chapter in *The Young Manhood of Studs Lonigan* [1934], in which Farrell crystallized his vision of the contemporary world in a scene that is like an epitome of all human depravity and evil. It is as if after such a catharsis the author had been forced to write at a lower pitch, to let the threads of the web draw in upon his hero in a somewhat relaxed manner. The result is a certain repetitiousness, an occasional lapse into the banal and irrelevant, a general prolixity in the rendition of the characters' thoughts and emotions. The truth is that, whether because of the decreasing novelty of the material for the reader or because of a decreasing interest in it on Farrell's part, this last volume does not, through its first three-quarters, approach the qualities of its two predecessors in the series [*The Young Manhood of Studs Lonigan* was preceded by *Young Lonigan* (1932)]. But this judgment must immediately be followed by the qualification that the last quarter, which is devoted to Studs Lonigan's illness and death, brings the whole series to a brilliant and momentous close.

The theme, when it does finally emerge, is not stated but implied— through a contrast of the most objective sort between materials belonging by every right to the completion of the canvas. Old Patrick Lonigan [Studs's father], melancholy over the bankruptcy of his business, the loss of his home, and the impending death of his son, is halted on his way home by an unusually raucous May Day demon- stration near the University of Chicago. As the long parade of workingmen, college students, and young pioneers files past, with their banners "Free Tom Mooney" [Mooney (1882–1942) was an American political activist and labor leader who was convicted of the San Francisco Preparedness Day Bombing of 1916 (in anticipation of the United States's imminent entry into World War I) and "Defend the Soviet Union," Patrick curses them for their brazenness, their youthful strength and good looks, their hopefulness. In one of the surest psychological passages that Farrell has ever written, he shows how all the voices of the old man's religious and patriotic loyalties rise up in protest, how all of them are drowned out by this strange new music, and how he can drive its din from his ears only by retiring to the nearest speakeasy. When Patrick returns home in a drunken state, followed by his younger son [Martin] in the same condition, Studs is already in his death agony [from pneumonia]; and a little later the reader is made to feel—what one feels only in the greatest works of fiction—that the individual catastrophe is but the symbolical parallel to some vaster and more consequential catastrophe in the world at large.

More than this implication will not be found at the close of the Studs Lonigan trilogy, which is a representation rather than an indictment of our culture. The distinction between these two nouns should, but probably will not, include the answer to the question whether or not James T. Farrell is to be classed as a writer of the proletarian revolutionary school, whether he is an artist or a propagandist. From one point of view, of course, no member of that school has written a more profoundly revolutionary novel. If it is revolutionary in a writer to project the experience of his time with such truth and vividness that a reader, imposing on it his own qualitative judgment, can only decide that such experience must be changed, then Farrell must be considered revolutionary. But Farrell is not this reader; he does not anywhere in his book impose such a judgment. "Here is a record of one large and important area of contemporary experience," Farrell seems to say. "It is as complete and honest and penetrating as I can make it. You make of it what you must." His direct concern, in other words, has been with truth, which for the artist is the truth of experience as he perceives it, not the truth that the mind in every age finds it necessary to impose on its experience.

As an artist, of course, Farrell is not without faults of the gravest kind; but the most serious of them, as it happens, is the defect of his greatest virtue. What distinguishes him from most recent American fiction writers is what may be called the wholeness or balanced sanity of his perception. He has steered a successful course between the Charybdis of contemporary subjectivism and the Scylla of Marxist orthodoxy. But one of the less fortunate consequences of the balanced view of life for the artist is the tendency to include more in his picture than is always necessary. In addition to a weakening of the power of selection, this brings with it a relaxation of intensity, since without a bias either of temperament or doctrine intensity must be supplied by the aesthetic process alone. Farrell's most serious defect at present is the all-too-common one of an insufficient control over his material. His need is to submit himself to a discipline that will enable him to do greater justice to the breadth and clarity of his perception. If he does manage to achieve such an aesthetic discipline within the next few years, there will be nothing to prevent him from becoming one of the truly great writers of our time.

30. "Radix Malorum" (1935)
The Treasure of the Sierra Madre, by B. Traven

It is not hard to understand why the two books to date of this author have enjoyed such an enormous vogue in the various European countries in which they appeared before being published in English. If B. Traven's first novel, *The Death Ship* [1926], has sold over a million and a half copies in Soviet Russia, and sold over 200,000 copies in Germany before it was banned by the Hitler government, the reason is to be found in the fact that it is based on a situation which, while realistically conceived and rendered, is actually a symbolical representation of much that is weighing upon the European mind at present.

Unlike Hans Fallada, Louis-Ferdinand Céline, and the majority of Marxist writers, B. Traven [a.k.a. Bruno Traven, Ret Marut, Otto Feige] thus is not so much concerned with expressing an abstract point of view toward the modern world as with offering an epitomized impression of that world so vivid and complete that the reader can arrive at a point of view of his own. Traven is almost entirely free from the greatest of all the vices of the contemporary fiction writer, which is to work from the idea to the experience. In both his books the experience constitutes the pattern, what T. S. Eliot once called the "objective correlative," for ideas and attitudes that are perhaps only incompletely formulated in the mind. The experience *is* the idea. And because of this building so solidly on the situation or experience or "story," Traven has to depend very little on style and the other idiosyncratic graces of the modern novelist. The virtues of his writing, construction and detail, suffer no loss in translation. The "objective correlative" that he supplies for the mood of self-inquiry that is passing over the Western world is comprehensible in every tongue. [B. Traven's twelve novels, collected short stories, and single book of reportage were published in German first, and their English editions appeared later; nevertheless, the author always claimed that the English versions were the original ones and that the German renditions were only their translations.]

The central situation in the present book, *The Treasure of the Sierra Madre*, is one of the oldest known to storytelling. It was old when Geoffrey Chaucer appropriated it for "The Pardoner's Tale" [*The Canterbury Tales*, 1387–1400] and with minor variations it has never ceased being used in narrative and drama. Yet Traven has filled in this situation with such an abundance of freshly imagined anecdote and detail that it produces the effect of a tale being told for the first time.

Three derelict Americans in Mexico set out on an expedition in search of a fabulous gold mine abandoned centuries ago by the

Spaniards when it was found to be under an Indian curse. After many hardships they discover the mine, work at it arduously for many months, and finally depart with their treasure. But on the journey home the oldest of the trio is forced to stay behind in an Indian village, trusting his share of the booty to his companions. One of these is gradually over-taken by the compulsion to kill his comrade and keep all the little bags of gold dust for himself. Forcing the other man into a forest clearing, he shoots him down in cold blood. A little farther on down the road, however, he meets with a band of Mexican bandits who deal him the same fate, severing his head from his body with a single stroke of a machete. The gold dust is scattered to the four winds.

It should be added that the main story is supported by a kind of anec-dotal history of all the stories of cruelty and bloodshed that have grown up around gold prospecting in Mexico, from the time of the Spanish to the present. The book itself is a mine of melancholy information about the effects of gold on races and individual men. *The Treasure of the Sierra Madre* includes also, without departing from the main subject, as profound an insight into the Mexican psychology as will be found in any recent work on the subject. But it is as a parable, in the broadest sense, of the impingement of greed on the whole of a man's character, as in the case of the rather ordinary young American in the story, that B. Traven's novel will appeal to a world that is becoming more and more aware of the importance of the theme. ["Radix malorum est cupiditas," or "The root of evil is greed."] It is certain to meet with the same popularity in Russia and the same disapproval in Germany as *The Death Ship*—and for precisely the same reasons.

31. "Footprints in Cement" (1935)
Lucy Gayheart, by Willa Cather

Years after the heroine of this novel has been found entrapped by a tree stump beneath the icy waters of a Midwestern river, her former admirer [Harry Gordon], now sole owner of the old Gayheart place at the end of town, gives instructions to one of his retainers: "Those marks there in the cement were made by [Jacob] Gayheart's daughter Lucy, when she was a little girl. I'll just ask you that nothing happens to those two slabs of walk—in my time, at least." Such a sentiment of the past, with its special commingling of the sacred and the common-place, is actually all that Willa Cather's new work, *Lucy Gayheart*—despite its elaborate preparation of character and back-ground—finally manages to communicate. The book has been only another and less memorable rendition of the theme that has occupied this novelist from the beginning.

Like the heroines of *The Song of the Lark* [1915], *O Pioneers* [1913], and *A Lost Lady* [1923], Lucy Gayheart is one of those exquisite "sports" that were thrown up at the close of the period of pioneer expansion in the West. She is too lovely, too intelligent, too responsive to the call of what is rhetorically designated as life to be content with anything which that period had to offer. Unlike Marian Forrester [the main character of *A Lost Lady*], however, she is unable to compromise, and that is the pathos of her situation. For a few hours she has known dangerous release in the arms of an aging and unhappy baritone [Clement Sebastian] in a dimly lighted studio in the Fine Arts Building [a.k.a. the Studebaker Building] in Chicago. After such a taste of abandonment, with all that it holds of classical music and continental passion and Romantic sorrow, the daily bread of Harry Gordon's too well-disciplined affections loses all its savor for her. After such a revelation, as a matter of fact, there can be no future for either Lucy or this novel. Cather would be hard put to dispose of such a character as Clement Sebastian elsewhere than in the picturesque depths of Lake Como. And Lucy Gayheart has made a choice that leaves her only the life-in-death of continued existence in the Platte Valley [Nebraska]. For Harry Gordon and the reader there can be only the perennial, if somewhat unsatisfactory, consolation of the footprints in the cement.

The outline of Cather's story, as given, is of course reducible to something that one has already seen many times and will see again in the Hollywood cinema. But to complain of its hackneyed simplicity is not to take account in this book of that other element of the novel form for which Willa Cather has been considered especially notable. The following is offered as a fair example of the style that is used to indicate or render subjective states on the part of the characters in *Lucy Gayheart*:

> She had never loved the city so much; the city which gave one the freedom to spend one's youth as one pleased, to have one's secret, to choose one's master and serve him in one's own way. Yesterday's rain had left a bitter, spring-like smell in the air; the vehemence that beat against her in the street and hummed above her had something a little wistful in it tonight, like a plaintive hand-organ tune. All the lovely things in the shop windows, the furs and jewels, roses and orchids, seemed to belong to her as she passed them. Not to have wrapped up and sent home

certainly; where would she put them? But they were hers to live among.

That this is not the best writing that has come to us from the author of *My Ántonia* [1918] and *A Lost Lady* is as evident from the sentimentally relaxed rhythms as from the stereotyped imagery. What it reveals even more profoundly than the naïvely Romantic pattern of her newest book is how completely this writer now permits the *élans* of her sensibility to rule over her intelligence. Where a Flaubert, troubled by much the same conflict between imagination and conscience, was able at the end to attain to the high detachment of *Sentimental Education* [1869], Cather surrenders to the temptation of facile sentimentalism, which has been her greatest temptation from the beginning. For those who had hoped that the archeological holiday of her last two novels [*Death Comes to the Archbishop* (1927) and *Shadows on the Rock* (1931)] might be followed by a return to the clearly envisaged experience of her earlier books about the West, *Lucy Gayheart* can only be a source of grave discouragement.

32. "A Matter of Quality" (1935)
"Flowering Judas" and Other Stories, by Katherine Anne Porter

In the five years that have passed since the almost surreptitious publication of the short story "Flowering Judas" [1930], Katherine Anne Porter has apparently written only four stories that she believes worthy of being included in the same collection. With such a record, obviously, this writer can hardly expect to attain to the titanic company of those recent fictionists who have been busily demonstrating the superiority of matter over mind in literary production. She offers no panoramic survey of modern society, no saga of the American or any other soil, no documentary materials for a study in the elephantiasis of the literary sensibility in our time. Porter cannot successfully be compared with Balzac, Tolstoy, or Proust—and Rabelais is quite out of the question. Confronted with her 285 widely spaced pages, the most popular of current standards—the standard of quantitative measurement—becomes as ineffectual as a yardstick in an Einsteinian universe. Quality rather than quantity being the only possible issue, criticism is suddenly made aware how little prepared it is for its task.

Nonetheless, it is possible to isolate the essential quality of these ten stories as an honesty that manages to steer a successful course between the two worst perils of the contemporary prose writer: artificiality and that self-conscious effort at sincerity which is a special kind of artificiality. "A spray of lantern light shot through the hedge, a single voice slashed the blackness, ripped the fragile layer of silence suspended above the hut." This passage from the story "María Concepción," with its too vivid parade of strong verbs, does come pretty close to being "literary." But it is just enough justified by the situation and there is no more of it than is necessary.

More often an effect depends on a single word so casually embedded in the sentence as to escape individual attention. María Concepción's friends "were around her, speaking for her, defending her, the forces of life were ranged invincibly with her against the beaten dead." Here the whole weight of the feeling is contained, with Flaubertian inevitability, in the one adjective toward the end. The same kind of force without emphasis is achieved when María Concepción looks down upon the dead body of her rival: "María Rosa had eaten too much honey and had had too much love." As it happens, María Rosa had been a beekeeper, so that even in this rare use of symbolism Porter does not depart from the literal: the fact and the symbol are one and the same.

And throughout these stories it is the same strict adherence to the fact for what the fact can produce that saves the author both from the rhetorical emphasis of Virginia Woolf and her followers and from the equally rhetorical understatement of the Hemingway school. This gift for making audible what might be called the overtones of fact is responsible for Porter's success in this collection over such a wide range of subjects. Whether it is the phonographic recording of a quarrel between two young people in the country, or the predicament of a young American schoolmistress in Mexico, or the incorrigible Bovaryism of an Irish immigrant woman on a Connecticut farm, Porter is able to secure richness without too much reliance on the brush.

The only objection that may be raised is that in certain of the stories, there is an insufficient crystallization of theme. In "Theft," by contrast, the tenuous mood is properly condensed in the "moral" attached at the close: "I was right not to be afraid of any thief but myself, who will end up by leaving me nothing." But in "Magic" and "He," as in "Hacienda" and "That Tree," no such definition is given to the experience that has been recorded. From this point of view, the most satisfactory items are "María Concepción" and "The Cracked Looking-Glass." If Katherine Anne Porter had written nothing but these two short narratives, she would still be among the most distinguished masters of her craft in America.

33. "The Critic's Job" (1935)
The Double Agent: Essays in Craft and Elucidation, by R. P. Blackmur

The fundamental defect of most literary criticism in our time is that its object has been too rarely the object that alone would guarantee its autonomy as a special form or mode of intellectual activity—the work of literature. Its object, when it has risen above mere gossip or entertainment, has usually proved to be situated in realms of discourse only remotely or obliquely related to the specific realm of literature—in history, in philosophy, in psychoanalysis, or, as more recently, in political economy. Even such critics as I. A. Richards and Kenneth Burke, who do keep close to the object most of the time, prove upon scrutiny, as R. P. Blackmur points out, to be really talking about linguistics or moral philosophy. Of critics like Samuel Johnson, Walter Pater, and Remy de Gourmont, to mention only more obvious examples of the literary critic *pur sang*, we have suffered a dearth since literature and the other arts were disqualified [as decadent] by all right-minded citizens during the scandalous 1890s.

The T. S. Eliot of *The Sacred Wood* [1920] was perhaps the last important critic in English to write about literature as literature and not as something else; and the eclectic nature of his reputation attested to the rarity of his approach. But Eliot, forsaking literature for theology, has now reduced criticism to a somnolent Sermon on the Devil. Criticism as a whole has become an aerial battleground for competing theologies, including the brand whose leading apologist in this country is Granville Hicks. The literary object, needless to say, has been left far below. And as literary criticism has drifted into the adjacent regions of speculation, it has lost its special role or function, its reason for existence. To put the matter more bluntly, it has lost its utility for those who happen to be most interested in literature when they are talking or reading about literature.

Blackmur is a young critic who brings to his task, in addition to "enough love and enough knowledge," enough real concentration on the object to make his essays in "craft and elucidation" very useful to the contemporary reader. The most useful items in his collection are precisely those in which the focus is most sharply on the text of the writers under discussion: "Notes on E. E. Cummings' Language," "Examples of Wallace Stevens," "The Method of Marianne Moore," "D. H. Lawrence and Expressive Form," and "The Masks of Ezra Pound." These are among the best, because among the most securely grounded, studies of these modern writers that will be found anywhere.

If Blackmur has gone to school to Eliot [about whom he writes in *The Double Agent,* in the essay "From *Ash Wednesday* (1930) to *Murder in the Cathedral* (1935)"], as is quite obvious from his method, what he has learned has been a method rather than a particular set of judgments. He has applied to certain important American poets of our day the same sort of rigorous textual analysis that Eliot used so successfully on the Elizabethans. And, as in Eliot, distinctions between the imagery used by two poets, between different kinds of imagery used by the same poet, or between the imagery and the intention in a given poem—such distinctions lead usually to some sort of generalized conclusion about a poet or about poetry in general.

The usefulness of R. P. Blackmur's fervently concentrated approach in this volume will be found in the amount of real light that it throws on the sometimes extremely difficult objects of modern literature, such as *The Cantos* [1925] of Ezra Pound or *The Bridge* [1930] of Hart Crane. [*The Double Agent* includes an essay on Crane and *The Bridge.*] But the conclusions in the essays mentioned above are nearly all safely within the sphere of literary form and style; that is, they do not involve any single and definite intellectual point of view. Technical criticism, like the philosophical, the psychological, and the political varieties, is also only a partial approach to the object. Its value, therefore, is limited.

It was inevitable, therefore, that Blackmur, again following Eliot, should recognize the desirability of relating his specific analyses to a larger frame of intellectual values. In a final essay the difficulties of such an undertaking are demonstrated in a style that is a reflection of a good deal of earnest confusion. (The trouble is partly that Blackmur has not yet decided whether T. S. Eliot or Henry James is to be the principal influence on his prose.) After reviewing most of the prevalent approaches to literature, Blackmur modestly offers his own, which turns out to be the "technical," although a much-qualified and indeed debilitated version of that approach. It is, we are told, only the facts about a literary work that can be examined; the rest can "only be known, not talked about." But even the facts, it appears, can be arrived at completely only by direct apprehension—mere technical scrutiny is not enough. Art is defined as "the looking-glass of the pre-conscious," and criticism as "the establishment and evaluation . . . of the modes of making the pre-conscious consciously available." In other words, the critic undergoes a kind of mystic immersion in the object, as a result of which he produces a few odd bits of elucidation.

The objection to this description, of course, is that it fails to provide the modern critic with what is his greatest need, a method for evaluating the fruits of the "pre-conscious." It reduces his role to that of a deep-sea diver who does not know what to do with the treasures that he brings up to the surface. He is still without a principle for relating his special perceptions to a larger frame of values, so that Blackmur has not really progressed in theory beyond the practice of his earlier and more useful essays [commencing in 1930, and several of which are included in the posthumous *Selected Essays of R. P. Blackmur* (1986), edited by Denis Donoghue]. What his stimulating book does most forcibly demonstrate, especially through its unresolved contradictions, is the immediate necessity of restoring to criticism a more intimate correspondence between what is talked about and what is known, between the literary object and the whole of our intellectual arrangement of experience. The critic's job is to learn once again how to combine the closest attention to the object with the most complete awareness of the world that surrounds it.

34. "On Being Contemporary" (1936)

When Ben Jonson said of his friend William Shakespeare that he was not of an age but for all time, he set the pattern for a kind of literary compliment that has caused much confusion from his time to our own. For as both writers recede into the past, it becomes evident how distinctly Shakespeare, as "Nature's child," was also the child of that tempestuous misalliance between the Middle Ages and the Renaissance which gives its peculiar character to the Elizabethan era. Shakespeare was also, as Jonson had apostrophized him a little earlier, "soul of the age!" ["To the Memory of My Beloved the Author, Mr. William Shakespeare and What He Hath Left Us" (1623)]. Undoubtedly a more accurate tribute would have been that Shakespeare gave such a profound expression to the dominant conflict of his time as it was rehearsed in his own personality that even his contemporaries could perceive the timeless quality of his work. He was for all time because he was so profoundly and completely of his own age. Nothing of the compliment is lost through the paradoxical restatement; in fact, we admire more the sensibility that could absorb so many diverse materials, the intelligence that could operate on them, and the imagination that could finally fuse them into a succession of enduring wholes.

One is reminded of the Jonsonian eulogy by the number of eloquent reassertions that we have had in recent months of the same belief in the extra-temporal nature of literature and the literary experience. Edmund Wilson, addressing a letter to the Russians on the subject of

Ernest Hemingway, deplores the so-called decadent elements in this writer's work—the bullfighting, the lion-hunting, and the rest—at the same time that he points out the coexistence of certain moral values, like courage and integrity, which are represented as timeless and therefore capable of being used over and over again. André Gide, describing how he spent one whole day of his life recently, offers what is really an apology for having turned from his social and political preoccupations to a reading of the *Odes of Pierre de Ronsard* [1550–52]. "Nothing could be less contemporary," he confesses. "Merely very beautiful verses, answering to no other need than that of filling the heart and mind with a species of dynamic and thoroughly wholesome joy." A little further on and this emotion is qualified by the phrase "extra-temporal." And then we have had in the pages of the *Nation* Joseph Wood Krutch's sharp reprimand to those reviewers and critics who are in the habit of referring to one living writer after another as belonging to the past. The objection to this habit, according to Krutch, is that it is "to render trivial the whole enterprise of literature by depriving it of one of its fundamental assumptions—the assumption, that is, that human intelligence and human feeling are characterized by a continuity in virtue of which it is possible for a man to say something that will continue to seem to the point some centuries, let alone some months, after it is said."

Certainly all three of these writers—Wilson, Gide, Krutch—are justified in stressing at this time the essential continuity of those elements of a literary work that are capable of being detached from its content. The relevance of their defense will be appreciated by anyone who has been following the current trend of literary criticism all over the world. But also the uncomfortable impression must strike some readers that these absolute values, this extra-temporal emotion, this intelligence and feeling are spoken of in a way to suggest that they float about, like Platonic essences, in a kind of purified literary arcanum. Certain qualities and effects have been isolated and then reduced to their proper abstractions by the mind. Further discussion of these abstractions would almost certainly require the critic to build up intellectual structures that would soon become quite independent of the particular and concrete work. We should be asked to pass, in other words, from the contemplation of the individual work to the more general problems of morality, aesthetics, and human psychology. Unquestionably the value of such criticism would be very great, for it would prove to us how much these problems are involved in every literary work. But its danger, perhaps, is to make us forget that every worthwhile work is in itself the solution of a problem, of a whole host of problems, all of which are embraced in the general problem of the

136

writer's relationship to his experience. A more practical program for the critic in any time would therefore be to determine, insofar as he is able, how those qualities of literature that are indubitably perennial and universal may be re-created in terms of the materials and ruling conceptions of his own age.

The problem is upon us today with such urgency that unless we do something to clarify it, we are going to have very little writing possessing form, values, and intelligence to bequeath to posterity. The most volatile and prolific movement in American poetry at the moment, for example, is operating on the theory that to be contemporary is to invoke the future. In fact, the general mass of revolutionary poetry turned out in the last few years provides an excellent example of just how much literary criticism can affect the writing of a period. This criticism has instructed the writer in the belief that he is most surely of his time when he gives expression to its aspirations for the future. It encourages him to mortgage his experience for an abstraction, with the result that his work falls into the didactic, the forensic, and the oratorical, all legitimate forms of discourse but none of them dependent for their effect on the kind of direct representation of experience that is essential to literature. Form is absent from most revolutionary poetry because form in literature arises from the conflict between intelligence and experience within the writer himself, and the conflict of the revolutionary poet is waged exclusively with society. As for "values," the rendition of these is projected, along with the experience that alone could give them any reality, into the abstract future. And the intelligence, when it is allowed to operate at all, is turned outward to ends beyond the work. The type of utopian revolutionary writer in every age offers such an unsatisfactory example of the contemporary because he offers us, in the first place, such an unsatisfactory example of the writer.

Yet the quality of his work is ultimately no worse, perhaps, than that of the more ubiquitous type of writer who for one reason or another is cut off from the vital currents of the life and thought of his time. Examples enough we have in the writer who persists in troubling ghosts that have already been laid, the writer who is too slow to recognize when a literary attitude or method has been at least temporarily exhausted, the writer who attempts to fan into life sentiments and beliefs that have perished with the social patterns to which they were attached, and the writer who disguises his timidity or distaste beneath a disingenuous archaism. If there are more examples of this type of writer than of any other, it is because the combination of courage and awareness that stimulated great literary energy is rare in any time and place. From the standpoint of the reader who looks for the "perennial and universal," the absence of this energy is felt not so much in any backwardness in ideas and theories as in the total quality of the experience revealed in the writing of those who remain behind or "outside" their time.

We are left, then, with the notion of the writer who is neither of the past nor of the future but quite simply of his own time. It should be evident, however, that it is never simple for the writer to be of his own time. It is much easier to stuff experience into the handy molds of the immediate past or to make statements about the future. Either evasion makes fewer demands on the energy than the attempt to render with precision a setting of experience that never has been, and never will be again, quite the same in all its features. To be contemporary in this sense is to maintain the kind of equilibrium that Ronsard was able to maintain in the fifteenth century, Shakespeare in the sixteenth, and every complete writer in the centuries that have followed. This equilibrium in the writer is of course between his consciousness of the changes going on in the social and intellectual life around him and his sense of duty to those things that we call the perennial and the universal. His awareness of the first is important because it is the measure of his energy, and while energy is not the sole measure of his merit, it is an indispensable perquisite to everything in his work. But this awareness can never be allowed to carry him to the point where he is led from his own object to objects outside his proper sphere. The object with which he is concerned must remain the unique expression of a unique complex of experience.

It may be added that perhaps one of the greatest handicaps to being truly contemporary is a too self-conscious effort of awareness. Among current American writers, for example, Archibald MacLeish has been particularly distinguished by the nervous concern that he has betrayed throughout his career over the necessity of being contemporary. This has led him into a succession of different versions, including, more recently, the revolutionary. It has even pressed him to the extent of composing a revision [1936] of Matthew Arnold's "Dover Beach" [1867], a poem that might be considered a classic illustration of the wrong way of being contemporary. Like Arnold, MacLeish merely convinces us that it is not by talking about one's time that one best expresses it. The consciousness of being of one's time becomes an idea that, like any other idea carried beyond its limits, gets very much in the way of that deep saturation of experience which alone can render someone the "soul" of his age.

35. "The Comic View" (1936)
"Bones of Contention" and Other Stories,
by Frank O'Connor

It is too bad that Frank O'Connor's books are not better known in this country, because they illustrate qualities likely to be forgotten in a period like the present. It is not only their humor, or their peculiar variety of humor, but also the qualities of sympathy and detachment. Sympathy is something that we have had in abundance, both as expansive self-pity and as aggressive championship of the lowly. But it is rarely to be found as a function of the writer's whole vision of experience—a vision so complete as to include the writer along with his characters. O'Connor is detached in the sense that he allows the observed experience to carry its own moral. And the moral is that anything less than a profound and all-inclusive charity is madness and death.

This is to put it very strongly, but such is actually the moral of the title story of O'Connor's first collection, *Guests of the Nation* [1931], in which a group of Irish revolutionaries is forced by political necessity to entice a friendly English hostage into a forest and shoot him. O'Connor's characteristic stories, to be sure, are not so harrowing, but there is always a burden of potential disaster. In the present collection, *Bones of Contention*, most of the tales are demonstrations of the triumph of nature over circumstance and are therefore comic: the theft of musical instruments by a disreputable street band ("Orpheus and His Lute"); an old peasant's preference of imprisonment to paying a fine, for the sake of humiliating a neighbor ("The Majesty of the Law"); and the communal loyalty of a whole village in protecting its own against the law ("Tears, Idle Tears" and "Peasants"). There is also the uproarious fantasy of the man who is literally paralyzed by life ["The Man That Stopped"]: he "stops" in the street one day and has to be removed by the police.

Beneath all this rich humor and light-hearted fantasy there is undoubtedly much suffering; but to those who would object to his acquiescence, O'Connor would probably reply that the comic writer is concerned, not with the separate elements, but with one possible pattern of experience. The comic pattern demands objectivity, and the technical success of the stories in *Bones of Contention* arises out of the strict, objective adherence to dialogue and situation. (When the attempt is made to present character from the inside, as in two or three instances, the result is less distinguished.) The language is a realization of improbable flights of Irish speech of a sort to make the more famous passages of John Millington Synge seem like the insincerities of a tired *littérateur*. The words grow on the page, sprouting into lush foliage out of the materials of the situation.

As for the situations themselves, they are rarely more than the commonplace crises of living in the Irish town and countryside. What the author does with them, of course, is a result of his gift and his vision—as in his novel *The Saint and Mary Kate* [1932], a realistic chronicle of puppy love in the Cork slums that becomes a hilarious parody of the Temptation of Saint Anthony. Frank O'Connor thus reminds us again how much the deepest values of narrative spring from an intensely perceived empirical experience. Perception alone is not enough; but perception, in an age given over to one mode of abstraction after another in its fiction, is necessary for the revival of such important things as wit, poetry, and understanding.

36. "Huxley Agonistes" (1936)
Eyeless in Gaza, by Aldous Huxley

Somewhere in *Eyeless in Gaza*, the hero quotes the closing lines of one of Gerard Manley Hopkins' six "sonnets written-in-blood" [a.k.a. "sonnets of desolation" or "terrible sonnets," 1885–86]:

> I see
> The lost are like this, and their scourge to be
> As I am mine, their sweating selves; but worse.
> [From the sonnet "I wake and feel the fell of
> dark, not day" (1885).]

And the thought occurs that with this novel, Aldous Huxley proves that his whole career has been moving toward a rediscovery of the truth, restated in the same sonnet, that "self-yeast of spirit a dull dough sours." At least it will seem true if we take the liberty of identifying an author with his hero, which is here somewhat more justifiable than usual in view of the fact that the hero is a prosperous sociologist, renowned for his ironic detachment and given to a kind of finicky distaste for any form of experience that is too unpleasantly concrete.

Anthony Beavis is the Huxley hero, the one and only Huxley hero, aged forty-three, and finally confronted with the ancient problem of salvation for himself and the world. He is a projection, that is to say, of everything that his creator has thought, felt, and read in the seven years since his last novel, *Point Counter Point* [1928]. (One may ignore the unhappy interruption of the fantasy that appeared in 1932 under the title *Brave New World*.) And to say that Beavis represents a distinct enlargement in every sense over his earlier self is one way of indicating the considerable advance that this book marks in Huxley's development as a fiction writer. Whatever else remains to be said about it, *Eyeless in Gaza* is the deepest, the most serious, and the most complete novel of his career.

After the erudite snickerings and Rabelaisian guffaws, after the admirable collection of protozoic analogies, after the tired fornications in Mayfair boudoirs, the Huxley hero has become a stern but ardent moralist. Just before this transformation, it is true, he has begun to have doubts about the existence even of his own personality; he has apparently been reading Marcel Proust; and there are several pages of denatured metaphysics for the readers of the lending libraries. But all such doubts are dissolved in the warm light of Beavis's recognition that he can no longer live irresponsibly, that he has "duties toward himself and others and the nature of things."

For twenty years he had thought such "responsible living" to be nonsense—"nonsense, in spite of occasional uncomfortable intimations that there might be a point, and that the point was precisely in what he had chosen to regard as the pointlessness, the practical joke." Beavis's shock is the result partly of the lesson of experience, partly of his meditations on society and its institutions, and partly of his friendship with a certain Dr. James Miller. Or it may be said that the doctrines of this spiritual reformer provide an interpretation, as well as a direction, for a life that would otherwise be without significance. Life and its interpretation are therefore presented simultaneously, so to speak, out of what may be called the drowning man's point of view in fiction.

This method, reminiscent both of the Jamesian "process of vision" and the movie flashback, involves a discarding of the normal time order of narrative for the more or less fortuitous order of the memory. For Huxley, translating the lesson of experience, such a method has the advantage of dispensing—like a physician administering an otherwise too saccharine fluid drop by drop over a period of time—no more of the lesson than the reader's preference for experience enables him to take in one sitting. Moreover, it has the advantage of distributing more equally the disquisitions that are the fruit of the hero's recent readings in biology, chemistry, sociology, and anthropology. But it may be questioned whether this willful playing with the normal sense of time is not really evidence of a last infirmity in a writer headed toward nobility.

The substance of Anthony Beavis's experience, as a matter of fact, is reducible to a single situation. It is that complication in his youth which caused him to betray the feelings of his best friend's fiancée in order to win an idle bet from his mistress. As a revelation of the "piddling, two-penny, halfpenny personality" of the modern man, this is a situation admirably suited to Huxley's general theme in *Eyeless in Gaza*. The remorse suffered by the hero is an adequate psychological explanation for his overeager surrender to the persuasive Dr. Miller, uttering from a mule-back in Mexico the immemorial formula of Buddhist redemption, "love and compassion."

To summarize the stages of speculative reasoning by which Beavis arrives at the same formula would be to give more order to his thought than Huxley himself has troubled to give it. We know that he is opposed to both fascism and communism because each sacrifices the means to the end. Revolution always fails of its aims because it operates from the wrong motives and puts the wrong people in power. It merely creates new institutions to enslave the individual and set him against his fellow men. Politically, therefore, Beavis—or Huxley—is an anarchist, unless the pacifism that we leave him practicing as well as preaching at the end can be considered a system. But "Millerism" is perhaps more strictly a spiritual and psychological discipline, like yoga or Christian Science. There is much talk of "the proper use of the self," and also a serious defense of vegetarianism.

Beavis's final meditations, to tell the real truth, read like the lucubrations of a Bloomsbury intellectual sunk irrevocably into the downy folds of the Buddhist heaven. These meditations do not read like the high strength of the Miltonic Samson struggling with real good and real evil, within and without, but instead like the "peace beyond peace" of Annie Besant [British socialist, theosophist, writer, and orator; see her 1885 autobiography]. It is perhaps the last irony of this novel that it will be most appreciated by the Stigginses and the Burlaps [Reverend Stiggins, from *The Pickwick Papers* (1837), by Charles Dickens; Denis Burlap, from *Point Counter Point*], by those accustomed to commit the greatest enormities in the name of love, by the sort of people that Huxley has grown famous in satirizing.

The report that, with *Eyeless in Gaza*, Aldous Huxley has turned sentimentalist will probably be little credible to many people. Sentimentalism implies lack of intelligence, and surely Huxley is among the most intelligent of living writers. Yet the contradiction may be somewhat diminished if it is admitted that the professional *homo sapiens*—the chimpanzee on the upper side of humanity, as it were—is more likely to be thrown off his base than the so-called average man.

[In this regard, see also Huxley's 1948 novel *Ape and Essence*.] Between his brittle intelligence and his sense of experience, between his intellect and his sensibility, there has always been in Huxley a breach that has prevented him from being a great imaginative writer. Confronted in mid-career with the reality of certain values to which he had hitherto paid little attention, his intelligence gives the reins to his sensibility with an abandonment that will shock some very much less "intelligent" individuals.

While a sense of the reality of human life does not make for any less love, it does render impossible a bubbling Romantic belief in the kind of disembodied human goodness and justice in which the author finally puts his faith. Such realism makes impossible any program for men or societies that is not based on some objective system of organization and control. But there is a sense in which Huxley, without undergoing a profound reorientation of mind and temperament, could have arrived at no other solution to his problem. From thinking too little of humanity the Romantic ironist has ended by thinking too much: the wheel has come full circle back to Jean-Jacques Rousseau.

37. "Aragon's Novel of Pre-War Europe" (1936) *The Bells of Basel*, by Louis Aragon

The timeliness of *The Bells of Basel*, the new work by Louis Aragon, will unquestionably overshadow all other aspects for the majority of readers at the moment. And certainly there is a sense in which this book is at least as timely as the last important news dispatch from abroad. The bells that toll through the closing paragraphs, the bells of the old cathedral of Basel that called liberals, Socialists, workingmen, and peasants to the gigantic peace congress in that city in November, 1912, are to be heard ringing at this instant in Washington, Brussels, Geneva, and Buenos Aires. In addition, the police scandals resulting from the celebrated Bonnot affair [the Bonnot Gang was a criminal anarchist group, led by Jules Joseph Bonnot, that operated in France and Belgium from 1911 to 1912], the vacillations of the liberal republican government in France, the tightening of imperialist rivalries in Africa, the numerous strikes and mass demonstrations of workers—all of these will give the reader the impression that he is following a pattern of events hardly distinguishable from what can be extracted from a hasty perusal of recent Sunday news items.

The timeliness of Aragon's novel resides neither in the sort of literary opportunism that serves up morsels of current history which tend to become cold before the ink has dried on the page, nor in the sort of fanciful prognostication that fails to disturb us very profoundly because it lands us safely in an unrealized future. Such timeliness resides, rather, in the ominous parallel that *The Bells of Basel* draws between a past that we have actually lived and a present in whose happenings and directions we are very much interested. The author is undoubtedly determined, in the particular picture that he gives of pre-war Europe, by his vantage point in time and by the consistency of his sociopolitical point of view. But it will have to be granted that he makes every effort to avoid the usual dangers of historical bias through the great richness of his documentation and the extreme objectivity of his method: the straightforward reporting of the great Paris taxicab strike of 1912, for example, might have appeared, with only occasional minor elisions, in any one of the conservative journals of the period. Only in the last few pages is this carefully preserved attitude of detachment allowed to break down in a manner corresponding to the hysterical disintegration of the European world on the eve of the last great war.

But to insist too much on the immensely fascinating, journalistic aspect of the book is possibly to distinguish it insufficiently from the great run of current novels whose interest is entirely journalistic. It must be recalled that before identifying himself with the group of revolutionary writers to which André Gide, Romain Rolland, André Malraux, and numerous other important writers in France have bound themselves [the Association of Revolutionary Writers and Artists (1932–39), under the auspices of the French Communist Party], Louis Aragon was one of the leading exponents of what used to be called "pure literature." A disciple of Arthur Rimbaud and Comte de Lautréamont [a.k.a. Isidore Lucien Ducasse], he began his career by pushing the doctrines of those pioneers in literary anarchism to their ultimate application in Dadaism and surrealism. By 1924 Aragon had made himself, in Regis Michaud's phrase, the terrorist of surrealism: "To death all those who live the lives of others. ★ ★ ★ To death those whose hands have been pierced by the pen, to death those who paraphrase what I say."

The advantage of this reminder is twofold. It helps us, first of all, to explain the intensity with which Aragon has adopted the cause of social revolution as an equal reaction to the fervor with which he plunged into the desperately anti-social Bohemianism of the postwar period. The incoherent and suicidal passion that was directed against so many objects it seemed at times to lack any object at all is here canalized into a disciplined prose that brings its author in line with the great tradition of French satire. And, secondly, Aragon's apprentice years in the studios of "pure literature," however stifling they may otherwise have been, are probably responsible for the strength of the distinctly literary values in this new work. Such are its qualities of form, selection, and style that they serve to make *The Bells of Basel* the most compelling piece of literature to come to us from France since the same translator [Haakon Chevalier] brought out his version of Malraux's *Man's Fate* [1933].

Although the bells of Basel may be heard faintly rumbling all through the narrative, it is not until the end that the larger consequences of the life that has been described are brought home to the reader. The general theme, of course, is that most of the ills of European civilization before the war, and by implication afterward as well, are traceable to the fundamental contradiction of capitalistic economics as represented by the class struggle. By limiting himself to the rendition of a particular aspect of this civilization, however, Aragon reduces the impact of such a diagrammatic statement of his theme. To wit: the enormous background of people and events is defined solely by the life experiences of three quite different types of women, whose names give the titles to three of the four sections of the book.

Diane de Nettencourt, the first of these women, is intended to represent the type of stupid, extravagant, and wholly parasitic heroine to which the imagination of the upper-middle-class male gave homage in the years before the war. She possesses little character apart from a total immunity from any moral sense and a charm that is subject to the current laws of supply and demand. The succession of men to whom she gives herself constitutes a gallery of worthies of the period—the cynical moneylender Brunel, the great automobile manufacturer Wisner, and the important military commander Dorsch. Through the interrelationships of this group, Aragon weaves the whole complex pattern of conflicting political and financial interests that lay behind the scenes of pre-war Europe. It must be admitted, however, that in this opening section he does not altogether triumph over the gravest peril of the satirical novelist—oversimplification.

This is not the case with the novelist's treatment of the second woman in his trio, Catherine Simonidze, daughter of nomadic Russians stranded in Paris, and a heroine more consistent with the traditional middle-class romances of chivalry. Through Catherine the special application of the theme, the position of women in a competitive society, is worked out both in action and in the views that she is made to express on the subject of her sex. Her wantonness, which is as considerable as that of the luxurious Diane, is the somewhat confused expression of a strongly sensual nature at odds both with itself and the world. Obviously Aragon himself is sympathetic to this character, both sensitive and articulate, through whom the revulsion of man's sensibility before the modern world can be delicately rendered.

But Catherine Simonidze is also made to illustrate the evils of anarchism both in social theory and in individual living; and we leave her at the end sitting alone in a London hotel with a copy of Marx and one more year of life in which to change her direction. Her portrait fades before that of the last and most sketchily limned of the three heroines, Clara Zetkin. The narrative closes, as a matter of fact, with a description of Clara's eyes—those eyes that cause the author to drop into the first person and address his reader in hortatory accents. For Aragon the eyes of the aged German revolutionist, whom he saw twenty years after the Congress of Basel at a meeting in Moscow, are "the eyes of all the women of tomorrow, the youth of the eyes of tomorrow."

As intimated earlier, *The Bells of Basel* becomes a work of explicit propaganda only in the closing pages, which describe not only the speech of Clara Zetkin in the German Reichstag after the war, but also, well before that, the tragically futile peace movement of 1912 and the assassination of Jean Jaurès on the eve of the French mobilization in 1914. Up to this point, Aragon has presented his narrative with a fidelity to the precise movements of historical fact that may even seem irrelevant to some of his readers. For a thorough appreciation of this part of the work, therefore, no acceptance of its fundamental thesis is required. But it would be dishonest as well as inaccurate to pretend that anything less than a complete endorsement of the novel's assumptions renders possible the kind of full literary response at which Louis Aragon has aimed and which only some readers will be able to give.

38. "New Rhetoric for Old" (1936)
The Philosophy of Rhetoric, by I. A. Richards

To readers unfamiliar with I. A. Richards' earlier works, the lectures comprising *The Philosophy of Rhetoric* are likely to seem fragmentary, limited in their preoccupations, and indefinite in their assumptions. Their purpose is to point the way toward "a persistent, systematic, detailed inquiry into how words work that will take the place of the discredited subject which goes by the name of Rhetoric." Richards is concerned with such specific matters as the definition of words, their interrelationships in context, and the nature of metaphor.

Both his tone and method are so polemical, however, as to make the hasty reader believe that he is involved in nothing more serious than a grammarian's squabble. This is because Richards was hardly able, within the limits of a few short papers, to do justice to the whole long career of thinking and experimentation that lies behind his present absorption with words. A few eloquent but undeveloped statements, a few ominous hints, and a few knotty quotations from Samuel Taylor Coleridge were probably all that reminded his listeners [at Bryn Mawr College] that behind his discussion of words lies a whole philosophy of rhetoric, and behind this in turn a whole philosophy of the universe.

What I. A. Richards failed to make perfectly clear in six lectures is even more impossible to make clear in a single review; and it will have to be enough to raise one or two points about the possible value and consequences of the inquiry that he has undertaken in *The Philosophy of Rhetoric*. Accepting without trouble the intuition, which Richards shares with Coleridge, that the literary work may best be compared to a plant, of which words would be the "parts and germinations," we may ask whether it is really possible to construct a "discussable science" that will formulate, like any proper science, the exact laws of its genesis, growth, and fruition? Is it possible to raise our "implicit recognitions" into distinctions so explicit that they may be imparted to others, presumably by schoolteachers to their pupils? This is the most general question that the book forces to the mind, and Richards' answer is to match quotations from Coleridge with others from Francis Bacon and Thomas Hobbes to the effect that the end of knowledge is power.

But another way of discovering an answer is to consult the author's own practice, where it will be noted that he is uniformly more engaged in showing us what rhetoric is *not* than what it is, where the approach is consistently negative. Much of the book, therefore, is necessarily directed against various ancient and modern theories—the "proper usage" criterion for words, meaning as onomatopoeia, and the treatments of metaphor offered by T. E. Hulme, André Breton, and Max Eastman. Here Richards is the brilliant and nearly always convincing dialectician. But let us look at some of the formulations set up against the various exploded notions—the definition of words, for example: ". . . what a word means is the missing parts of the contexts from which it draws its delegated efficacy." The "context" is a cluster of recurrent events in the mind; the word is "delegated" to take over the duties of parts that can then be omitted from the recurrence. The only trouble with this definition is that neither the context nor the process of abridgement by which a part stands for a whole can be established; we come up against "the limits of knowledge."

The same impasse is struck when we consider the interrelationships between words in a given literary context, what is here called their "interinanimation." This excellent new term enables us to label a phenomenon but it does not unfold the principles of its operation. Similarly, after breaking down metaphor into a "tenor" and a "vehicle," Richards is forced to admit that the relations between these two cooperating uses are limitless, that their interpenetration is of the integral and organic character of life itself. In his handling of each of these problems, he actually gives the effect of proving just the opposite of his thesis. He convinces us, rather, that since every rhetorical unit has meaning only in relation to a particular context, and since every context is really a unique event, no single set of generalizations as to "how words work" can possibly be drawn up.

This is not to deny the value of Richards' criticism, which will continue to be, on its strictly negative side, of extreme service to contemporary writing. It is only when he insinuates that the scientific method can conjure up a new rhetoric on the ruins of the old that the dry wind of Alexandria seems to blow through his pages. It is only when his disciples write studies titled *Seven Types of Ambiguity* [1930, William Empson] and then illustrate all seven types in their verse that the dangers of his method are revealed. In brief, it is only when Richards introduces the scientific criterion of "use" that his criticism becomes something different from the unique interpretation of a unique literary event.

On its negative side, his criticism further constitutes a warning not only to students of literature but also to everyone who uses language for purposes of communication. In its emphasis on the organic nature of communication, on the relationship of words to a whole, and on the relationship of this whole to the whole of our mind and personality, such criticism should prevent us from falling into those "springs and snares" that John Donne warns about [in "Sermon 116: Preached to the Nobility" (1611)] in detaching sentences from Scripture [Proverbs 13:14; Psalm 141:9]. Above all, it should discourage us from even contemplating the possibility of a new Manual of Rhetoric.

The real contradiction in Richards' position, if one had time to examine it, would prove to be between a philosophy that is intuitive, contemplative, and organic and one that is experimental, pragmatic, and mechanical. As Coleridge put it, without necessary qualifications, it is the difference between Plato and Aristotle; and no more than Coleridge himself is Richards likely to effect the reconciliation. If he follows Coleridge in his interpretation of literature, he follows Bacon and Hobbes in deciding that something must be "done" with this interpretation; and these influences, classical to Romantic, stand for opposite directions of the mind. It is this tension, however, that makes I. A. Richards one of the liveliest, most stimulating, and most rewarding of contemporary critics.

39. "The Poetry of Doom" (1936)
Absalom, Absalom!, by William Faulkner

Much confusion will be saved if one applies to William Faulkner's new book, *Absalom, Absalom!*, not the usual standards of the realistic novel but whatever standards we are accustomed to apply to lyric poetry of the most subjective sort. All writing is personal, to be sure, and in the last analysis so-called objective fiction represents just as temperamental a view of the facts as the frankest lyric. But in fiction usually there is some line of demarcation between the facts and the writer's vision of them, some pretense of establishing a norm or mean in their presentation. Leaving aside obvious examples of the realistic or documentary, we need only turn to such a work as *Wuthering Heights* [1847, Emily Brontë], which Faulkner's book helps us recall, to recognize how safely we are removed from the tempestuous center of feeling by the device of a narrator who is a model of sober and balanced vision. Even in Henry James, through his "frames" and his politely colloquial style, and in Marcel Proust, through his sustained abstract logic, we are permitted within the work itself something like a normal or social angle on the facts.

Nothing so distracting is allowed us by William Faulkner. From first to last we are plunged into the same world, and everything that we see and feel and think is saturated with the special atmosphere of this world. Through neither the form nor the style do we escape from the closed universe of his intensely personal vision. Despite the elaborate orchestration—the story is told through at least a half-dozen voices—the voice that we hear throughout is always the same. Whether it is Miss Rosa Coldfield, frustrated Southern belle of 1866, or Shrevlin McCannon, matter-of-fact Harvard undergraduate of 1910, rhythm and vocabulary are identical; all the characters have fallen under the influence of Faulkner's later prose style. The method of multiple point of view, borrowed from James and Joseph Conrad, thus does not have any real justification in this novel. It does not give us those contrasts of perception for which it was invented nor is it actually required for aesthetic order. At best it adds a little factitious intensity to a work already sufficiently fraught with intensity of the most genuine sort. The aggravating ventriloquism of method does not disguise the fact that everything in it is the product of the same unrelieved and unrelieving vision of existence.

Through the uniformity of his image-laden and mournfully cadenced style, Faulkner gives most reason for being considered as a poet rather than as a novelist, but there is also the peculiar operation of his imagination. Given a view of living here as "one constant and perpetual instant when the arras-veil before what-is-to-be hangs docile and even glad to the lightest naked thrust," he is more concerned with the potentials than with the actualities of experience. Life being a very bad dream in which anything might happen, his imagination posits isolated people, actions, gestures, even speeches, broods upon them until they take the full shape of his vision, and then attempts to relate them in some sort of pattern. The reader will be struck by the recurrence of phrases like "Just imagine," "Conceive only," and "Listen," all springing from the passion to make us realize, in the most literal sense, the unique person or event. Young Tom Sutpen turned away from the front door by a Negro butler, Henry's throwing the dead body of his sister's fiancé at her feet, old Tom Sutpen killed by a rusty scythe—each of these scenes is something separate, complete, and detachable. Each is a symbol of the same uniform vision. The work is put together not out of a logical sequence of such symbols, for the imagination does not recognize the pattern of logic, but according to an order of ascending horror. Even to speak of pattern or order is perhaps inaccurate. It is rather the scale or gamut of all possible human misery and depravity.

Faulkner's imagination, that is to say, does not operate by filling in some design that has been constructed by the rational mind. It will be disappointing, for example, to try to discover in the career of Thomas Sutpen—who migrated from West Virginia by way of the West Indies to Mississippi, where he acquired a hundred miles of land and built an enormous mansion, only to be defeated in his effort to found a family by the intervention of the Civil War and bad luck with his sons—a demonstration of the social and economic contradictions of the Old South. Nor is it possible to stop at the explanation that his domestic troubles are all traceable to a social attitude that regards miscegenation as a more heinous crime than incest. Undoubtedly these circumstances of history and geography affect the *form* of the Sutpen saga, but its meaning will be found in a much deeper and broader interpretation of life as a whole. According to this interpretation, everything that has happened could have happened anywhere else in the world. The little drop of Negro blood that runs through Sutpen's destiny then becomes no more than the symbolical materialization of that irrational element that exists to thwart the most carefully planned designs of the human will. The ultimate cause of everything in *Absalom, Absalom!* is that "sickness somewhere at the prime foundation of this factual scheme," that sickness inherent perhaps in the imagination itself, which always sets before it more than it can ever accomplish and enjoy.

It is because of the depth and the scale and the cumulative grandeur with which Faulkner presents his intuition that this book seems not only the best that he has yet given us, but also one of the most formidable of our generation. His vision of existence, which is a product of temperament, will be ultimately accepted or rejected according to the temperament of the reader. But to reject the vision is not necessarily to reject the book. T. S. Eliot refers somewhere to the mark of the great poet as the ability to understand and communicate the essential strength and weakness of the human soul. For most readers, Faulkner will fail of this mark through giving us too much of the weakness and not nearly enough of the strength. Unquestionably, his book will suffer from the limitations of his vision. But there is also no question that it owes most of its astonishing qualities to these same limitations. *Absalom, Absalom!* possesses the awful impressiveness that comes from exhausting any attitude or vision, however wrong and one-sided, of its last measure of intensity.

40. "Two Small Books" (1937)
The Sacrilege of Alan Kent, by Erskine Caldwell
Three Times Three, by William Saroyan

Neither of these two slender volumes is likely to affect one way or another our impression of the fundamental qualities of their respective authors. The Caldwell item, *The Sacrilege of Alan Kent*, written several years ago [but published only in 1936] in a since abandoned style, is quite obviously intended for the back pages of *Publishers' Weekly*. Collectors of American "firsts" will find much to appreciate in the printing and in the numerous wood engravings by Ralph Frizzell. Of the latter it may be said that it is almost a question of whether they were made for the text or the text for them.

Caldwell unfolds the spiritual biography of his hero through a series of sharply etched vignettes, or poetic snapshots, some of them only a sentence or two long, and all possessing the black and frozen quality of the illustrations. The effect is of moving too rapidly through a picture gallery—more exactly, a gallery of horrors. For famine, rape, and murder, as well as the more naïve modes of depravity so leisurely detailed in Caldwell's later works, are here concentrated within a few bare images. Also, the pressure of the formal scheme results in an over-intensification of style in the individual sections that comes close to both the banal and the grotesque. What this experiment must have proved to Caldwell was that he could not treat his particular kind of subject matter with the usual Romantic lyricism, that he could balance its exaggerated violence only with a correspondingly exaggerated simplicity of language. The story is therefore, for anyone interested in the problems of writing, a very valuable lesson in the disadvantages of overstatement.

The stories in William Saroyan's collection, *Three Times Three*, are all of recent origin; and it would be possible to show that he is in about the same stage of technical improvement that Erskine Caldwell was in when he wrote *The Sacrilege of Alan Kent*. Saroyan is indeed in a some-what worse predicament, for he has not only not found his proper idiom but he has also not found an adequate subject. All that he still has in great abundance is feeling; but while feeling can fill up the whole universe, it may not be enough to fill up one very short story. Thus far, Saroyan has succeeded only in convincing a number of people that talking about life, art, America, and William Saroyan is the same thing as re-creating these somewhat indefinite realities.

In the present book he carries the bluff a step farther by burdening each of the items with an introduction describing the source of his inspiration, the condition of his health, the trouble with communism, and the rest. But remarks, as he should have overheard Gertrude Stein telling Ernest Hemingway, are not literature; and there is no good permanent disguise for the writer who fails to work out and establish an objective equivalent for whatever may be his feeling. Fortunately, there are two indications in the current volume that a recognition of this elementary truth may be on the way.

The first is to be found in "The Man with the Heart in the Highlands," which is rightly labeled "goofy and tragic and comic and classic." Upon examination, its success will be found to derive from the fact that it is a single incident built around the personality of a character who is not William Saroyan. It is the one clean-cut example of objec-tivity in the book. The other successful item is "Public Speech," in which the set conventions of American oratory, as well as the whole surrounding situation, serve as a framework to contain the otherwise self-consuming indignation and despair. It is quite as good in its way as the much-imitated "Address for a Prize Day" in W. H. Auden's *The*

Orators [1932]. If Saroyan can come to realize that these triumphs are the result not of luck but of shifting the writer's focus from the self to the work, he may still live to put his admirers to shame.

41. "Revolution by Poetic Justice" (1937)
On This Island, by W. H. Auden
Forward from Liberalism, by Stephen Spender

It is no secret that the group of young English poets that includes W. H. Auden, C. Day-Lewis, Michael Roberts, and Stephen Spender has caused almost as much embarrassment to the orthodox Marxists as to the bourgeois enemy against whom they wage guerrilla warfare in their verse. The response to Auden's recent volume, *On This Island,* for example, demonstrates this ambiguity to a marked degree. Those critics who do not deplore the shock tactics adopted in certain of the poems in the collection discover in certain others a retreat into the private vision that amounts to something like religious backsliding. Obviously Auden is being completely pleasing to nobody just at present; and the sharp division in his verse can only suggest that he himself is still rather undetermined as to his precise function as a poet. On the one hand, he is a satirist of such vigor, freshness, and ingenuity that at first glance it seems impossible not to recognize him as a militant revolutionist. But his satire is strongest on the purely negative side; it is the satire of "The Vision of Judgment" [1822, Lord Byron] rather than that of "The Hind and the Panther" [1687, John Dryden]. It is clearer to what things the poet is opposed than to what things he gives allegiance.

On the positive side, the values are but dimly implied through a rhetoric that never finds symbols as definite and compelling as those that are made to stand for the rejected order. Moreover, these values do not operate in the only way in which they could prove their complete reality for a poet—through an aesthetic ordering that is a reflection of an ordering of the whole personality. In W. B. Yeats's phrase, Auden gives the impression of quarreling with his neighbors without having made sure that everything is perfectly all right at home. [In *The Celtic Twilight* (1893), Yeats wrote, "Out of the quarrel with others we make rhetoric; out of the quarrel with ourselves we make poetry.] It is understandable enough why the churchgoing Communist has found something distinctly suspect in the centrifugal quality of the communism emanating from this verse. It is communism not only without benefit of clergy but without any very fixed points of reference in the mind. And like any contemporary attitude that becomes too detached from intellectual support, it is continually dissipating into a wholly negative and morally self-consuming Romanticism. (It is irrelevant that Auden has just reported in Spain: the final test of values in a poet is not in action but in poetry.)

As for the other sort of poetry that Auden writes, the personal love lyrics in the current volume, it possesses a distinction of line and surface that is all too rare in our time. But its connection with the attitudes elsewhere expressed in his work is either too general or too remote to be established without considerable sophistry. Eda Lou Walton has pointed out that the influence of Gerard Manley Hopkins on Auden has been discarded for that of A. E. Housman; and there is a more than technical interest in the shift. It may signify a temporary abandonment of the effort toward complete self-integration around an idea, of which Hopkins provided the example, for the more limited notations of the unattached sensibility.

The incertitude that is merely implicit in Auden's poetry is quite explicit in the work of other members of his group, particularly Stephen Spender, who has just written what he calls an act of will, an assertion in behalf of two things that he very much cares for: justice and poetry. The book, *Forward from Liberalism*, is a bewildering farrago of historical information, political theory, personal autobiography, and unamalgamated emotion. The whole first part is an account of liberalism along the lines drawn by Harold J. Laski and John Strachey; and this is, of course, an account of liberalism that will be thoroughly familiar to readers of liberal journals. Liberalism is again represented as a smokescreen ideology promoted by the middle class during the last two centuries to conceal its real motives from itself and from others. And the thesis is that since political freedom without economic freedom has proved inadequate to all but a privileged few in the modern world, democracy must immediately be replaced by communism.

In the third section of *Forward from Liberalism*, which is a journey in space as the first has been a journey in time, we are taken on a political Cook's Tour through England, fascist Italy and Germany, and the Webbs' [Sidney and Beatrice] two-volume version of Soviet Russia. It is true that these final chapters were written before the Spanish Civil War and the last Moscow Trials. But presumably, since Spender was prepared for the former event and at least reconciled to the previous set of show trials, these events do not alter his fundamental picture. From the first and third sections we are expected to receive an impression of the external facts of social and political reality presented to the disinterested "liberal-idealist" observer.

In the middle section, which is titled "The Inner Journey," Spender is concerned not so much with facts as with his own attempt to achieve an emotional orientation in regard to them. He submits himself to an inner catechism, asking himself disconcerting questions concerning the authenticity of his conversion, the relationship between his role as poet and his role as propagandist, and the problem of the freedom of the individual. Here we are brought to the core of those problems that are treated elsewhere in the book only through the clichés of current political analysis. And it is here that we can detect more than once evidence of the deep personal confusion that is responsible, among the members of his group, for the increasing breach between their declared allegiance and their poetic practice.

For Spender justice, freedom, and equality correspond not to moral or intellectual values but to emotions: "To me Beethoven's *Fidelio* [1805] has a greater emotional appeal than any other music, because the music of that opera is dominated by the excitement of one idea, one word, one musical phrase—*Freiheit* [freedom]." There would be nothing suspect about this utterance if it were immediately followed by an identification of the sentiment with an objective set of values outside the individual. But Spender persists in retaining a distinction between the individual capable of having such a feeling and communism as a dogma. This is evident in the conclusion that "the only integrity is personal integrity. Therefore, whilst it is right to demand absolute loyalty from the individual to his group, it is wrong to try and transform his mind into a generalized group mind." Such a separation of individual integrity from the integrity of the group offers another classic example of the irrepressible Romantic ambition to have one's cake and eat it too.

But the separation is made even more vivid in the distinction between poetry and prose, which are represented as "two separate ways of exercising one's consciousness." Prose of the propagandist sort is concerned with problems of the will; but poetry with the problem "of crystallizing and contemplating a given situation, a situation that is permanent and yet contains within itself inescapable truth, which is a seed of energy, planted in the mind of the reader." Logically, of course, this amounts to that divorce between morality and aesthetics which leftist critics so bitterly denounce in the writers of the last century. Problems of will—of which social action is here the most prominent— are segregated in one section of the personality, and creative activity in another. The only thing that could possibly unite them would be some body of dogma common to the poet and his society; but Spender is opposed to dogma. "Principles are more important than dogma, because principles develop, whilst a dogma is static. . . . The real leaders, the true loyalists, stand above the Party code."

It is hardly necessary to point out that what all this amounts to is a religion without a church. (How enthusiastically, it may be asked, would this last statement be welcomed in Moscow?) The "principles" for which Spender stands are not in their broadest sense different from those of Romanticism, which was also a religion without a church. And Romanticism, it will be recalled, is intimately bound up with that liberalism which Spender is so busily exposing throughout his volume. In the final analysis the motivation behind his group is indistinguishable from what we find in Byron, Shelley, and the other English poets of the early nineteenth century. Leaving aside comparisons of a strictly literary nature, there is the same rejection of external authority, the same failure to relate the individual to the social will, and the same belief in progress. It is communism with a distinctly English accent. That is to say, it is the old ideal of Anglo-Saxon Protestantism recovering from the effects of its alliance with nineteenth-century liberalism and ready to fall into the arms of a communism from which all external curbs have been carefully removed.

Another way of putting this would be to say that W. H. Auden, Stephen Spender, and the rest are indulging in the emotional satisfaction to be derived from communism as a revolutionary movement without undertaking the moral and intellectual responsibilities involved in its acceptance as a dogma. Communism is either a new label for a set of unanchored emotional attitudes, which makes it identical with Romanticism, or it is a self-contained body of objective ideas, which makes it at least comparable to an orthodox church. Unless these writers submit their minds to such alternatives, their work is certain to vacillate between either an expansive rhetoric or a negative satire and the "narrow strictness" of the personal lyric, between problems of will and problems of poetry. Such an effort of the intellect, it may be added, is itself a moral struggle of the greatest fertility for poetry, as Hopkins demonstrated in his strenuous attempt to reconcile his sensibility with his theology. And the point is here made because such an effort, in the case of poets with their almost excessive vulnerability to contemporary experience, is a necessary condition to their further development.

42. "Gloried from Within" (1937)
The Notebooks and Papers of Gerard Manley Hopkins, edited by Humphry House

It has long been known that Hopkins' interests included music, architecture, drawing, science, and of course the philosophy and theology that went with his calling [the Catholic priesthood]. But not until the publication of *The Notebooks and Papers of Gerard Manley Hopkins* has it been possible to appreciate how completely all these fields of interest were brought to a synthesis in his thought and feeling. It is now clear that, as he believed everything in nature fell into that centripetal order or design which he called "inscape," he intended that everything in his personality should be "to one purpose wrought."

If Hopkins possessed a sensibility that could only be matched by a John Keats or a William Wordsworth or a Walt Whitman, he also possessed powers of observation and generalization that might have made him a great figure in the century of experimental science. He was not a Leonardo da Vinci, but his mind was motivated by the same passion concerning *ersi universale* [universal being], the same search for a common principle for man and nature. (It is not surprising to find him equally obsessed by the human skeleton—"the bones sleeved in flesh.") It is to make modest claims for these notebooks to say that they might have been written by a Keats with a better developed intellect or by a Samuel Butler with an infinitively richer sensibility. And this is to say that they are continually taking us to the frontiers of knowledge both of ourselves and of our world.

The early notebooks belong to the eve of Hopkins's conversion to the Catholic Church and include a number of hitherto unpublished poetic fragments as well as several undergraduate essays. The impact of the physical world on his senses during this period of spiritual and intellectual crisis may be judged from the following:

> Drops of rain hanging on rails, etc. seen with only the lower rim lighted like nails (of fingers). Screws of brooks and twines. Soft chalky look with more shadowy muddles of the globes of cloud on a night with a moon faint or concealed. Mealy clouds with a not brilliant moon. Blunt buds of the ash. Pencil buds of the beech. Lobes of the trees. Cups of the eyes; gathering back the lightly hinged eyelids. Bows of the eyelids. Pencil of eyelashes. Juices of the eyeball. Eyelids like leaves, petals, caps, tufted hats,

handkerchiefs, sleeves, gloves. . . . Juices of the sunrise. Joints and veins of the same.

The journal proper, begun in 1868 and continued almost up to Hopkins' death [in 1889], is made up of close analytical notations of natural phenomena. Some of these are accompanied by drawings, like the one on page 165, which features the following note: "The curves of the returning wave overlap, the angular space between is smooth but covered with a network of foam, etc." Most of the notations are instances of "inscape," like the one describing the flag flower from bud to bloom: "Each term you can distinguish is beautiful in itself and of course if the whole 'behavior' were gathered up and stalled it would have a beauty of all the higher degree." Moreover, the design in natural objects is often related to the forms of art: the eyes of opened peacock feathers are likened to "the flowing cusped trefoil" of architectural decoration. Trees and pigeons, "trim and symmetrical and gloried from within," remind him of the lilies in the coat of arms of Eton College.

Sometimes, though not often, the religious application is made explicit, as when the strength and grace of the bluebell are compared to "the beauty of the Lord." For Hopkins everything in nature, even the snow swept to one side of a path, assumed an inner pattern that corresponded to that principle of individuation in the human personality for which he found the philosophical explanation in the neglected Duns Scotus [a.k.a. John Duns, generally considered to be one of the three most important philosopher-theologians of Western Europe in the High Middle Ages, together with Thomas Aquinas and William of Ockham]. It need hardly be pointed out how perfectly Hopkins made this view apply both to the theme and to the structure and style of his later verse. But it might be noted how closely such a view anticipated, except for the final theological parallel, the direction of the most recent biological research.

Hopkins kept, along with this record of his intellectual observations, another journal that traced his spiritual and psychological development through the same period. But this was either destroyed or has been lost. Part of the loss is compensated by the intensely confessional tone of his "Comments on *The Spiritual Exercises of St. Ignatius Loyola* [1548]," a piece that is invaluable to the future study of Hopkins' poetry.

First and last, it must be said, Gerard Manley Hopkins has suffered much from the devotion of his friends, and the present expensive and laboriously edited [by Humphry House] volume is another instance. It is to be regretted that the Oxford University Press did not bring out this material in a form offering fewer obstacles to the general reading public.

43. "The Symbolism of Zola" (1937)
Germinal, by Émile Zola

Whatever the motive behind the re-issue of this particular novel of Émile Zola's at the moment, it does force us to mark off more carefully the different stages in his career, to distinguish between Zola the salesman for naturalism and Zola the man of action, between Zola the indefatigable charter of "forces" and Zola the artist into whom he now and then permitted himself to lapse.

To put it rather naïvely, *Germinal* [1885], which represents one of the more conspicuous of these lapses, is something better than one had remembered Zola, even at his best, capable of doing. Whether or not it is his most powerful novel, as Matthew Josephson maintains [in the introduction to the 1937 re-issue of the novel by Knopf], it is likely to be found the most successful of his novels that one has been able to get through. And one may improve on Josephson's compliment—that *Germinal* can stand as a model of the *social* novel—simply by making certain claims for it as a novel: it is not, as a whole, in need of any such restrictive label. The point of this review, as a matter of fact, will be that it succeeds when it does succeed in spite of, rather than because of, naturalism, or the attempt to make of literary art the overworked drab of a mechanical philosophy. It will be seen as an example of quite another sort, a triumph of quality over quantity, of imagination over "forces," of mind over lumpy nineteenth-century matter. And in all these respects *Germinal* will be seen as a particularly timely example.

From such a point of view its weaknesses, to consider these first, are easily demonstrable as effects of the inherent unsuitability of naturalism, a system of causality based on quasi-scientific principles, to the practice of literature, a matter of grasping wholes of intelligible experience. Despite his determination to be "just" to the Hennebeaux, the Grégoires, and the Dansaerts, the middle-class types required by the scheme, Zola never succeeds in making them as credible as his miners, putters, and other dwellers in the pit. Their conversations at dinner, their attitudes and sentiments, such as the incident of the delivery of bakery goods at one of their doors immediately after a show of mob violence, all possess that sharpness of contour which means that they

159

are more the products of an intellectual necessity than of a creative process. The will toward artistic justice dissolves before the greater will to apply the law of the primacy of economic forces.

The single exception among these people is Deneulin, who is ruined by the marauding strikers, although he has always been a "good" employer. Up to a point Zola can ignore this man's role as member of the owning class; he can place him outside the diagram; but since he cannot make him too real without making him seem too sympathetic, he is forced to line him up with the other "pawns" on the flat table of his doctrine. Irony is an uncomfortable mode for the doctrinaire; having blundered into it, Zola retraces his steps as quickly as possible.

The greatest weakness in the novel, however, is the characterization, or rather lack of characterization, of the central figure of Étienne Lantier, through whom Zola reveals his own most profound embarrassment. For to Étienne is given the impossible role of demonstrating the laws of heredity—a relative of the Macquarts, he is cursed with alcoholism and insanity—and of being an inspiration to the miners to exert their will sufficiently to throw off their chains. A dim phenomenon, arriving from nowhere and returning to the same place, moving like a somnambulist among the distraught miners but persuading them no more than the reader of his reality, he reflects the essential contradiction of his creator's career. That contradiction, of course, was how belief in any great creative movement, whether of literature or life, could be reconciled with a philosophy that gives to the individual so little control of the sources of creation.

It will be a transition to more positive aspects to suggest that, in his practice, Zola admirably transcends the theoretical recommendations of naturalism in regard to the handling of crowds and the use of detail. Documentation was the name that the naturalists gave to the concrete vehicle that literature had always had, and must always have, in order not to possess a body without substance. The peculiarity of naturalism was not in its fondness for details but in its peculiarly inorganic use of them, which at times amounted to detail for detail's sake. Zola, a notorious offender, has here achieved some relevance because, as will be noted in a moment, most of his details are fused around a dominating symbol.

As for his actual rendering of crowds, it is something different from the reference to vague "social masses" in his notes. A crowd is a notion, an abstraction, a language symbol for an aggregate of separate realities. To become a symbol for art or literature it must take on the concretion that derives from its physical mass, as in the plastic arts, or from metaphor and partial individuation, as in literature. Otherwise, it retains its abstract character, as in the Greek chorus, the anonymous and depersonalized voice of the collective code. Zola *realizes* the crowd that teems through the middle sections of the book through a wealth of metaphors that would repay close study. But what really makes it come alive is our previous familiarity with everything that need be known about the Maheus, Pierrons, and others who make it up on the plane of intensive personal relationships.

Zola is probably so successful in treating these people because their experience approximated his own so closely that he could render them without the paralyzing interference of his system. There is also Josephson's point that he had spent some seven months in close contact with them in the mining region of the Loire valley. This desertion of the *longueurs* of his Medan villa was tantamount not only to an exchange of theory for experience but also to a profound alteration of method. For the humbler characters in *Germinal* are not the "pawns" of anything but life itself; they are symbols of a deep and sympathetic intuition of the nature of human experience. This is true not only for individual creations, like old Maheu and the wanton Mouquette, but also for the relationships between them and the whole structure of the work.

The most moving of the novel's relationships undoubtedly is the love affair between Étienne and the girl Catherine, whose last moments, in the depths of the collapsed mine, bring us back to an atmosphere and a meaning at least as old as the story of Orpheus and Eurydice. For what is the mine itself but a re-integration of the Hades-Hell symbol? The immediate and particular social situation is contained within the larger pattern of a universal recrudescence: "the seeds of a new order sown underground." Étienne emerges from his journey underground to *la vita nuova* of his own and of social experience. Both the title and the heavily rhetorical final pages give support to the idea that in this work Zola was striving to integrate the theme of social revolution with the great tradition of literature—which is, first and last, symbolical.

Chronologically, *Germinal* belongs late in the author's career, as part of that long cycle of twenty novels [Rougon-Macquart (1871–93), of which *Germinal* is number thirteen] in which he sought to compete with Matter, and at the moment when Huysmans and others were turning from naturalism to the equally blind alley of decadence. It came too late to stem the reaction that Zola's own earlier excesses had made inevitable. Symbolism itself came to mean the isolation of one of the several elements of the ancient pattern that he had attempted to revive in modern terms. But it may not be too late, in light of both naturalism and symbolism, for the writer of today to profit from his effort.

This would seem to be the lesson: if literature is to be effective, it had better be literature and not something else, and it is more effective when dealing with symbols than with theorems. To the reminder that "symbolism" is a discredited movement, the only answer can be that since literature cannot dispense with symbols, the trouble must have been with the nature of the symbols and the particular use of them by the members of this movement. Émile Zola has indicated the manner in which they might be recharged and reordered for our time.

44. "Quintessence of Dust" (1943)
Shakespeare and the Nature of Man,
by Theodore Spencer

To say that this is a very timely book will surprise only those who believe that discussion of Shakespeare, not to mention the nature of man, should be out for the duration. For others it is bound to possess a deeper relevance than the latest war journal or the latest blueprint for the future. Like recent volumes by W. T. Stace, W. M. Dixon, Reinhold Niebuhr, and other hard-working amateurs of the human, *Shakespeare and the Nature of Man* attempts, among other things, to throw some light on what is happening in the world at present by some consideration of the human past. Man, in the abstract, has become in certain quarters quite the rage. It is a rare radio address of any dimensions that can refrain from frequent invocation of his dignity. What Theodore Spencer's book does is not only to restate what once was meant by this abstraction, but also to suggest the very careful and difficult redefinitions that we must make if it is to regain any real content.

The main difference between Shakespeare's age and our own, according to Spencer, is that the first "was breaking into chaos, while our age is trying to turn chaos into order." William Shakespeare was born into an age that had an inherited, and therefore largely unconscious, system of order that took care of all man's most important relations—to God, to nature, to society, and to himself. It was a hierarchical order in which every movement of the human organism was inevitably involved in the movement of the universe as a whole. By quoting from a number of lesser known sixteenth-century writers, Spencer makes us aware how much this conception of the parallel between the human order and the separate orders of the cosmos, Nature, and the State was part of the general mind.

Spencer's thesis is that while such a view—the Elizabethan world view—is essentially an optimistic one, in its emphasis on the very special role that man plays as the connecting link between the higher and lower realms of being, it led in time to a gloomy insistence on the inadequacy with which most men fulfilled the role. It led to the mood of Hamlet's "What a piece of work is a man!" And, indeed, this conflict at the Renaissance between the theoretical and the actual, between what men pretended to be and what they are, finds its culmination "as Shakespeare presents the discovery of the evil actuality under the good appearance, and describes the individual passion or weakness that has to be destroyed before order can prevail once more."

Even more spontaneously, one feels, Spencer is concerned with showing the relation of the explicit beliefs and attitudes operative in the Elizabethan age to Shakespeare's use of the dramatic medium and expression of his final vision of life. Like most modern scholars, he agrees that it was no accident that tragedy should have appeared in England at this particular moment: concern over "the paragon of animals"—in this case, a revival of the medieval sense of sin and limitation in protest against the over-inflated humanism of the early Renaissance—has always, everywhere, been the motive behind formal tragedy. The Elizabethan age was fortunate in having at hand for its purposes the well-developed tradition of the medieval morality play. And Shakespeare, too, was fortunate in being able to turn the familiar and generally accepted conventions of this form to the uses of his own development as a poet and a man of his age.

Most of the analysis of the separate plays in *Shakespeare and the Nature of Man* is centered on the problem of appearance and reality, as it is evaded, confronted, or resolved by the tragic heroes. In the early dramas the problem is suggested but not really treated: Romeo's idealized passion is shown for what it is, youthful lust, but not by Romeo himself; the tragedy of *Romeo and Juliet* [1595] has an external cause— the stars. The Renaissance difficulties over good and evil are talked about but not put "inside" the hero so that they tear his consciousness to pieces. In the great plays of the middle period these difficulties constitute the whole action, and in *Hamlet* [1601], *King Lear* [1606], and *Othello* [1604] a resolution occurs when the hero is made to see both the real evil beneath the apparent good and the real good beneath the apparent evil. Dramas like *Coriolanus* [1609] and *Timon of Athens* [1607] correspond to a period when Shakespeare seems to have abandoned himself to the vision of mankind as irredeemably evil. To Spencer they are a deathlike prelude to the free and life-affirming mood of *The Tempest* [1611].

Unfortunately, however, to the discussion of this late play the author allows too little space; one feels that it is not enough simply to say that

here "is a rebirth, a return to life, a heightened, almost symbolic, awareness of the beauty of formal humanity after it has been purged of evil—a
blessed reality under the evil appearance." We are left with too many
final questions—not only about *The Tempest* but also about
Shakespeare in general. Is he, as George Santayana and others maintain, devoid of any qualified intellectual attitude toward life or
experience? How is his of view of man distinguishable from the
Romantic one, which is still so much with us? Does Shakespeare offer
us any new system of ordered belief to take the place of the old, whose
disappearance he records?

To raise these questions is not to demand answers but to indicate
the pertinence of such a study as this to an age in which the moral bewilderment that racked Shakespeare's heroes has been extended to every
department of human activity—and on a worldwide scale. We, too, are
making heavy payments for having failed consistently in our imagination to make the right discriminations between the real good and the
real evil. What was tragic vision in Shakespeare has become for us
historical actuality. And re-examination of the nature of man becomes
a matter not of philosophical but practical necessity. Theodore
Spencer's is the most up-to-date work on Shakespeare in every sense
of the word—in its method of approach, in its synthesis of all the best
recent work on the subject, and in its implications.

45. "The New Parnassianism and Recent Poetry" (1944)

I

Beyond any doubt, and it has been evident for some time, we are in the
midst of what may be described, at the risk of indulging in rather large
words, as another Poetic Renaissance. The evidence is overwhelming:
the number of anthologies and separate volumes pouring from the
presses, the little magazines devoted largely or exclusively to verse, and
the increasing lip service being rendered poetry by the older and more
conservative book-supplements. The phenomenon is common to
England and America, and in America it is common to almost every
region of the country.

Interesting as it might be to venture some explanation for the occurrence of a poetic renaissance at this particular moment, theorizing of
this sort is outside the present scope. Besides, not many people are
likely to forget how the Romantic movement paralleled the French
Revolution and the Napoleonic epoch; how the French symbolists

wrote in the shadow of the Franco-Prussian War [1870–71]; and how the last important generation in European poetry—the generation of William Butler Yeats, Paul Valéry, Rainer Maria Rilke, and T. S. Eliot—reached its fulfillment in the decade following the First World War. What must concern us, in the presence of such a vast quantity of new verse, is as always the more immediate and general question of quality. And, more particularly, we are challenged into examining the nature and quality of this verse's much stressed and usually self-labelled "newness."

To say anything about poetry is, of course, to say pretty much everything; and, although this discussion must limit itself to the problem of language, it is not possible to get very far with this problem without some remarks concerning the situation to which all such new verse is a response. Let us begin by noting that the situation reflected in it is uniform and even monotonous: it is a poetry of doom. But here a few distinctions must be made: the poetry of the Pound–Eliot generation was also a poetry of doom; it was overcast not only by the searing memory of a recent historical experience but also by a foreboding of an even more shattering and destructive event. It was concerned with a crisis in human values—moral, spiritual, and intellectual—on a worldwide scale. The tone was prophetic: Eliot found his archetype in the blind Teiresias in the wilderness; this was actually a poetry of pre-doom. In the generation that followed, History took on an ever more menacing actuality; it was knocking on the door with an urgency that only the poets themselves seem to have detected with any degree of clearness and alarm. But, in the work of W. H. Auden, Stephen Spender, C. Day-Lewis, and their numerous American disciples, prophecy gave way most of the time to exhortation—the silent monologue to the Class Oration. Not only were these writers thoroughly imbued with the sense of disaster but they also sought to make poetry a practical means of averting it. This was a period in which History was conceived as providing the poet not only with background and materials but also with a public role; a period in which imagination all too often retired before the compulsions of social conscience.

Now the newest crop of poets are writing after the long predicted and unsuccessfully averted Event has materialized; they are writing *in* the Event. It is possible to name names and name places; a whole demonology and topography of disaster are available to their purposes. In particular, the names of cities—Guernica, Nanking, Prague, and Vienna, replacing the Venice and Byzantium of their elders—echo through their pages like blasts from the Last Judgment. Auden had set the example of the poet as globetrotter; but some of these poets would be Baedekers not only to a continent but to the universe, as well. This is from one of George Barker's *Pacific Sonnets* [1944]:

> And in these islands hung on the fringe of Asia
> The herbaceous border of the Siberian waste,
> Where I move giddily in disgust or aphasia
> Straddling the huts of paper and paste,
> Here in this vacuum where goldfish float
> Between transparent planes of mental negation
> But are called thoughts, here on this glass
> I see reflected the mechanism of fate
> Evolving the instruments of destruction
> For all that I've left; the Europe that was,
> Whose historical frieze, in its seizure,
> Shrieks with the voice of Sibelius, crying
> Like a violin in the middle of the sea,
> "I am dying!"

Frederic Prokosch himself never tires of taking us on these Grand Tours, as in "The Festival" [1937]:

> Far to the east extend the ancient seas,
> The dear Danubian banks, the archaic trees
> Among whose pillars still the restless dead
> Dispel their homesick odors on the breeze;
>
> Crete blows the night across her wicked floors
> And Sicily now locks her little doors,
> And up the Adriatic leap the clouds
> And hurl a shadow on her sucking shores,
>
> And northward through the benches of the park
> Stealthily moves the thin conspiring dark;
> The thieves and fairies huddle by the bridge
> And hear the sickly hounds of Brussels bark.

To their common situation the younger poets are responding as variously as might be expected—on a scale that ranges from hysterical panic and indignation to something like the first tentative steps toward a rediscovery of the tragic. It is here that we come sharply upon our subject: for in the attempt to express oneself in an epoch of broken communications, the major problem is that of language; and for the poet the problem of language is the problem of metaphor. The general type of metaphor predominating in most of this writing should already be evident; but a few more examples may be offered, as in Howard Nemerov's "Notes on a New England Writer" [1941]:

> From the cold streets of Cambridge
> The lapis and basalt of St. Paul's
> Makes disturbing division, a golden
> And Byzantine disarray. Hath not
> Some golden Paleologus of the City Council
> Ordained this disorderly splendor?

The second example, from W. R. Rodgers' "White Christmas" [1942], has the advantage of being also an unmistakably explicit statement of what is a quite frequent response:

> But punctually tomorrow you will see
> All this silent and dissembling world
> Of stilted sentiment suddenly melt
> Into mush and watery welter of words
> Beneath the warm and moving traffic of
> Feet and actual fact. Over the stark plain
> The stilted mill-chimneys once again spread
> Their sackcloth and ashes, a flowing mane
> Of repentance for the false day that's fled.

Certainly this device of juxtaposing words nostalgic of the cultural past with words from the context of modern industrial urban society is familiar enough to any reader of modern verse. Not to be missed, because commented upon, is Nemerov's contrast between "the cold streets of Cambridge" and the Oriental "lapis and basalt," between the "golden Paleologus" and the "City Council." And the second quotation, with its matter-of-fact, frontal attack on its subject, would not approximate poetry at all without the contrast between "mill-chimneys" and "sackcloth and ashes," although the "flowing mane" does confuse matters somewhat. Of course this is the sort of thing that Ezra Pound, Eliot, and Wallace Stevens, through their borrowing from the French symbolists, made available to a whole generation of their admirers. Originally an attempt by the modern poet to resolve verbally the conflict between his obsessions with the past and the actualities of a present for which he had little sympathy and even less respect, the device has had a rather checkered career. But before noting the particular changes that the more recent poets have been able to ring on it, we must consider certain dangers that have always been inherent in its use.

In the first place, such a device makes exceptional demands on the poet, requiring not only a thoroughgoing immersion in the cultural tradition but also unrelaxed awareness of everything that is most real and important in the general life of his time. It is not enough to keep up with the morning newspapers or to take a course in the History of Ideas. Without an equally strong grasp of both past and present, there can be no authentic conflict, or only a reduced conflict, and hence a reduced poetry. Such a combined sense Charles Baudelaire possessed, and Arthur Rimbaud in his last writings, and in our own time Eliot and, to an even greater extent, James Joyce, who should properly be considered in this whole tradition. The absence of a combined sense of past and present leads to a particularly transparent variety of factitiousness—the substitution in the poem of daily headlines and odds-and-ends of bogus or second-hand erudition for the experience of which they should be properly merely the vehicle. It leads to that ever lurking danger for the artist—insincerity.

The second trouble with the device differs from the first only in being of a strictly technical order. It arises from the fact that because it must always depend on a contrasting or antithetical set of references, it requires two word-symbols rather than the one characteristic of the classical metaphor. What the classical metaphor represents is an already completed fusion of an indefinite number of diverse associations in a single word. In Cleopatra's speech following Antony's death, in William Shakespeare's *Antony and Cleopatra* [1607], the whole rhetorical effect of "Ah, women, women, look! / Our lamp is spent, it's out" is staked on a single, rather commonplace image. While it is true that this is reinforced and controlled by other light-images throughout the play—"sun" and "candle," for example—it is not dependent on them or on any external set of images. It is self-sufficient.

In William Blake's stanzas composing "The Sick Rose" [1794], furthermore, the two highly conventionalized symbols "rose" and "worm" are capable of being comprehended and responded to separately. Indeed, they must be if we are to follow their order in the poem, which is an imaginative order:

O Rose, thou art sick!
The invisible worm
That flies in the night,
In the howling storm,

Has found out thy bed
Of crimson joy;
And his dark secret love
Does thy life destroy.

Now in the device that we have been discussing, the effect is obtained by no such temporal ordering of words, each with its independent secretion of associations; we are talking now about an effect of simultaneity, the setting side-by-side of words with calculated differences of association. The metaphorical force resides not in order but in collision—a collision that is made to occur on the surface of the poem, and indeed may be, as in Pound's *Hugh Selwyn Mauberly* [1920], the poem itself. Besides the difference in time-order, there is a difference in the direction of the poetic impulse: the one is unitive, the other analytical. This is not to say that the analysis implied by the second type of metaphor is never absorbed into the imagination in the better modern poets; but in the wrong hands, it is open to the same essential objections that Samuel Taylor Coleridge raised against the fancy. It can become the work of will and intellect rather than of the imagination. (Parallels in modern painting are to be found in certain of the imitators of Giorgio de Chirico and Pablo Picasso.) It can degenerate, in short, into a rather cheap registering of shock for shock's sake.

II

Both dangers are merely inherent in the technique; not all who have used it have been undone; and every method has its dangers. Returning to the younger poets, we must note first of all significant shifts of emphasis in the particular *choice* of imagery. For one thing, there is more dependence on physical science and the machine than in their immediate predecessors, as in the following apparently (and perhaps aptly) anonymous lines of verse:

O dancer's realm where the difficult transposition of thought
Grows the easy act of the oiled, fluid joint,
The limb obeying even the crook of the dream.

Not always is the identification of human beauty with the beauty of the machine (whatever one may think of such an identification) so fluidly attained. In John Ciardi's "George Washington Bridge" [1941], even the meter is reduced to stream-lined mechanics:

And arc and piers and highway soar from steel
Into a swinging web of flying sound.
A gull's geometry, a flashing keel,
A flowering ceremony of the ground.

The men who climbed like birds to trap that wire,
Like birds were born to know what song and flight meant:
The tempo of an arc, curve of a choir,
The eye's adagio and the blood's excitement.

More often than not, as in George Barker's "Munich Elegy No. 1" [1941], scientific imagery is used to provide a contrast between the public disaster and the individual plight:

Those occasions involving the veering of axles
When the wheel's bloody spikes like Arabian armaments
Release Passchendaele on us because it is time, bring
Also with blood to the breast the boon to the bosom:
I saw it happen, had near me the gun and the tear.
Those occasions are all elegiac. The wheel and the wish
Turn in a turtle the chaos of life. It is death,
Death like a roulette turning our wish to its will.

But there is nothing in all this that is fresh or perceptibly modified; it is in Rimbaud and Jules Laforgue; and it is everywhere in Hart Crane, who in this, as in other respects, is a favorite influence.

Nor altogether novel is that exorcism of the world of commonplace objects that has come to be a contemporary form of the pathetic fallacy. It is a long way back to Stéphane Mallarmé; but undoubtedly from his fans, handkerchiefs, and hallucinated *meubles* [household articles], Rainer Maria Rilke developed the conceit; and Auden has acknowledged in verse his debt to Rilke. In "The Double Shame" [1940], Stephen Spender states clearly enough what lies behind the current cult of *Dinglichkeit* [thing-ness or materiality]:

Solid and usual objects are ghosts
The furniture carries great cargoes of memory,
The staircase has corners which remember
As fire blows most red in gusty embers,
And each empty dress cuts out an image
In fur and evening and summer and gold
Of her who was different in each.

170

Among the ghosts at work in Spender's "The Double Shame," it may be noted, is the author of *Swann's Way* [1913, volume 1 of *Remembrance of Things Past* (1913–27)], Marcel Proust. More addicted than anyone else to this brand of ghostly pathos, Randall Jarrell, in "Children Selecting Books in a Library" [1942], analyzes the manner in which the actual process of animization takes place:

> The little chairs and tables by a wall
> Bright with the beasts and weapons of a book
> Are properties the bent and varying heads
> Slip past unseeingly: their looks are tricked
> By our fondness and their grace into a world
> Our innocence is accustomed to find fortunate.

Very closely related, if not identical, is the persistent resuscitation of the world of childhood. And here we are led into examining some of the responses to what has been described as the general situation. At least half of this verse must be haunted by recollections of the nursery or the schoolroom. Some of the titles are, in addition to "Children Selecting Books in a Library," the following: "Ode for School Convocation" (Ciardi, 1941), "The Christmas Roses" (Jarrell, 1941), "Boy at a Christmas Tree" (John Nerber, 1941), and "The Schoolboy's Complaint" (Malcom Lowry, 1942). At their simplest the poems in this category are little more than sentimentally ironic comments, on the part of the "tricked, bitter boys" (to use Jarrell's phrase from "Children Selecting Books in a Library"), on the disparity between "the rigmarole of private life's belongings" and what appears to be, from a child's point of view, a world without form. Sometimes this poetry rises from irony to a shrilly uncontrolled *saeva indignatio* [cruel indignation], which is the note struck by Barker in "Epistle to D. T." [1937]:

> I know what it was, he said, that you were beginning;
> The rigmarole of private life's belongings.
> Birth, boyhood, and the adolescent baloney. So I say
> Good go ahead, and see what happens then.
> I promise you horror shall stand in your shoes,
> And when your register of youth is through
> What will it be but about the horror of man?
> Try telling about birth and observe the issue.

Actually, Dylan Thomas, the most metaphysical and in all respects the most passionate of these poets, himself does some "telling about birth"; he takes us right back to the embryonic state itself in "Twenty-Four Years" [1938], in which the poet crouches "like a tailor / Sewing a shroud for a journey / By the light of the meat-eating sun."

But let us not draw too obvious conclusions; these young people are not only acquainted with Sigmund Freud and C. G. Jung but are also aware of the limitations of modern psychoanalysis. Most of them know what they are doing: they are much less the dupe of the unconscious than the symbolists, for example, or even Rilke himself. What the Freudians call "the traumatic experience" and "the genetic history of the individual" becomes for them a deliberate metaphysical framework for the emotion provoked by the general catastrophe. And what this amounts to for the poet, of course, is the attempt to construct a myth for himself out of the materials of his own past. As Jarrell puts it, again in "Children Selecting Books in a Library,"

> One taste of memory (like Fafnir's blood)
> Makes all their language sensible, one's ears
> Burn with the child's peculiar gift for pain.

As myth, such poetry is also the effort to comprehend by analogy with the life of the individual what has been the peculiar destiny of a whole culture. But this is such a powerful direction in other departments of recent literature—in the epic novels of Joyce and Thomas Mann, for example—that no more need be said about it here.

How successfully myth of this kind is being realized in verse is another matter; the more ambitious and self-conscious exercises in self-mythologizing have been embarrassing. Only in a very few lyrics do we detect first signs of that self-knowledge-cum-acceptance which belong to the truly tragic emotion. It is hollow and not quite persuasive in Lloyd Frankenberg's "Hide in the Heart" [1939], an echo of Matthew Arnold's "Dover Beach" [1867]:

> Hide in the heart. There is no help without.
> The strong winds ramp about the world tonight.

It is a little too oratorical in Stephen Stepanchev's "The Poet Leaves a Burning City" [1941]:

> Weakness no one honors, historians merely
> Explain it, and it is late for anger, sir.

There is room for pride and purpose only, spirit
Freed from the fingering ruin and its wretched last.

Muriel Rukeyser expresses the same stoicism with a more memorable compactness in the line "the sure magnificent music of the defeated heart, " from "River Elegy" [1940]. But Randall Jarrell, at the end of a long and uneven monologue titled "The Difficult Resolution" [1945], comes close to the proper note:

Remember what you learned then: that you are powerless
Except to know that you are powerless, to learn
Your use and your rejection, all that is destroying you—
And to accept it: the difficult resolution.

III

In an 1864 letter to his friend A. W. M. Baillie, Gerard Manley Hopkins writes,

I think then the language of verse may be divided into three kinds. The first and highest is poetry proper, the language of inspiration. The word inspiration need cause no difficulty. I mean by it a mood of great, abnormal in fact, mental acuteness, either energetic or receptive, according as the thoughts which arise in it seem generated by a stress and action of the brain, or to strike into it unasked. . . . But I need not go into this; all that is needful to mark is, that the poetry of inspiration can only be written in this mood of mind, even if it only last a minute, by poets themselves. Everybody of course has like moods, but not being poets what they then produce is not poetry. The second kind I call *Parnassian*. It can only be spoken by poets, but is not in the highest sense poetry. It does not require the mood of mind in which the poetry of inspiration is written. It is spoken *on and from the level* of a poet's mind, not, as in the other case, when the inspiration which is the gift of genius, raises him above himself. . . . Parnassian then is that language which genius speaks as fitted to its exaltation, and place among other geniuses, but does not sing in its flights . . .

It is unnecessary to mention the third kind of language that Hopkins distinguishes later in this passage; the second kind, or Parnassian, is what interests us. But, before proceeding to examine the second kind of language, it may be well to point out what Hopkins, although he was undoubtedly aware of the fact, does not mention—namely, that, rather than being the label of a particular movement or school, Parnassianism represents a *phase* or *stage* in the evolution of some important poetic style. (It should not, for example, be confused with the movement of the same name in France toward the middle of the nineteenth century.) It can occur only after a period of considerable energy, with its accompanying technical innovations and experiments, has run its course.

In the letter quoted, Hopkins uses some lines of Alfred Tennyson as an example of the Parnassian; we know that he was reacting also against William Morris, Dante Gabriel Rossetti, and Edward Burne-Jones; and there is little disagreement today that what these mid-Victorian poets actually represent is the liquidation of the great Romantic movement of the beginning of the century. (Hopkins' own verse was an attempt to escape the contagion by a return to an earlier metrical tradition.) One might go on to suggest that much of the poetry produced in England in the sixteenth century is hardly more than a crude Parnassian version of a style that had already reached its decadence on the continent. Perhaps Edmund Spenser is our supreme Parnassian poet. And there is the dreadful probability that the bulk of Roman literature (including even the great Vergil) should really be treated, in relation to its Greek models, as no more than a vast triumph of the Parnassian spirit.

From some of these examples it might seem that what Hopkins has in mind is no different from what we mean by classicism or neoclassicism. But classicism usually includes much more—a specific body of historical reference and a particular attitude, usually Romantic, toward the past, as well as a style possessing certain characteristic features. Parnassianism refers to a particular state or condition of health in *any* language or style. Moreover, it is not to be mistaken for the merely derivative and imitative, which is always with us. Parnassianism has its own degrees of excellence; it has its own "beauties": Tennyson's *Tithonus* [1860] and *Ulysses* [1833], for example, are gems of the species. It is, to quote Hopkins again, from an 1881 letter to Richard Watson Dixon, "the language and style of poetry mastered and at command but employed without any fresh inspiration." Indeed, it is because the original burden of inspiration has fallen on others that this style can afford to concentrate almost exclusively on surfaces. Deeply involved in our response is the element of recognition, as Hopkins describes in the Baillie letter: "It is a mark of the Parnassian that one could conceive oneself writing it if one were the poet." But this is a quickly exhausted delight: "I believe that when a poet palls on us,"

Hopkins observes in the same letter, "it is because of his Parnassianism. We seem to have found out his secret."

Now it should be no secret that what is here being insinuated is that the work of too many of our "new" poets is subject to the same objections to be raised against the Parnassian. Actually, the great movement in Anglo-American verse that stemmed from the French symbolists had lost its greatest energy and was technically rather tired by the time the newer poets arrived on the scene. There had intervened, for example, the tragic and instructive career of Hart Crane, who should have demonstrated the impossibility of making out of verbal shock-tactics, which are at best a means, a sufficient poetic end. Apparently temptation was too great, however, and with only slight modifications of imagery, the "new" poets have taken over the more important metaphorical devices by means of which their chosen ancestors sought to express the tension that marked their experience. What has been forgotten is just this irrefrangible relationship between language and experience—the fact that Baudelaire, Rimbaud, Eliot, and the rest really *earned* their language. Because of our conviction of the incontrovertible reality of their conflict, these poets are saved, at their best, from the twin dangers of artifice and insincerity.

From neither of these weaknesses is much of the recent work entirely free. It is spoken, for the most part, in Hopkins' phrase, "on and from the level of a poet's mind"—a hardworking, disingenuous mind. This applies equally to the two opposite tendencies represented: the tendency toward a prolix and hysterical rodomontade, on the one hand, and toward a calculated flatness of prose-statement, on the other. In the case of the first, we feel that however desperate the current situation, the poet himself proves nothing by carrying on in such a way; he cannot hope to compete with History. His is language "mastered and at command" only in the sense that it is a deliberate appropriation from known and more convincing sources—the agonized violence of the Rimbaud-Crane strain in modern verse. That such a style should ever have developed into a Parnassian phase may seem anomalous; for the Parnassian is ordinarily characterized by a kind of ironed-out gentility of diction and rhythm. But when the tradition happens to be violence, it can be put to Parnassian uses like any other; it can lead to work that gives away its "secret." More easily comparable to the Parnassians of the past are those poets who stuff their verse with the paraphernalia of the familiar, for an effect that is rarely more than that of a sustained facility and cleverness. Here especially do we have the illusion that *we* are writing the poem—putting it together out of the well-worn spelling blocks that clutter the nursery floor.

It has not been possible to describe the metrical and rhythmical qualities of this verse; and, without some such description, its Parnassian character cannot perhaps be appreciated. But from certain quotations it should be clear with what reluctance these poets seem to engage the niceties of the ear in their verse. Too many of them relax into a deliberate sloppiness of melodic line, into what Conrad Aiken has somewhere called [in the essay "Back to Poetry" (1940)] an "anti-poetry"—a looseness of syntax, a fondness for the declarative mood, and a frivolous predilection for internal and off-rhymes. Nor has it been possible to enumerate certain other prevailing influences—Hopkins on rhythm, for example, or Yeats on both rhythm and imagery, in neither case altogether fortunate because what is most essential in these two poets is just what is most inimitable—on the seriousness of this poetry's controlling feeling. But perhaps enough evidence has been offered to suggest that a revival and study of Hopkins' Parnassian label may not be out of order.

IV

This is a conclusion that will seem too severe; so let it be said that it is an excellent thing that poetry is being written at all, and impressive that it is being written with such abundance. Most of the verse of any period is haunted by the immediate past and is of a fairly monotonous texture. But it is indeed in no carping spirit that the present characterization is made. Rather, it is out of the conviction that poetry has at the moment at least as great a function as at any moment in history. The current interest itself can only correspond to a need for the kind of drastic self-honesty that poetry alone makes possible in a period of historical anguish and confusion. For this reason we have the right more than ever to make the necessary discriminations, to look carefully at the scales. For poetry is the ultimate measure—the ringing-board on which the false or the impure resounds with an unmistakable clarity. It is a measure, first of all, for the poet—of his seriousness and devotion; for the rest of us, of all the values to which we like to pay service.

46. "Stephen Dedalus—in the Rough" (1945)
Stephen Hero, by James Joyce

For admirers of James Joyce, for students of modern literature generally, this is bound to be, in an altogether unhackneyed sense of the word, the most important literary event of the year. And indeed there is hardly an exact parallel for it in all our literary history. Through the joint enterprise of the Harvard University Library and New Directions Press, we have here, in *Stephen Hero*, about one-third of the hitherto unpublished first draft of one of the most influential novels of our time: *A Portrait of the Artist as a Young Man* [1916].

Earlier versions of lyric poems and short stories we have had frequently in the past, but never of a full-length novel of any significance. Not only does the present manuscript throw much light on Joyce's own individual development as an artist, filling in lacunae of thought and experience obscure in his later work, but it also provides invaluable laboratory material for anyone interested in the technique of the novel.

Detailed comparison with the sections of *A Portrait* to which it corresponds—the period of Dedalus's college years in Dublin—will make bright the labors of the scholars and critics of the future. It will be noted that certain members of his family—his mother, his sister Isabel, and his brother Maurice—play a much more extensive part in this version than does his father. And it will probably be explained that it was only in the interim that the father-son relationship, the basis of Joyce's work from *Dubliners* [1914] to *Finnegans Wake* [1939], had become a dominating obsession.

There is also in *Stephen Hero* a much more analytical and dramatically immediate rendition of the love affair that is merely hinted at in *A Portrait of the Artist as a Young Man*. Moreover, we see Stephen (Joyce) in a somewhat greater social role, attending parties in the shabby, confused, puritanical Dublin world into which he is born, and even contributing his fine voice to the entertainment. In a purely quantitative sense, there is much more of everything that we are curious to know about in this version. But that is at the same time a measure of its inferiority.

What did Joyce learn about his profession between the two drafts of his first novel? Primarily he learned, as Gertrude Stein once observed to Ernest Hemingway, that "remarks" do not make literature. He learned selection, concentration through the telescoping of disparate materials in some single concrete symbol or situation, the beauty that comes from controlled relations. Novel-writing was not to be just "talking into a typewriter"; the novel was not a catch-all for whatever passed through a writer's head; as an art it had to be grounded in the intelligible and not the abstract. The medium of this art being words, and the essence of art discipline, the discipline of the novelist lay in the appropriate use of words.

And in his choice of title for this "schoolboy's production," Joyce leaves no doubt that because of this discipline he conceived the role of the dedicated artist in our society as preeminently heroic. In Greek the word Stephen means "the crowned one," whether applied to the filleted animal brought to sacrifice or to the garlanded athlete of the Olympic Games. Above all else, then, *Stephen Hero* is a touching and impressive statement of faith on the part of one of the truly educated writers of our age.

47. "The Passion and the Task" (1948)
The Notebooks of Henry James,
edited by F. O. Matthiessen & Kenneth B. Murdock

By this time anyone who has not actually read *The Notebooks of Henry James* will have become acquainted with its general content, scope, and importance. All that can now be done is to add one's own support to the widely expressed conviction that there is nothing quite like it in the whole range of our literature. There are in existence plenty of journals, memoirs, and notebooks by eminent artists in all fields—Leonardo da Vinci, Eugène Delacroix, Nathaniel Hawthorne, the Goncourts [Edmond and Jules], and André Gide, among many others. But for the most part these are made up of impressions, observations on experience, or opinions on large subjects. Fyodor Dostoevsky, writing in his journal, will tell us of seeing one Sunday afternoon a forlorn-looking workingman taking a stroll with a small child, and of how the sight stirs him to reconstruct the whole background of the man's life. But only John Keats in his letters and Gerard Manley Hopkins in his own notebooks provide the excitement that comes from an account of the "divine process" itself, the eternal romance that the dedicated artist carries on with his muse.

Romance is neither too far-fetched nor too sentimental a word to describe what Henry James himself called, in a 1902 letter to H. G. Wells, this "interminable garrulous letter addressed to my own fancy." In this rare and unprecedented colloquy, James's fancy becomes something personified—even apotheosized—that is to say, something *outside* himself. Like Arthur Rimbaud [in an 1871 letter to Paul Demeny], he seems to say, "*Je est un autre*" ["I is somebody else"]; and the limited, fallible, tormented creature who is the artist is someone, some other, through whom a great unspeakable force is striving to get itself realized. We are, of course, reminded of Plato and the demonic possession, of the even more ancient and primitive concept of the poet as the vehicle or mouthpiece of superior powers. What we have here, in fact, is the furthest application of the ideal of aesthetic detachment that James inherited from the tradition of Gustave Flaubert.

But all this is perhaps to emphasize the anguish of estrangement at the expense of the tender and intimate satisfactions that are also part of any grand Romantic affair. Writing from Coronado Beach, California, in a moment of discouragement, James invokes

> my familiar demon of patience, who always comes, doesn't he?, when I call. He is here with me in front of this green Pacific—he sits close and I feel his soft breath, which cools and steadies and inspires, on my cheek. Everything sinks in: nothing is lost; everything abides and fertilizes and renews its golden promise.

This is indeed the very ecstasy of love! And there is also James's habit in these notebooks of using certain terms of endearment: "Ah, things swim before me, *caro mio*, and I only need to sit tight, to keep my place and fix my eyes, to see them float past me in the current into which I can cast my little net and make my little haul." Here is the most sustained of these amorous lyrical outbursts: "I come back, I come back, as I say, I all throbbingly and yearningly and passionately, oh, *mon bon*, come back to this way that is clearly the only one in which I can do anything now."

In short, it is this unbroken dramatic tension between art and life, form and experience, that will make these notations for some people as exciting as any of James's novels themselves. In particular there is a passage, too long to quote, that bears comparison with the finest in the whole body of his work. Rarely in his notes does James permit himself to go "to smash on the rock of autobiography." But, late in life, returning to the Cambridge [Massachusetts] of his youth, he pays a visit to the "unspeakable group of graves" in the family cemetery. In the act of presenting the emotion, the consequent emotion, of this "accident," he tells us what it is to be a *master*. First of all, the *mise-en-scène*:

> It was late, in November; the trees all bare, the dusk to fall early, the air all still . . . with the western sky more and more turning to that terrible, deadly, pure polar pink that shows behind American woods. . . . It was the moment; it was the hour; it was the blessed flood of emotion that broke out at the touch of one's sudden vision and carried me away.

Approaching his sister Alice's tomb, with its lines from Canto 10 of Dante's *Paradiso* (1320, third and final part of *The Divine Comedy*)—*ed essa da martiro | e da essilio venne a questa pace* ["after long exile and martyrdom, she came to this peace"]—inscribed on the gravestone, James is so overcome by the *rightness* of the whole occasion that he is filled with "an anguish of gratitude." He writes: "Everything was there, everything *came*; the recognition, stillness, the strangeness, the pity and the sanctity and the terror, the breath-catching passion and the divine relief of tears." How is this to be *expressed*, why does his pen not drop before "the infinite pity and tragedy of all the past? It does, poor help-less pen, with what it meets of the ineffable . . . of the cold Medusa-face of life, of all the life *lived*, on every side."

Much might be written about this passage. Tracing as it does the whole process from the experience to the emotion, from the emotion to at least its partial re-creation and weighted significance, its action is the creative act itself. The prose, in its fitting of syntactical rhythm to blended thought and feeling, is of a kind rarely to be found in English since the seventeenth century. It is prose *doing* the thing about which it is talking. Lastly, such a passage should give the lie forever to those who would still insist that James was unable to plumb the depths.

If nothing has been said here of the practical aspect of the notes, their inestimable *utility* to students or writers of fiction, it is because the editors do such a superb job in this regard. Taken together with James's *The Art of the Novel: Critical Prefaces* [1934], *The Notebooks of Henry James* constitutes the best manual of the art of fiction in existence. Murdock and Matthiessen help make this claim possible by their intelligent and tactful arrangement, selection, and commentary.

48. "The Rebirth of Allegory" (1949)
The Plague, by Albert Camus
Caligula and *Cross Purpose*, by Albert Camus
The Blood of Others, by Simone de Beauvoir
Modern French Short Stories, edited by John Lehmann

When the so-called existential movement—with its internal splinter-ings, its transparent intrigues, and its political reverberations—is finally seen with some perspective, it will be found to bear an odd resemblance to a whole school of writing that flourished late in the Roman decadence. Of Prudentius [a.k.a. Aurelius Prudentius Clemens] and the other poets of this period we have no more fascinating account than is to be found in Helen Waddell's little book *The Wandering Scholars* [1927]. Like them, Jean-Paul Sartre, Albert Camus, and Simone de Beauvoir are engaged in producing variations on the general form of the *psychomachia*—the battle of the soul with the body. The form of the novel in their hands becomes that of a dialogue on most of the classical problems of philosophy—freedom and necessity, truth and illusion, and especially, of course, essence and existence.

Certainly *The Plague* [1949], the second of Camus's novels, is hardly more than a string of such dialogues, interspersed with long passages of naturalistic detail reminiscent of but never quite equaling in power Daniel Defoe's *Journal of the Plague Year* [1722]. De Beauvoir's *The Blood of Others* [1945] does not rely on the same kind of large, controlling symbol but is based on an extended and repetitious interior monologue on the subject of being and guilt. This is to say that the existential novel continues to assume more of the character of a treatise than of the modern European novel as we have known it. It is closer, in its existentialism, to a medieval allegorical work like *The Romaunt of the Rose* [a partial translation into Middle English of the French allegorical poem *The Romance of the Rose* (1230–75)] than to anything by Flaubert or Dostoevsky or Henry James.

Although regarded in some quarters as perhaps the last word on the novel, the existential novel actually turns the clock back as far as fiction technique is concerned and casts aside nearly all the aesthetic gains that the novel has made in the last hundred years. Indeed, it is rather paradoxical that these believers in "existence," in the superiority of real or concrete *lived* experience over whatever abstract constructions our minds make of it, should be so little gifted in endowing their works with either reality or concreteness. Body is pared down to essentials to humor soul: the dust-cover of Camus's book shows one skeletal figure crouched over another, and this is as descriptive an advertisement of it as might be conceived.

The Latin poems of the *psychomachia* type themselves appeared at a moment of universal world-weariness, when the imagination of Western Europe had been drained white. So obvious are the parallels with our own time that they need scarcely be described. What is important is how influential the pattern of the existential novel will be upon the whole direction of the novel. Paris, at least in these matters, is our Rome, and as Paris goes usually goes the rest of our literature. Is the novel to undergo the same formal analysis that it suffered under naturalism, which was also the substitution of ideas *about* life for a re-creation of its immediacy and felt values? Perhaps the existential novel will justify its name and take on existence; in the meantime, it is a pretty lean kind of ghost.

The trouble with the allegory in Camus's novel is the trouble with all allegory—monotony. One of the characters in the book is playing a phonograph record:

> "Rather boring record," Rambert remarked. "And this must be the tenth time I've put it on today."
> "Are you really so fond of it?"
> "No, but it's the only one I have." And after a moment he added: "That's what I said 'it' was—the same thing over and over again."

The "it" to which he refers is the plague; and that is exactly what *The Plague* becomes for us. Once one has the key, or the general "idea," the book loses any strong principle of development, becoming no more than a hard-working demonstration, in Camus's admirable prose, of the resemblance between human existence on this planet and plague conditions in a large North African city. "Yes, plague, like abstraction, was monotonous," the narrator himself admits; and we share the sentiment only too well. Exactly the same kind of aesthetic objection may be raised (by those honest enough to register it) against the writer who has most influenced Camus and his group—Franz Kafka.

For the revival of allegory there are reasons enough, to be sure, and the greatest of them is that we are in our time reduced, morally and spiritually, to an "extreme situation." We at last have been forced to cut away the *accidentia* of our distressful historical situation and concentrate upon the inherent terror involved in the human substance. This leads to an ever sharper definition of the terms of our plight; definition is abstraction; and abstraction spells allegory. In the nineteenth century, *The Brothers Karamazov* [1879] and *Moby Dick* [1851] were great works of literature capable of being interpreted on the allegorical plane. But Dostoevsky and Melville were still interested enough in individual character in all its full-blooded contradictoriness to give us an image of life as well as a statement about it. In both of these works the philosophical and psychological are inseparable; the former grows out of the latter before our eyes. If none of the existentialists has so far created a single character of any dimensions, it may be because our age demands not the unique but the "extreme," not the individual but the typical. We require a diagram of our calamity.

The two plays by Camus, *Caligula* [1944] and *Cross Purpose* [a.k.a. *The Misunderstanding*, 1943], are of earlier composition and do not reflect the ultimate tenderness achieved in *The Plague*. Camus's Caligula is even more disastrous than the historical model, since he is constructed on the hypothesis that a human individual might really desire to attain absolute freedom. The play is largely chatter and bombast, its final meaning equivocal. *Cross Purpose* is better dramatically, at least must be quite harrowing on the stage, and through the feelings of the mother at the end does restore us to the humanly plausible. But neither play engages in us the kind of credulity that we expect from serious drama.

Insofar as Camus has any positive philosophy, it is stated midway in *The Plague*:

> The evil that is in the world always comes of ignorance, and good intentions may do as much harm as malevolence, if they lack understanding. On the whole men are more good than bad. . . . But they are more or less ignorant, and it is this that we call vice or virtue: the most incorrigible vice being that of ignorance that fancies it knows everything and therefore claims for itself the right to kill . . . and there can be no true goodness or true love without the utmost clear-sightedness.

With this conclusion we cannot but agree; it puts Camus clearly on the side of the angels. And if the book is read for what it is, a discourse on matters touching us all everywhere today, it should give much satisfaction to readers stifled by the moral emptiness of most recent fiction—especially in this country.

De Beauvoir's novel, *The Blood of Others*, is also filled with what we call "fine feelings." It has a splendid theme: "the curse of being" by which our freedom of action is purchased only at the cost of some evil effect upon someone else, even someone whom we love. But the theme is vaguely handled: the hero, a worker in the Resistance, is technically responsible for sending his mistress to her death, but he had no choice in the matter. The Dostoevskian formula that "each of us is responsible for everything and to every human being" is reiterated throughout the night he spends watching at the dying girl's bedside. But it remains a formula rather than a truth evolving from a pattern of action.

The only items of interest in the collection *Modern French Short Stories* are Sartre's "The Wall" [1939] and "The Room" [1938], and these, which were written before this writer's declaration of a "positive humanism" [in *Existentialism Is a Humanism*, 1946], are infused with that virulent *delectatio morbosa* which places him closer to Louis-Ferdinand Céline than to Camus. Of all the members of the existentialist group, Sartre is least endowed with the narrative gift, coldest in feeling, and most expert in sophistry.

49. "Poetry and 'The Non-Euclidian Predicament'" (1949)
Collected Poems of William Empson,
by William Empson

In this country at least, in which, in the *Collected Poems of William Empson*, his verse is published for the first time, Empson is not nearly so well known for his poetry as for his criticism, although he is as accomplished in the one as in the other. Nor are his poems likely to be received with too much appreciation or respect. They are strenuous beyond those of almost any modern poet who comes to mind—not in the manner of Ezra Pound or T. S. Eliot, for example, so largely the business of identifying quotations and allusions. There are few linguistic pyrotechnics or syntactical hijinks here. In fact, nearly all of these poems observe rigorously classical metrical and stanzaic patters. Several of the most successful, like the one beginning "It is the pain, it is the pain endures," are in the villanelle form [and, in this case, actually bears the title "Villanelle"]. As for Empson's use of the couplet, some of the best of his might have been written by John Dryden:

> This lost pain for the damned the Fathers found:
> They knew the bliss with which they were not crowned. ["This
> Last Pain"]

The difficulty in William Empson is that of reference to fields of knowledge and discourse that have rarely, and perhaps never with the same degree of intensity, been introduced into poetry. Mathematics, the new physics, biochemistry, and entomology are only a few such fields into which the poet makes his reader jump, like Douglas Fairbanks from motor to express ["Express and motor, Doug can jump between," from "Earth Has Shrunk in the Wash"]. Of course modern science, both as a background for imagery and as theory, has been boring its way into modern poetry for a long time. (This last statement was not intended as an Empsonian ambiguity!) But it has been largely for occasional effects of historical irony (the early Pound and Eliot out of Jules Laforgue) or for rhetorical décor, as in Hart Crane. In William Empson's work, a concept from modern physics is inseparable from the development of meaning in the poem. To be unacquainted with the concept is to miss the meaning.

Just so, here is a stanza that, in physical terms, resolves the situation described at the beginning of the poem:

Matter includes what must matter enclose,
Its consequent space, the glass of firmament's air-holes.
Heaven's but an attribute of her seven rainbows.
It is Styx coerces and not Hell controls. ["Plenum and Vacuum"]

For the reader who, like this reviewer, is innocent of even the major propositions of modern physics, there are of course the twenty-five pages of notes at the back of the volume, from which we get the following concerning the stanza quoted above:

Matter *includes* space on relativity theory, in a logical not spatial sense, because from a given distribution of matter you might calculate the space-time in which it seems to move freely. . . . Then the space not in our space-time, which we cannot enter, is thought of as glass with the universe as a bubble in it.

Unfortunately, not all the notes are even as helpful as these; for Empson's prose, although fascinating, is often as full of ambiguities as his verse. From the notes, moreover, one derives the impression that in certain of the poems, especially the earlier ones, the ambiguities are *too* calculated, the work of the will rather than the imagination, like the paintings of some of the surrealists. Of the line "Taught and quivered strung upon the bend" (from "Bacchus"), for instance, we are informed that "taught is what he did, but he is now 'taut.'" Did Empson think of this before, during, or after the composition of the poem? But there is artifice in all poetry; and when the poetry is as brilliant as it so often is here, the artifice can be condoned more easily than the spontaneities of other poets. That said, the later poems in this volume move toward greater forthrightness of utterance and simplicity of feeling. Of these the longest and most moving is "Autumn on Nan-Yueh," the most hilarious is "Just a Smack at Auden."

What is to be said of Empson's style is just about the best that can be said about that of any artist: it is his own. Such, alas, is seldom the case with most of the members of his own generation or the slightly younger one. Insofar as this signature can at all be defined, it is in the almost constant stressing of the caesura:

> My stare drank deep || beauty that still allures.
> My heart pumps yet || the poison draught of you.
> Poise of my hands || reminded me of yours. ("Villanelle")

What, then, is the final burden of meaning in this extraordinary collection? As might be expected, it is not unrelated to the kind of metaphor to which we have seen Empson addicted. It would have something to do with man in his "non-Euclidean predicament" ("Letter I"), with the pathos of his lost communications on every level of his being, of which the cosmological is merely the symbol. In this sense, "Earth Has Shrunk in the Wash" is the revelatory title of one of the most difficult poems in what is a difficult but rewarding volume.

50. "Limits of the Intrinsic" (1950)
Theory of Literature, by René Wellek & Austin Warren

Theory of Literature is a book for which there has long been an urgent need if only as a necessary job of fumigation, written by two scholar-critics, René Wellek and Austin Warren, eminently qualified. Broad in scope, too broad for strategic purposes, it is a thoroughgoing examination into the state of modern literary criticism and of the teaching of literature in our colleges and universities. In method it is at once historical, theoretical, and analytical (if any true distinction can be made between these last two terms); it is actually a *history* of the theory of literature through the ages, with a prescription at the end for its correction and refinement in our time. For these and other reasons this is an unusually difficult tome to read, as it must have been to write, making great demands on our patience with all the foolishness that has accumulated around its subject.

For example, the main structure of the book's argument (after a preliminary, rather superfluous and too academic résumé of basic "Definitions and Distinctions") is based on a sharp differentiation between two approaches to literature: the "extrinsic" and the "intrinsic." By their first term the authors seem to mean very much what I. A. Richards, Kenneth Burke, and John Crowe Ransom call the "reductive." In the section devoted to it they describe and evaluate all of its major forms—the biographical, the psychological, the socio-economic, and the ideological. Much of this is informative, but to anyone except a student too immature to have followed all the controversies that have arisen out of these separate modes of anesthetizing the literary organism in recent decades, the critical objections raised against them become rather tiresome. The operations performed on the Freudian and Marxist schools especially seem like mere floggings of dead horses.

The question then arises as to whom *Theory of Literature* is really addressed—to the neophyte in criticism or teaching (a category that would include the genial abstraction known as "the general reader"), or to the established practitioner in either of these fields? If to the first, the book is perhaps too overburdened with scholarly reference and analytical improvisation to be easily available. If the volume is addressed to the professional teacher or critic, it runs into two different kinds of risk. For someone (like this reviewer) who is already in unqualified agreement with its main position, and with most of its special judgments, *Theory of Literature* can provide only the pleasure of corroboration. But by those to whom it should be the most enlightening, whose number is legion, it is likely not to be understood at all.

Here we must turn to the section dealing with what Wellek and Warren call the "intrinsic" approach. This section begins with a clearcut and today largely heterodox statement of the authors' credo: "The natural and sensible starting point for work in literary scholarship is the interpretation and analysis of the works of literature themselves." There follow eight strenuous chapters devoted to what they believe to be the proper analysis of the literary work of art, involving among many other things consideration of such technical elements as "Euphony, Rhythm, Meter," such pervasive linguistic matters as "Style and Stylistics," such teasing problems as those of "Image, Metaphor, Symbol, Myth." These chapters are the most erudite as well as the most penetrating in the book, and they should be the most helpful.

But throughout *Theory of Literature* one feels that Wellek and Warren are fighting a losing battle. For anyone ungifted from birth with some susceptibility to these "intrinsic" elements—with an ear for rhythm, let us say, or the ability to respond to symbols—is unlikely to be convinced by anything they have to say. All the talking in the world, the dagger-like definitions and the ardent explanations, will not remedy what is congenital misfortune. And it is the pathos (if not indeed the tragedy) of so many engaged in the teaching of literature in America at present that they have so little natural endowment or aptitude for the task. Without it we have what we have, and what the authors of this volume know that we have: the Ph.D. programs in English of the various graduate schools across the nation and the annual meetings of the Modern Language Association of America.

This is a disheartening way to conclude a review of what, on the part of René Wellek and Austin Warren, is a valiant effort to improve the situation. But these tears are shaken from a wrath-bearing tree.

Bibliographical Record of William Troy's Uncollected Literary Criticism, including the contents page of *The Bookman: William Troy on Literature and Criticism, 1927–1950*

1. "White Lightning"
Hippolytus Temporizes, by H.D.
New Republic, August 24, 1927: 24–25.

2. "A Family Affair"
The Grandmothers, by Glenway Wescott
New Republic, September 14, 1927: 105.

3. "Crisis in the Novel"
The Figure in the Carpet: A Magazine of Prose,
October 1927: 11–15.

4. "Comedy of Time"
Orlando: A Biography, by Virginia Woolf
New Republic, November 21, 1928, pp. 23–24.

5. "A Defense of the Occident"
Defense of the West, by Henri Massis
New Republic, April 18, 1928: 277–278.

6. "Gusto and Literature"
The Figure in the Carpet: A Magazine of Prose, May 1928: 7–13.

7. "A Modern Apocalypse"
Solitaria, by V. V. Rozanov
New Republic, May 2, 1928: 329.

8. "Critical Writing"
The Hogarth Essays, edited by Leonard & Virginia Woolf
New Republic, November 14, 1928: 357.

9. "Red Dusk in Ireland"
The Assassin, by Liam O'Flaherty
New Republic, January 30, 1929: 306

"The Position of Liam O'Flaherty"
The Bookman, March 1929: 7–11.

"*Two Years,* by Liam O'Flaherty"
The Bookman, November 1930: 322–323.

"O'Flaherty's Development"
The Martyr, by Liam O'Flaherty
The Nation, August 9, 1933: 165.

10. "Lost Jehovah and Six Poets"
The Earth for Sale, by Harold Monro
Retreat, by Edmund Blunden
The Black Rock, by John Gould Fletcher
The Lost Sail, by Alfred Kreymborg
Lost City, by Marion Strobel
Cry of Time, by Hazel Hall
The Bookman, February 1929: 691–693.

11. "Poetry in Vacuo"
Contemporaries and Snobs, by Laura Riding
A Survey of Modernist Poetry, by Laura Riding & Robert Graves
New Republic, February 6, 1929: 328.

12. "Literature or History"
The Reinterpretation of American Literature, by Norman Foerster
New Republic, June 19, 1929: 131–132.

13. "The Story of the Little Magazines, I"
The Bookman, January 1930: 476–481.

"The Story of the Little Magazines, II"
The Bookman, February 1930: 657–663.

14. "Fiction"
The Governor of Massachusetts, by Elliot Paul
The Bookman, September 1930: 79.

15. "Proof Positive"
The Proof, by Yvor Winters
The Bookman, October 1930: 190–191.

"The Iron Maiden"
Primitivism and Decadence, by Yvor Winters
The Nation, February 20, 1937: 216.

16. "Fiction"
The Erl King, by Edwin Granberry
The Bookman, November 1930: 312.

17. "James Joyce and His *Ulysses*"
James Joyce's Ulysses: *A Study*, by Stuart Gilbert
New York Times Book Review, January 18, 1931: 1 & 27.

"Stephen Dedalus—in the Rough"
Stephen Hero, by James Joyce
New York Times, February 11, 1945.

"To So Little Space"
Fabulous Voyager: James Joyce's Ulysses, by Richard M. Kain
Partisan Review, Fall 1947: 424–426.

18. "Nathan's Testament"
Testament of a Critic, by George Jean Nathan
New Republic, February 18, 1931: 25.

19. "Symbolism as a Generating Force in Contemporary Literature"
Axel's Castle, by Edmund Wilson
New York Times Book Review, February 22, 1931: 2.

20 "Biography"
The Life of Robert Burns, by Catherine Carswell
The Bookman, March 1931: 89.

21. "Fiction"
Blind Man's Mark, by Martin D. Armstrong
The Bookman, March 1931: 82.

22. "Fiction"
The Little Town, by Heinrich Mann
The Bookman, April 1931: 190–191.

23. "Biography"
Abraham Cowley: The Muse's Hannibal, by Arthur H. Nethercot
The Nation, April 15, 1931: 426–427.

24. "A Study of the Imagist Group of Poets"
Imagism and the Imagists, by Glenn Hughes
New York Times Book Review, April 19, 1931: 9.

25. "Biography"
Rousseau: The Child of Nature, by John Charpentier
The Bookman, May 1931: 298.

26. "Moore's Pure Novel"
Aphrodite in Aulis, by George Augustus Moore
New Republic, May 27, 1931: 50.

27 "Biography"
Schopenhauer: Pessimist and Pagan, by Vivian J. McGill
The Bookman, June 1931: 419.

28 "Fiction"
The Dogs, by Ivan Nazhivin
The Bookman, June 1931: 414.

29 "Henry James and Young Writers"
The Bookman, June 1931: 351–358.

30 "An Irish Boyhood"
The Garden, by L. A. G. Strong
The Forum, August 1931: ix.

31. "Fiction"
"Many Thousands Gone" and Other Stories, by John Peale Bishop
The Bookman, August 1931: 636.

32. "A Varied Self"
The Contemporary and His Soul, by Irwin Edman
The Bookman, October 1931: 212.

33. "Rimbaud, 'The Literaturicide'"
A Season in Hell: The Life of Arthur Rimbaud, by Jean-Marie Carré
New York Times Book Review, November 8, 1931: 9.

34. "The New Intellectual"
North American Review, April 1932: 333–340.

35. "A New Talent"
Midsummer Night Madness, by Sean O'Faolain
The Nation, April 27, 1932: 495–496.

"Sean O'Faolain"
A Nest of Simple Folk, by Sean O'Faolain
The Nation, January 24, 1934: 105–106.

"Gerontion in Cork"
Bird Alone, by Sean O'Faolain
The Nation, September 12, 1936: 307.

36. "Apocalypse of the Word"
The Nation, June 29, 1932: 723–724.

37. "Economics and Fiction"
Inheritance, by Phyllis Bentley
The Nation, October 5, 1932: 313–314.

38. "Technique Is Not Enough"
The Twentieth-Century Novel, by Joseph Warren Beach
The Nation, December 14, 1932: 593–594.

39. "Cummings' Non-Land of Un-"
Eimi, by E. E. Cummings
The Nation, April 12, 1933: 413.

40. "Fragmentary Ends"
Death in the Woods, by Sherwood Anderson
The Nation, May 3, 1933: 508.

41. "Four Newer Novelists"
Miss Lonelyhearts, by Nathanael West
Sing Before Breakfast, by Vincent McHugh
Not to Eat, Not for Love, by George Weller
Thunder Without Rain, by Clifton Cuthbert
The Nation, June 14, 1933: 672–673.

42. "Pathos Is Not Enough"
Pity Is Not Enough, by Josephine Herbst
The Nation, July 12, 1933: 52–53.

43. "Bundles of Fragments"
The Best Short Stories of 1933, edited by Edward J. O'Brien
Twentieth-Century Short Stories, edited by Sylvia
    Chatfield Bates
The Nation, July 26, 1933: 110–111.

44. "Literary Trapezist"
Orphée, by Jean Cocteau
The Nation, August 30, 1933: 244–245.

45. "The Romantic Agony"
The Romantic Agony, by Mario Praz
The Nation, October 11, 1933: 417–418.

46. "Hemingway's Opium"
Winner Take Nothing, by Ernest Hemingway
The Nation, November 15, 1933: 570.

47. "Studs Lonigan's World"
The Young Manhood of Studs Lonigan, by James T. Farrell
The Nation, February 28, 1934: 252.

"Portrait of an Age"
Judgment Day, by James T. Farrell
The Nation, May 1, 1935: 513.

48. "T. S. Eliot, Grand Inquisitor"
After Strange Gods: A Primer of Modern Heresy, by T. S. Eliot
The Nation, April 25, 1934: 478–479.

49. "The Worm i' the Bud"
Tender Is the Night, by F. Scott Fitzgerald
The Nation, May 9, 1934: 539–540.

50. "Flower of Manhattan"
A Backward Glance, by Edith Wharton
The Nation, May 23, 1934: 598.

51. "The James Credo"
The Elder Henry James, by Austin Warren
Alice James: Her Brothers, Her Journal, edited by Anna Robeson Burr
The Nation, June 13, 1934: 682.

"The Passion and the Task"
The Notebooks of Henry James, edited by F. O. Matthiessen &
Kenneth B. Murdock
Partisan Review, March 1948: 377–378.

52. "Schoolmaster's Holiday"
Black Monastery, by Aladar Kuncz
The Nation, September 26, 1934: 357–358.

53. "The Conversion of André Gide"
The Nation, October 17, 1934: 444–447.

54. "Jules Romains's Progress"
The Proud and the Meek, by Jules Romains
The Nation, October 31, 1934: 513–514.

55. "More Romains"
The World from Below, by Jules Romains
The Nation, October 2, 1935: 387.

"Romains Again"
The Boys in the Back Room, by Jules Romains
The Nation, April 10, 1937: 416.

55. "Dostoevsky Street"
Dostoevsky: An Interpretation, by Nicholas Berdyaev
Dostoevsky: A Life, by Avrahm Yarmolinsky
The Nation, December 12, 1934: 682, 684.

56. "Nada and 'Diamat'"
Literature and Dialectical Materialism, by John Strachey
The Nation, January 9, 1935: 51.

57. "Priapus in Georgia"
Journeyman, by Erskine Caldwell
The Nation, February 13, 1935: 192, 194.

"Two Small Books"
The Sacrilege of Alan Kent, by Erskine Caldwell
Three Times Three, by William Saroyan
The Nation, January 16, 1937: 76–77.

58. "Anatomy of Dickens"
The Sentimental Journey, by Hugh Kingsmill
Dickens, by André Maurois
The Nation, March 6, 1935: 282.

59. "New Country"
Collected Poems, 1929–1933, by C. Day-Lewis
Vienna: A Poem, by Stephen Spender
Cry of Time, by Hazel Hall
The Nation, March 13, 1935: 311–312.

60. "And Tomorrow"
Pylon, by William Faulkner
The Nation, April 3, 1935: 393.

"The Poetry of Doom"
Absalom, Absalom!, by William Faulkner
The Nation, October 31, 1936: 524–525.

61. "Twilight of the Dolls"
The Wolf at the Door, by Robert Francis
The Nation, June 19, 1935: 715–716.

62. "Radix Malorum: B. Traven"
The Treasure of the Sierra Madre, by B. Traven
The Nation, July 17, 1935: 79–80.

63. "Realism—Old Style"
The Furys, by James Hanley
The Nation, July 31, 1935: 135.

64. "Footprints in Cement"
Lucy Gayheart, by Willa Cather
The Nation, August 14, 1935: 193.

65. "Allegory for Our Time"
Land Under England, by Joseph O'Neill
The Nation, August 28, 1935: 248.

66 "Between Two Worlds"
Europa: The Days of Ignorance, by Robert Briffault
The Nation, September 11, 1935: 304–305.

67. "Race, Environment, and Time"
Literature and Society, by Albert Guerard
The Nation, October 23, 1935: 475–476.

68. "A Matter of Quality"
"Flowering Judas" and Other Stories, by Katherine Anne Porter
The Nation, October 30, 1935: 517–518.

69. "Macedonian Cycle"
Express to the East, by A. Den Doolard
The Nation, November 13, 1935: 572–573.

70. "The Critic's Job"
The Double Agent: Essays in Craft and Elucidation, by R. P. Blackmur
The Nation, December 4, 1935: 656.

71. "In Search of Havelock Ellis"
From Rousseau to Proust, by Havelock Ellis
The Nation, December 11, 1935: 683–684.

72. "What Is Americanism?"
Partisan Review, April 1936: 12–13.

73. "On Being Contemporary"
The Nation, April 22, 1936: 511–512.

74. "The Comic View"
"Bones of Contention" and Other Stories, by Frank O'Connor
The Nation, April 29, 1936: 556–557.

75. "Tradition for Tradition's Sake"
Reactionary Essays On Poetry and Ideas, by Allen Tate
The Nation, June 10, 1936: 747–748.

"The British Genius"
The Language of Poetry, edited by Allen Tate
Partisan Review, March 1942: 169–170.

76. "Huxley Agonistes"
Eyeless in Gaza, by Aldous Huxley
The Nation, July 11, 1936: 49–50.

77. "Louis Aragon's Novel of Pre-War Europe"
The Bells of Basel, by Louis Aragon
New York Times Book Review, September 27, 1936: 2 & 20.

78. "Russian Style"
Bitter Victory, by Louis Guilloux
The Nation, November 21, 1936: 608.

79. "Shorter Notice"
All Brides Are Beautiful, by Thomas Bell
The Nation, November 28, 1936: 640.

80. "New Rhetoric for Old"
The Philosophy of Rhetoric, by I. A. Richards
The Nation, December 26, 1936: 765–766.

81. "Behind the Lines"
Invasion, by Maxence van der Meersch
The Nation, January 30, 1937: 130.

82. "Revolution by Poetic Justice"
On This Island, by W. H. Auden
Forward from Liberalism, by Stephen Spender
The Nation, March 27, 1937: 354–356.

83. "Buck Mulligan's Memoirs"
As I Was Going Down Sackville Street, by Oliver
    St. John Gogarty
The Nation, April 17, 1937: 441.

84. "Variations on a Theme"
The Years, by Virginia Woolf
The Nation, April 24, 1937, pp. 473–474.

85. "Gloried from Within"
The Notebooks and Papers of Gerard Manley Hopkins, edited by
Humphry House
The Nation, May 1, 1937: 511–512.

86. "Roads to Tragedy"
The Agamemnon of Aeschylus, translated by Louis MacNeice
Ion of Euripides, translated by H.D.
The Nation, June 12, 1937: 681–682.

87. "The Symbolism of Zola"
Germinal, by Émile Zola
Partisan Review, December 1937: 64–66.

88. "Literature of the Will"
New Writing, edited by John Lehmann
New Letters in America, edited by Horace Gregory
Poetry, January 1938: 206–209.

89. "Quintessence of Dust"
Shakespeare and the Nature of Man, by Theodore Spencer
New Republic, March 8, 1943: 324–325.

90. "The New Parnassianism and Recent Poetry"
Chimera, Winter-Spring 1944: 3–16.

91. "Selections from the Poetry of Aloysius Bertrand"
Gaspard de la Nuit, translated by William Troy
Chimera, Spring 1945: 29–42.

92. "The Rebirth of Allegory"
The Plague, by Albert Camus
Caligula and *Cross Purpose*, by Albert Camus
The Blood of Others, by Simone de Beauvoir
Modern French Short Stories, edited by John Lehmann
Hudson Review, Winter 1949: 587–589.

93. "Poet and Mystifier"
Yeats: The Man and the Masks, by Richard Ellmann
Partisan Review, February 1949: 196–198.

94. "Poetry and 'The Non-Euclidian Predicament'"
Collected Poems of William Empson, by William Empson
Poetry, July 1949: 234–236.

95. "Permutations of a Myth"
The Hero with a Thousand Faces, by Joseph Campbell
Partisan Review, September 1949: 952–955.

96. "Limits of the Intrinsic"
Theory of Literature, by René Wellek & Austin Warren
Hudson Review, Winter 1950: 619–621.

Table of Contents to
William Troy: Selected Essays. Ed. Stanley Edgar Hyman.
New Brunswick, N.J.: Rutgers University Press, 1967. 300 pp.

Memoir, by Allen Tate, p. ix
Introduction, by Stanley Edgar Hyman, p. 3

1. Perspectives in Criticism
"Time and Space Conceptions in Modern Literature," p. 19
"A Note on Myth," p. 35
"Myth, Method, and the Future," p. 40

2. British and American Literature
"The Lesson of the Master," p. 45
"The Altar of Henry James," p. 58
"Virginia Woolf and the Novel of Sensibility," p. 65
"Stephen Dedalus and James Joyce," p. 89
"Notes on *Finnegans Wake*," p. 94
"D. H. Lawrence as Hero," p. 110
"The Lawrence Myth," p. 120
"A Note on Gertrude Stein," p. 134
"F. Scott Fitzgerald," p. 137

3. Continental Literature
"Stendhal: In Quest of Henri Beyle," p. 149
"On Reading Balzac: The Artist as Scapegoat," p. 171
"Proust's Last Will and Testament," p. 183
"Three Novels by André Malraux," p. 192
"Paul Valéry and the Poetic Universe," p. 201
"Myth as Progress," p. 210
"Thomas Mann: Myth and Reason," p. 213

4. Tragedy
"Thoughts on Tragedy," p. 251
"*Antony and Cleopatra*: The Poetic Vision," p. 279

Bibliography, p. 291
Index, p. 295

Index

Abraham Cowley: The Muse's Hannibal, 192

Absalom, Absalom!, 149–151, 196

Accent, 6

Adam, Villiers de l'Isle, 64, 67

Adams, Léonie, ix, 1, 51

"Address for a Prize Day" (Auden), 152

Æ: see "Russell, George William"

Aeschylus, 34, 199

Aestheticism, 8, 21, 23–25, 52–53, 64–66, 70, 73, 75–76, 86, 127, 136, 149, 153, 155, 179, 181–182

After Strange Gods: A Primer of Modern Heresy, 104–107, 194

Agamemnon, 199

L'Âge d'or, 13

The Age of Innocence, 109

Agrarians (Southern), 4

Aiken, Conrad, 51, 176

Albertine disparue (Albertine Gone): see *Remembrance of Things Past*

Alexandrianism, 18

Alice James: Her Brothers, Her Journal, 195

Alighieri, Dante, 11, 24, 27–28, 93, 180

All Brides Are Beautiful, 198

Allegory, 5, 180–184, 197, 199

All's Well, 49

The Ambassadors, 8, 70, 73

American Field Service (Intercultural Programs), 1

Americanism, 11, 197

Anderson, Margaret, 44–45, 55–56

Anderson, Quentin, 6

Anderson, Sherwood, 44, 52, 59, 91–92, 94, 193

André Gide: His Life and His Work, 114–115

"Animula" (Eliot), 93

Antony and Cleopatra, 1, 168, 201

Ape and Essence, 143

Aphrodite in Aulis, 192

Apollonianism, 21

The Apple, 54

Aquinas, Thomas, 158

The Arabian Nights, 93

"Araby" (Joyce), 96

Aragon, Louis, 143–146, 198

Aristippus the Elder of Cyrene, 63

Aristotle, 148

Armstrong, Martin D., 192

Arnold, Matthew, 138, 172

"The Art of Fiction" (James), 74, 76–77

The Art of the Novel: Critical Prefaces, 180

Ash Wednesday, 66, 134

As I Was Going Down Sackville Street, 198

The Assassin, 34–37, 190

Association of Revolutionary Writers and Artists (France), 144

Astor family, 109

"At Baia" (H.D.), 18

The Atlantic Monthly, 56, 67

Auden, W. H., 2, 7, 121, 152–154, 156, 165, 170, 198

"Audience to Poet" (Hall), 123

Augustanism, 18

Austin, Alfred, 42

Austrian Civil War, 122

Autumn Leaves, 114
"Autumn on Nan-Yueh"
  (Empson), 185
Axel, 67
Axel's Castle, 64–67, 191
"The Azure" (Mallarmé), 73

"Bacchus" (Empson), 185
"Back to Poetry" (Aiken), 176
A Backward Glance, 109–111, 195
Bacon, Sir Francis, 62, 147–148
Baedeker, Karl, 166
Baillie, A. W. M., 173–174
"The Ballad of Dead Ladies"
  (Villon), 51
Balzac, Honoré de, 4, 6, 8, 10–12,
  28, 110, 131, 201
Barker, George, 166, 170–171
Barnes, Djuna, 44
Baroque, 93
Bates, Sylvia Chatfield, 94, 96, 194
Baudelaire, Charles, 30, 40, 67, 81,
  168, 175
Baugh, Hansell, 80
Beach, Joseph Warren, 193
Beach, Sylvia, 45
Beauvoir, Simone de, 180–181,
  183, 199
Beethoven, Ludwig van, 155
Beinecke Rare Book and
  Manuscript Library (Yale
  University), ix
Bell, Thomas, 198
The Bells of Basel, 143–146, 198
"Below the Battle" (Bourne), 46
Bennington College, 1–3, 7–8
Bentley, Phyllis, 193
Berdyaev, Nicholas, 195
Bergson, Henri, 83
Bergsonianism, 66, 83
Berry, Walter, 110
Bertrand, Aloysius, 199
Besant, Annie, 142
The Best Short Stories of 1933, 94–
  95, 194
"Beyond Desire" (S. Anderson),
  91

Bird Alone, 193
"Birth" (O'Flaherty), 37
Bishop, John Peale, 192
"Bisons" (Winters), 60
Bitter Victory, 198
Black Monastery, 195
Blackmur, R. P., 2, 6, 57, 133–135,
  197
The Black Rock, 190
The Black Soul, 38–39
"The Bladder" (O'Flaherty), 37
Blake, William, 11, 168
Blast, 43, 47, 53
Blind Man's Mark, 192
The Blood of Others, 180–181, 183,
  199
Blues, 53
Blunden, Edmund, 190
Bodenheim, Maxwell, 42, 44
Bogan, Louise, 51
Bohemianism, 53, 81–82, 144
"The Bomb Shop" (O'Faolain), 99
*"Bones of Contention" and Other
  Stories*, 139–140, 197
Bonnot, Jules Joseph, 143
Bonnot Gang, 143
The Bookman, 2, 13, 80, 189–193
Boon, 68
Boucicault, Dion, 33, 100
Bourget, Paul, 110
Bourne, Randolph, 45–46
Bovaryism, 132
"Boy at a Christmas Tree"
  (Nerber), 171
Boyle, Kay, 58
The Boys in the Back Room, 195
Brave New World, 141
Breton, André, 147
The Bridge, 134
Bridges, Robert, 42
Briffault, Robert, 197
Brontë, Emily, 149
Brooks, Cleanth, 2
Brooks, Van Wyck, 2, 45, 68–69,
  71
Broom, 54
"Brother Death" (S. Anderson), 92

The Brothers Karamazov, 182
Broun, Heywood, 86
Browne, Maurice, 40
Brunetière, Ferdinand, 11
Bruno, Giordano, 10
Bruno's, 49
Bryn Mawr College (Pa.), 147
Buddhism, 66, 142
Buffon (Georges-Louis Leclerc,
    Comte de Buffon), 113
Bunin, Ivan, 46
Buñuel, Luis, 13
Burke, Kenneth, 2–3, 6, 46, 133,
    186
Burne-Jones, Edward, 174
Burr, Anna Robeson, 195
Butler, Samuel, 157
Byron, George Gordon "Lord,"
    153, 156

Cabell, James Branch, 62, 76
Caldwell, Erskine, 94, 103,
    119–121, 151–152, 196
The Calendar of Modern Letters, 53
Calico Shoes, 102
Caligula, 180, 182–183, 199
Calverton, V. F., 57
Calvinism, 112
Campbell, Joseph, 200
Camus, Albert, 2, 180–183, 199
Candide, 32
The Canterbury Tales, 128
The Cantos, 134
Capitalism, 86, 90, 145
Carré, Jean-Marie, 78–80, 193
Carswell, Catherine, 191
Carter, Nicholas, 49
Cather, Willa, 2, 129–131, 197
Catholicism, 5, 12, 29, 89,
    101–102, 105, 112, 157
Céline, Louis-Ferdinand, 128, 183
Celticism, 12, 33, 65, 95, 103
The Celtic Twilight, 153
César Birotteau, 10
Cézanne, Paul, 40
Chaplin, Charles, 49
Charles I (King of England), 32

Charpentier, John, 192
Chaucer, Geoffrey, 128
Chesterton, G. K., 40
Chevalier, Haakon, 145
"Chicago" (Sandburg), 47
Chicago Little Theatre, 40
Chicago Renaissance, 82
"Children Selecting Books in a
    Library" (Jarrell), 171–172
Chimera, 199
Chirico, Giorgio de, 97, 169
Christianity, 79
Christian Science, 142
"The Christmas Roses" (Jarrell),
    171
Ciardi, John, 169, 171
"Civil War" (O'Flaherty), 35
Civil War (a.k.a. War Between the
    States), 150
Clark, Emily, 53
Classicism, 5, 18, 48, 56–57, 61,
    66, 113, 130, 149, 152, 155,
    168, 174, 181, 184
Claudel, Paul, 79–80
"A Clean, Well-Lighted Place"
    (Hemingway), 98
Close Up, 55
Coady, Robert J., 49–50
Cocteau, Jean, 2, 96–97, 194
Coleridge, Samuel Taylor,
    147–148, 169
"The Collapse of American
    Strategy" (Bourne), 46
Collected Poems, 1929–1933
    (Lewis), 11, 121–122, 196
Collected Poems of William Empson,
    200
Colon, Dolores, ix
Columbia University, 1, 86
Comedy, 28, 31, 85, 139, 152,
    189, 197
"Comments on *The Spiritual
    Exercises of St. Ignatius Loyola*"
    (Hopkins), 158
Communism, 57–58, 86, 112, 114,
    142, 152–156
Communist Party, 86, 144, 156

Conrad, Joseph, 34, 149
Contact, 55
Contemporaries and Snobs, 190
The Contemporary and His Soul, 193
Contemporary Verse, 51
Contempo: A Review of Books and Personalities, 97
Convention and Revolt in Poetry, 30
Cook, George Cram ("Doc"), 82
Cook, Thomas: see "Cook's Tour"
Cook's Tour, 154
Corbière, Tristan, 65
Corday, Charlotte, 43
Corelli, Marie, 43
Coriolanus, 163
Corydon, 112
Coryell, John R., 49
The Counterfeiters, 113–114
Cowley, Malcolm, 2, 46, 52
"The Cracked Looking-Glass" (Porter), 95, 132
Crane, Hart, 44, 50, 52, 58, 134, 170, 175, 184
The Criterion, 54, 57
Criticism, film, 1, 13
Criticism, literary, 1–13, 24, 31–32, 42, 45–46, 57, 63, 66, 72, 104–105, 131, 133–137, 148, 153, 155, 177, 184, 186–187, 189–191, 197, 200
Cross Purpose, 180, 182–183, 199
Cry of Time, 122–124, 190, 196
Cubism, 43
Cummings, E. E., 2, 46, 89–91, 133, 193
Curtius, Ernst Robert, 66
Cuthbert, Clifton, 194
Cyrenaism, 63

Dadaism, 30, 44, 96, 144
D'Annunzio, Gabriele, 76
Dante: see "Alighieri, Dante"
Darantière, Maurice, 45
Davidson, Donald, 4
Davidson, Jo, 66

Day-Lewis, C., 11, 121–122, 153, 165, 196
Death Comes to the Archbishop, 131
Death in Venice, 7
Death in the Woods, 91–92, 193
The Death Ship, 128–129
Debussy, Claude, 40
Decachord, 51
Decadence, 133, 136, 161, 174, 180, 191
The Decline of the West, 84
Deconstruction, 2
Defense of the West, 189
Defoe, Daniel, 181
Delacroix, Eugène, 11, 178
Demeny, Paul, 178
Dey, Frederick van Rensselaer, 49
The Dial, 39, 46–47, 99
Dichtung und Wahrheit (*Poetry and Truth*), 30
Dickens, Charles, 142, 196
Dickinson, Emily, 123
"The Difficult Resolution" (Jarrell), 173
Dill Pickle Club (Chicago), 82
Dionysianism, 21, 112, 121
"Disorder and Early Sorrow" (Mann), 96
Dissociations, 108
The Divine Comedy, 27–28, 93, 180
Dixon, W. M., 162
Dixon, Richard Watson, 174
Documentary, 4, 95, 131, 149
The Dogs, 192
Donne, John, 148
Donoghue, Denis, 135
Doolard, A. Den, 197
Doolittle, Hilda, 18–19, 25, 42, 189, 199
Dos Passos, John, 62, 118
Dostoevsky, Fyodor, 34, 93, 118, 178, 181–183, 195
The Double Agent: Essays in Craft and Elucidation, 133–135, 197
The Double Dealer, 53
"The Double Shame" (Spender), 170–171

"Dover Beach" (Arnold), 138, 172
The Dream Life of Balso Snell, 93
Dreiser, Theodore, 52, 62, 76
Dreyer, Carl-Theodor, 13
Dryden, John, 81, 153, 184
Dubliners, 176
The Duchess of Malfi, 34
Dujardin, Édouard, 20, 80
Dumas (*père*), Alexandre, 73
Dunsany, Lord (Edward Plunkett), 42
Duns Scotus (John Duns), 158

The Earth for Sale, 190
"Earth Has Shrunk in the Wash" (Empson), 184, 186
Easter Rebellion, 101
Easter Rising: see "Easter Rebellion"
Eastman, Max, 55–56, 147
Edenism, 8
Edman, Irwin, 193
The Education of Henry Adams, 94
The Egoist, 42–43, 47, 53
Eimi, 89–91, 193
Einstein, Albert, 131
The Elder Henry James, 195
Eliot, T. S., 2, 6, 24, 27–30, 43–44, 51, 54, 57, 65–67, 80, 93, 104–107, 115, 119, 122, 124, 128, 133–134, 151, 165, 167, 175, 184, 194
Elizabeth I (Queen of England), 32
Elizabethanism, 21, 24, 35, 88–89, 134–135, 162–163
Ellis, Havelock, 197
Ellmann, Richard, 200
Empson, William, 2–3, 148, 184–186, 200
Enemy, 50
Les Enfants terrible (*The Holy Terrors*), 97
"Epistle to D. T." (Barker), 171
The Erl King, 191
Esperanto, 59
Ethan Frome, 110
Eton College (U.K.), 158

Euclidianism, 184, 186, 200
Euripides, 18–19, 199
Europa: The Days of Ignorance, 197
Exile, 41, 50
Existentialism, 12, 180–181, 183–184
Existentialism Is a Humanism, 183
Experiment, 54
Express to the East, 197
Eyeless in Gaza, 140–143, 198

"The Fable" (Winters), 61
Fabulous Voyager, 191
Fairbanks, Douglas, 184
The Fairy Goose, 37
Fallada, Hans, 128
Farce, 85
Farrell, James T., 102–104, 125–127, 194
Fascism, 105, 118, 122, 142, 154
"Fathers and Sons" (Hemingway), 98
Faulkner, William, 2, 98, 103, 124–125, 149–151, 196
February Uprising: see "Austrian Civil War"
Feige, Otto: see "Traven, B."
Fergusson, Francis, 6
Fernandez, Ramon, 10, 12, 66, 114
"The Festival" (Prokosch), 166
Fidelio, 155
Fiedler, Leslie, 6
"Fifty Grand" (Hemingway), 56
The Figure in the Carpet: A Magazine of Prose, 52, 189
Film Nation: William Troy on the Cinema, 1933–1935, 13
Fine Arts Building (a.k.a. Studebaker Building, Chicago), 130
Finger, Charles J., 49
Finnegans Wake, 3, 59, 101, 176, 200
"Fire and Ice" (H.D.), 18
"The First Autumn" (Caldwell), 94

First World War: see "World War I"
Fitts, Norman, 50
Fitzgerald, F. Scott, 2, 4–7, 12, 107–109, 195, 200
Fitzgerald, Moira, ix
Fitz-James, Comtesse de (Rosalie von Gutmann), 110
Flaubert, Gustave, 25, 75, 112, 131–132, 179, 181
Fletcher, John Gould, 190
"Flowering Judas," 131
"Flowering Judas" and Other Stories, 131–132, 197
Foerster, Norman, 190
Folio, 52
"For a Broken Needle" (Hall), 123
Ford, Ford Madox, 43, 54
Foerster, Norman, 190
Forge, 51
Forster, E. M., 53
Fort, Paul, 41
The 42nd Parallel, 118
The Forum, 192
Forward from Liberalism, 154–155, 198
Four Years, 96
Francis, Robert, 196
Franco-Prussian War, 165
Frank, Joseph, 2
Frank, Waldo, 45
Frankenberg, Lloyd, 172
Franz Ferdinand (Archduke of Austria), 43
Frazer, J. G., 10
French Revolution, 164
Freud, Sigmund, 9–10, 13, 20, 83, 172
Freudianism, 9, 68, 172, 187
Frizzell, Ralph, 151
From Rousseau to Proust, 197
Frost, Robert, 41
The Fruits of the Earth, 113
Fugitive, 41, 51, 53
"Fugue" (O'Faolain), 99
Fulbright, J. William, 1
The Furys, 196

Futurism, 43

Gaelicism, 33
Galsworthy, John, 40
"The Gambler, the Nun, and the Radio" (Hemingway), 98
The Garden, 192
Gas-House McGinty, 102
Gaspard de la Nuit, 199
Gaudier-Brzeska, Henri, 44
George, W. L., 42
"George Washington Bridge" (Ciardi), 169
Georgianism, 43
Germinal, 6, 12, 159–162, 199
Gide, André, 2, 8, 75, 111–115, 136, 144, 178, 195
Gilbert, Stuart, 191
Glaspell, Susan, 82
"Goatherds" (Winters), 60
"God Rest You Merry, Gentlemen" (Hemingway), 98
God's Little Acre, 119
Goethe, Johann Wolfgang von, 30
"Going into Exile" (O'Flaherty), 37
Gold, Michael, 62
Goldberg, Isaac, 61
The Golden Bough, 10
The Golden Bowl, 8
Golden Galleon, 53
The Golden Hind, 54
Goncourt, Edmond, 75, 178
Goncourt, Jules, 75, 178
Gosse, Edmund, 54, 113
Gourmont, Remy de, 21, 108, 133
The Governor of Massachusetts, 191
Granberry, Edwin, 191
The Grandmothers, 189
Graves, Robert, 190
The Great Gatsby, 108
The Great War: see "World War I"
Greco, El (Doménikos Theotokópoulos), 49
Gregory, Horace, 97, 199

Guardian, 53
Guerard, Albert, 197
Guests of the Nation, 139
Guilloux, Louis, 198
Gulliver's Travels, 32
Gurdjieff, George, 85
Gurdjieffism, 85
Gypsy, 54
Gyroscope, 53

"Hacienda" (Porter), 132
Hall, Hazel, 190, 122–124, 196
Hamlet, 163
"Hand in Sunlight" (Hall), 123
Hanley, James, 196
Harbaugh, Thomas, 49
Harris, Frank, 49
Hart, Henry, 97
Harvard University, 86
Harvard University Library, 176
Hawthorne, Nathaniel, 178
Hazlitt, Henry, 57
H.D.: see "Doolittle, Hilda"
"He" (Porter), 132
Heap, Jane, 45
Hecht, Ben, 44
Hemingway, Ernest, 2, 13, 54–56, 59, 94, 97–99, 124–125, 132, 136, 152, 176, 194
Henry IV, Part I, 88
Herbst, Josephine, 194
The Hero with a Thousand Faces, 200
Hicks, Granville, 133
"Hide in the Heart" (Frankenberg), 172
"The Hind and the Panther" (Dryden), 153
Hippolytus Temporizes, 18–19, 189
Hitler, Adolf, 128
Hobbes, Thomas, 147–148
The Hogarth Essays, 190
Hollywood, 107, 130
Homer, 51
"A Hope for Poetry" (C. Day-Lewis), 122

Hopkins, Gerard Manley, 7, 84, 122, 140, 154, 156–159, 173–176, 178, 199
Hound & Horn, 53, 57
House, Humphry, 158, 199
Houseman, A. E., 154
The House of Mirth, 109
Howells, William Dean, 70
Hudson, Stephen, 53
Hudson Review, ix, 199–200
Hueffer, Ford Madox: see "Ford, Ford Madox"
Hughes, Glenn, 12, 192
Hugh Selwyn Mauberly, 169
Hugo, Victor, 24
Hulme, T. E., 44, 147
The Human Comedy, 28
Humanism, 2, 5, 62, 85, 163, 183
Huneker, James Gibbons, 40
Huxley, Aldous, 51, 124, 140–143, 198
Huysman, Joris-Karl, 161
Hyman, Stanley Edgar, 2, 200

If It Die, 113
Ignatius of Loyola, Saint, 158
The Iliad, 51
Illuminations, 80
Imagism, 12, 43, 60, 192
Imagism and the Imagists, 192
Impressionism, 76
The Informer, 35–36
Inheritance, 193
In Our Time, 97
"In a Strange Town" (S. Anderson), 92
Intellectualism, 46, 81–89, 124, 193
Invasion, 198
Ion, 199
The Irish Statesman, 38
Irony, 4, 12–13, 21, 24, 27, 124, 140, 142, 160, 171, 184
"I wake and feel the fell of dark, not day" (Hopkins), 84, 140

James, Alice, 180

James I (King of England), 32
James, Henry, 2, 6, 8, 11, 20,
    43–44, 52, 67–77, 92, 110,
    134, 149, 178–181, 192, 200
Jammes, Francis, 41
Jarrell, Randall, 171–173
Jaurès, Jean, 146
Jesuitism, 1
Johnson, John, 97
Johnson, Samuel, 133
Jolas, Eugene, 21, 58
Jonson, Ben, 135
Joseph and His Brothers, 9
Josephson, Hannah, 80
Josephson, Matthew, 52, 80, 159,
    161
Journal of the Plague Year, 181
The Journals of André Gide, 111
Journeyman, 119–121, 196
Joyce, Isabel, 177
Joyce, James, 1–2, 5–6, 8–9, 12,
    19–23, 27–29, 32–33, 43–45,
    47, 55, 59, 65, 80, 84, 90–91,
    95–96, 99–101, 103, 118, 168,
    172, 176–178, 191, 200
Joyce, Maurice, 177
Judaism, 52, 105
Judgment Day, 102, 125–127, 194
Jung, C. G., 9–10, 13, 172
"Just a Smack at Auden"
    (Empson), 185

Kafka, Franz, 182
Kain, Richard M., 191
Keats, John, 94, 157, 178
King Lear, 163
Kingsmill, Hugh, 196
Kirstein, Lincoln, 57
Knight, G. Wilson, 8
Knopf, Alfred A., 159
Kozlenko, Vladimir, 61
Kreymborg, Alfred, 51, 54, 190
Krutch, Joseph Wood, 136
Kuncz, Aladar, 195

Laforgianism, 124
Laforgue, Jules, 65, 80, 170, 184

Land Under England, 197
Lang, Fritz, 13
"The Language of Night" (Jolas),
    58
The Language of Poetry, 198
Lariat, 51
Laski, Harold J., 154
The Last Tycoon, 7
Laughing Horse, 53
Les Lauriers sont coupés (*The Laurels
    Are Cut*), 20
Lautréamont, Comte de (Isidore
    Lucien Ducasse), 110, 144
Lawrence, D. H., 3, 7–8, 53, 106,
    133, 200
Leavis, F. R., 3
Lehmann, John, 180, 199
Lenin, V. I., 115
"Letter I" (Empson), 86
Lever, Charles, 33, 100
Lewis, Janet, 53
Lewis, R. W. B., 2
Lewis, Wyndham, 43, 47, 50, 54
Lewisohn, Ludwig, 62
Liberalism, 45, 143, 154–156, 198
"The Liberators" (Preston), 39
Life and Letters, 54
The Life of Robert Burns, 191
Lindsay, Vachel, 41
*Literature and Dialectical
    Materialism*, 196
Literature and Society, 197
Little magazines, 39–60, 190
Little Review, 39, 41, 44–45, 47,
    55–56
The Little Town, 192
The London Aphrodite, 54
Lost City, 190
A Lost Lady, 130–131
"The Lost Novel" (S. Anderson),
    91
The Lost Sail, 190
Lowell, Amy, 12, 41
Lowes, John Livingston, 30
Lowry, Malcolm, 171
Loy, Mina, 51
Loyola Academy (Chicago), 1

Lucy Gayheart, 129–131, 197

M, 13
Macbeth, 34
Machine Age, 44
MacLeish, Archibald, 54, 138
MacNeice, Louis, 199
Macpherson, James, 39
Madame Bovary, 13, 95
"Magic" (Porter), 132
The Magic Mountain, 5, 7, 9
"The Majesty of the Law"
    (O'Connor), 139
Mallarmé, Stéphane, 65, 73, 79,
    170
Malraux, André, 3, 6, 12, 144–145,
    201
Manichaeism, 116
Mann, Heinrich, 192
Mann, Thomas, 5, 7–11, 46, 96,
    118, 172, 201
Man's Fate, 6, 145
Mansfield, Katherine, 42
"The Man That Stopped"
    (O'Connor), 139
The Man with the Heart in the
    Highlands" (Saroyan), 152
*"Many Thousands Gone" and Other
    Stories*, 192
"María Concepción" (Porter), 132
"Marina" (Eliot), 119
Maritain, Jacques, 105
The Martyr, 190
Marut, Ret: see "Traven, B."
Marx, Karl, 11, 110, 146
Marxism, 4, 6, 11, 114, 127–128,
    153, 187
Massis, Henri, 113, 189
Masters, Edgar Lee, 41, 49
Matthiessen, F. O., 2, 178, 180,
    195
Maurois, André, 196
Maurras, Charles, 105
McDonald, Maria, 58
McGill, Vivian J., 192
McHugh, Vincent, 194
Measure, 51

Meissonier, Ernest, 11
Melodrama, 34–36
Melville, Herman, 12, 182
Mencken, H. L., 1, 49, 52–53, 62
Menelik II (King of Ethiopia), 80
Men of Good Will, 116, 118–119
Metaphysical criticism, 7–8
Metropolitan Opera House (N.Y.),
    109
Michaud, Regis, 144
Middle Ages, 5, 135, 158
Midland, 53
Midsummer Night Madness, 99, 193
"Milking Time" (O'Flaherty), 37
Milton, John, 82
Miltonism, 142
Mirandola, Pico della, 10
The Mirror: see *Reedy's Mirror*
Miss Lonelyhearts, 92–93, 194
Mr. Gilhooley, 37
The Misunderstanding: see *Cross
    Purpose*
Moby Dick, 182
Mockel, Albert, 6
Modern French Short Stories, 180,
    183, 199
Modernism, 6–8, 10, 12–13,
    18–22, 24–25, 27–31, 33–25,
    38–41, 43–44, 46, 51–57, 61,
    64, 68, 78, 80, 84, 87–89, 93,
    96, 99, 102–107, 112, 115,
    121–122, 128, 131, 133–134,
    142, 145, 147, 154, 161, 163,
    167, 169, 172, 175–176,
    180–181, 183–186, 189–190,
    194, 199–200
Modern Language Association of
    America, 187
The Modern Quarterly, 57
The Modern Review, 53
Monro, Harold, 51, 190
Monroe, Harriet, 41, 50
Mooney, Thomas, 126
Moore, George Augustus, 192
Moore, Marianne, 51, 133
Moore, Thomas, 100
Morley, Christopher, 93

Morris, William, 174
Moscow (Show) Trials, 154
Mother, 13
"The Mother of a Queen"
    (Hemingway), 98
Mudie, Juliet, 42
Mudieism, 42
Mumford, Lewis, 2
"Munich Elegy No. 1" (Barker),
    170
Munson, Gorham B., 50, 52, 62
Murder in the Cathedral, 134
Murdock, Kenneth B., 178, 180,
    195
Murry, John Middleton, 42
Muse and Mirror, 51
Mushrooms, 51
My Ántonia, 131
Mystery plays (Middle Ages), 5
Myth criticism, 3, 5–7, 9–11, 172,
    200–201

Napoleonism, 164
Nathan, George Jean, 2, 61–64,
    191
The Nation, ix, 1, 3, 13, 136,
    190–199
National Book Awards, 1
"A Natural History of the Dead"
    (Hemingway), 98
Naturalism, 4, 20, 64, 66–67,
    75–76, 85, 159–161, 181
Nazhivin, Ivan, 192
Nemerov, Howard, 167
Neoclassicism, 174
Nerber, John, 171
A Nest of Simple Folk, 99–102, 193
Nethercot, Arthur H., 192
The Newcomes, 73
The New Coterie, 53
New Criticism, 2
New Directions Press, 176
New Historicism, 2
New Humanism, 62
New Leader, 6
New Letters in America, 199
New Playwrights, 62

New Psychology, 83
New Republic, ix, 64, 80, 189–192,
    199
New School for Social Research
    (N.Y.), 1–2, 5, 10, 52
New Writing, 199
New York Times, ix, 191
New York Times Book Review,
    191–193, 198
New York University, 1–2
Niebuhr, Reinhold, 162
Nietzsche, Friedrich, 7, 21,
    112–113
1919, 118
1924, 52
North American Review, ix, 193
"Note and Digression" (Valéry),
    28
*The Notebooks and Papers of Gerard
    Manley Hopkins*, 157–159, 199
The Notebooks of André Walter, 113
The Notebooks of Henry James,
    178–180, 195
"Notes on a New England Writer"
    (Nemerov), 167
Notes on Novelists, 69, 71–72, 76
Not to Eat, Not for Love, 194
La Nouvelle Revue française, 114
"November" (Winters), 60

O'Brien, Edward J., 94–96, 194
Ockham, William of, 158
O'Connor, Frank, 100, 139–140,
    197
"Ode for School Convocation"
    (Ciardi), 171
Odes of Pierre de Ronsard, 136
O'Donnell, Peadar, 100
Odyssey, 22
Oedipus complex, 9
O'Faolain, Sean, 99–102, 193
O'Flaherty, Liam, 33–39, 100,
    190
"The Old Hunter" (O'Flaherty),
    37
O'Neill, Eugene, 62, 82
O'Neill, Joseph, 197

"One Reader Writes"
(Hemingway), 98
On This Island, 153–154, 198
O Pioneers, 130
Oppenheim, James, 45
The Orators, 153
Orlando: A Biography, 31–32, 189
Orphée, 96–97, 194
"Orpheus and His Lute"
(O'Connor), 139
Ossian: see "Macpherson, James"
Othello, 163
Others, 41, 51
Owen, Wilfrid, 122
The Owl, 54
Oxford University Press, 159

Pacific Sonnets, 166
Pagany, 41, 53
Palms, 51
Palo Verde, 51
Paradiso: see *Divine Comedy*
"The Pardoner's Tale" (Chaucer),
128
Parnassianism, 9, 64, 164–176,
199
Parnassus, 51
Partisan Review, 11, 191, 195,
197–200
Pascal, Blaise, 113
The Passion of Joan of Arc, 13
The Pastoral Symphony, 114
Pater, Walter, 133
Pathos, 13, 107, 114, 130,
170–171, 186–187, 194
Paul, Elliot, 58, 191
Pearson's, 49
"Peasants" (O'Connor), 139
"Perhaps Women" (S. Anderson),
91
Phantasmus, 53
Phelps, William Lyon, 50, 62
Philistinism, 4, 98
Phillips, Stephen, 51
The Philosophy of Rhetoric,
146–149, 198
Picasso, Pablo, 97, 169

The Pickwick Papers, 142
Pierre-Quint, Léon, 114–115
The Pilgrimage of Henry James, 68
Pirandello, Luigi, 46
Pitoëff, Georges, 96
Pity Is Not Enough, 194
The Plague, 180–183, 199
Plato, 148, 178
Platonism, 136
"Plenum and Vacuum" (Empson),
185
Poe, Edgar, Allan, 12, 65
"The Poet Leaves a Burning City"
(Stepanchev), 172
Poetry Bookshop (London), 51
Poetry: A Magazine of Verse, ix, 41,
44, 47, 50, 56, 199–200
The Poetry Review, 51
Point Counter Point, 141–142
Pope, Alexander, 94
Porter, Katherine Anne, 94–95,
131–132, 197
*A Portrait of the Artist as a Young
Man*, 9, 23, 43, 99, 176
The Portrait of a Lady, 68
Post-colonialism, 2
Post-structuralism, 2
Pound, Ezra, 41, 43–44, 50, 67,
133–134, 165, 167, 169,
184
Pragmatism, 148
Prairie Schooner, 94
"Prayer" (H.D.), 25
Praz, Mario, 113, 194
"A Preface to Modern Literature"
(Wilson), 64
Preston, Keith, 39
Primitivism and Decadence, 191
Prokosch, Frederic, 166
Proletarianism, 86, 92
Prometheanism, 113
The Proof, 13, 60–61, 191
Propaganda, 127, 146, 155
"Protest" (Hall), 123
Protestantism, 101, 112–113, 156
The Proud and the Meek, 116–119,
195

Proust, Marcel, 3, 8, 12, 62, 65–66, 84, 86,103, 110, 112, 114, 118, 131, 141, 149, 171, 201
Provincetown Theater (N.Y.), 82
Prudentius (Aurelius Prudentius Clemens), 180
Prufrock and Other Observations, 43
Psychoanalytic criticism, 6
Psychomachia, 181
"Public Speech" (Saroyan), 152
Publishers' Weekly, 151
Pudovkin, Vsevolod, 13
Purgatorio, 93
The Pursuit of the Lucky Clew, 49
Pylon, 124–125, 196

The Quintessence of Nathanism, 61

Rabelais, François, 47, 131
Rabelaisianism, 141
Racine, Jean, 19
Ransom, John Crowe, 2, 186
Rationalism, 64
Reactionary Essays On Poetry and Ideas, 198
Realism, 75, 119, 140, 143, 149, 196
The Red and the Black, 7
Reedy, William Marion, 48
Reedy's Mirror, 49
The Reinterpretation of American Literature, 190
Remembrance of Things Past, 62, 66, 84, 103, 171
Renaissance, 35, 78, 135, 163
Renoir, Jean, 13
Republicanism (Irish), 101
Resistance (French), 183
Retreat, 190
"The Return" (S. Anderson), 91
Return from Chad, 112
The Reviewer, 53
Rhetoric, 146–149
Rhythm, 42
Rhythmus, 51
Richards, I. A., 2, 133, 146–149, 186, 198

Riding, Laura, 190
Rilke, Rainer Maria, 96, 165, 170, 172
Rimbaud, Arthur, 12, 30, 67, 78–81, 144, 168, 170, 175, 178, 193
"River Elegy" (Rukeyser), 173
Roberts, Michael, 153
Roderick Hudson, 68
Rodgers, W. R., 167
Rolland, Romain, 144
Romains, Jules, 116–119, 195
The Romance of the Rose, 181
The Romantic Agony, 113, 194
Romanticism, 4, 38–39, 48, 51, 56–57, 59–60, 64, 66–67, 78, 101, 112–113, 125, 130–131, 143, 149, 152, 154–156, 164, 174, 179, 194
Romany Marie (Marie Marchand), 82
The Romaunt of the Rose, 181
Romeo and Juliet, 163
Ronsard, Pierre de, 138
"The Room" (Sartre), 183
Roosevelt family, 109
Rosenfeld, Paul, 2
Rossetti, Dante Gabriel, 174
Rougon-Macquart cycle (Zola), 118, 161
Rousseau, Jean-Jacques, 143
Rousseau: The Child of Nature, 192
Rozanov, V. V., 189
Rubens, Peter Paul, 96
Rukeyser, Muriel, 173
Russell, George William, 38
Russian Revolution, 90
Rutgers University Press, 200

Sacred and Profane, 49–50
The Sacred Wood, 133
The Sacrilege of Alan Kent, 151–152, 196
Sage, Robert, 58
The Saint and Mary Kate, 100, 140
St. John Gogarty, Oliver, 198

Saint John's Vision of the Mysteries of the Apocalypse: see *Sacred and Profane*
Salient, 52
Sand, George (Amantine Lucile Aurore Dupin), 25
Sandburg, Carl, 42, 47, 49
San Francisco Preparedness Day Bombing of 1916, 126
Santayana, George, 46, 164
Saroyan, William, 152–153, 196
Sartre, Jean-Paul, 12, 181, 183–184
Sassoon, Siegfried, 53
Satanism, 8, 113
Satie, Erik, 40
Satire, 21, 27, 32, 52, 111, 121, 142, 144–145, 153, 156
Saturday Evening Post, 94
Sawyer, Eugene T., 49
Schnitzler, Arthur, 46
"The Schoolboy's Complaint" (Lowry), 171
Schopenhauer: Pessimist and Pagan, 192
A Season in Hell (Rimbaud), 79
A Season in Hell: The Life of Arthur Rimbaud, 79, 193
Seaver, Edwin, 52
Secession, 52
Second World War, 2
"The Secular Masque" (Dryden), 81
Seillière, Ernest, 10
Seldes, Gilbert, 46
Selected Essays (Troy), 1–2, 5, 8, 10, 200
Selected Essays of R. P. Blackmur, 135
Semiotics, 2
Sentimental Education, 131
Sentimentalism, 36, 38, 49, 80, 91, 96, 106, 118, 129, 131, 142, 155, 167, 171, 178, 182, 196
The Sentimental Journey, 196
"Sermon 116: Preached to the Nobility" (Donne), 148
Seven Arts, 45–47

Seven Types of Ambiguity, 148
S4N, 50
Shadows on the Rock, 131
Shakespeare, William, 1, 8, 34, 67, 88, 135, 138, 162–164, 168
Shakespeare and the Nature of Man, 162–164, 199
Shaw, George Bernard, 33, 40, 42, 65
Shelley, Percy Bysshe, 156
"The Sick Rose" (Blake), 168
"Simplex Munditiis" (Winters), 61
Sing Before Breakfast, 194
Sitwell, Edith, 51
Sitwell, Osbert, 51
Sitwell, Sacheverell, 51
"The Small Lady" (O'Faolain), 99
The Smart Set, 49
"The Sniper" (O'Flaherty), 35
Socialism, 122, 142–143
Societé Internationale Forestière et Minière du Congo (Belgium), 111
Socraticism, 112
The Soil, 49
Solitaria, 189
The Song of the Lark, 130
"Sonnets of Desolation" (Hopkins): see "Sonnets Written-in-Blood"
"Sonnets Written-in-Blood" (Hopkins), 140
Sontag, Susan, 4
Sorbonne University (Paris), 1, 6
Southern Review, 53
Spanish Civil War, 154
Spectricism, 43
Spencer, Theodore, 162–164, 199
Spender, Stephen, 122, 153–156, 165, 170–171, 196, 198
Spengler, Oswald, 46, 83–84
Spenser, Edmund, 174
The Spiritual Exercises of St. Ignatius Loyola, 158
The Spoils of Poynton, 69, 72, 75
Spoon River Anthology, 49
Spring Sowing, 37

"Spring Sowing" (O'Flaherty), 37
Spurgeon, Caroline, 8
Stace, W. T., 162
Star-Dust, 51
Stein, Gertrude, 5, 32, 46, 49, 55, 59, 65–66, 98, 110, 118, 152, 176, 200
Stendhal (Marie-Henri Beyle), 4, 6–9, 11–12, 201
Stepanchev, Stephan, 172
Stephen Hero, 176–178, 191
Stephens, James, 42
Sterne, Laurence, 32
Stevens, Wallace, 42, 51, 133, 167
Stork, Charles Wharton, 51
Story, 94
Strachey, John, 154, 196
Strachey, Lytton, 59
Strobel, Marion, 190
Strong, L. A. G., 192
Structuralism, 6
Studs Lonigan Trilogy (Farrell), 125–127, 194
The Sun Also Rises, 97
Surrealism, 29, 80, 144, 185
A Survey of Modernist Poetry, 190
Swann's Way: see *Remembrance of Things Past*
"Sweeney among the Nightingales" (Eliot), 44
"Sweeney Erect" (Eliot), 44
Swift, Jonathan, 32–33
Symbolism, 6, 8, 10, 29, 64–67, 80, 132, 159, 161–162, 164, 167, 172, 175, 191, 199
Symons, Arthur, 54, 97
Synge, John Millington, 33, 140

Taggard, Genevieve, 51
Tambour, 55
Tarr, 43
Tate, Allen, 2, 21, 198, 200
"Tears, Idle Tears" (O'Connor), 139
The Tempest, 163–164
Tender Buttons, 66

Tender Is the Night, 4, 107–109, 195
Tennyson, Alfred "Lord," 174
The Tent, 37
"Terrible Sonnets" (Hopkins): see "Sonnets Written-in-Blood"
Testament of a Critic, 61–64, 191
Thackeray, William Makepeace, 73, 110
"That Tree" (Porter), 132
The Theatre of George Jean Nathan, 61
Theory of Literature, 186–188, 200
"This Last Pain" (Empson), 184
This Quarter, 55
Thomas, Dylan, 172
"Three Lambs" (O'Flaherty), 37
The Three Musketeers, 73
Three Times Three, 152–153, 196
Thunder Without Rain, 194
Thurber, James, 93
Thy Neighbour's Wife, 34
Time Regained: see *Remembrance of Things Past*
Timon of Athens, 163
Tithonus, 174
Tobacco Road, 119
Tolstoy, Leo, 73, 131
"To the Memory of My Beloved the Author, Mr. William Shakespeare and What He Hath Left Us" (Jonson), 135
"Tract on Living" (Hall), 123
Tragedy, 5–7, 19, 21, 34, 37, 68, 73, 85, 146, 152, 163–164, 166, 172, 175, 180, 187, 199, 201
The Tragic Muse, 73
The Transatlantic Review, 54–55
transition, 21, 55, 57–60
Travels in the Congo, 112
Traven, B., 128–129, 196
Traven, Bruno: see "Traven, B."
The Treasure of the Sierra Madre, 128–129, 196
Trilling, Lionel, 3
Tristram Shandy, 32

The Triumph of the Egg, 92
Troy, Camilla, 5
Turbyfill, Mark, 42
Turgenev, Ivan, 76
Twain, Mark, 71
The Twentieth-Century Novel, 193
Twentieth-Century Short Stories, 96, 194
"Twenty-Four Years" (Thomas), 172
"Twilight of Idols" (Bourne), 46
Twilight Sleep, 110
Two Years, 190

Ulysses (Joyce), 20–23, 27–28, 44–45, 59, 84, 89, 95, 100, 103, 174, 191
Ulysses (Tennyson), 174
Unanimism, 29
University of Bordeaux (France), 1
University of Chicago, 126
University of Grenoble (France), 1
University of New Hampshire, 1
University of Pittsburgh, 86
University of Rennes (France), 1
U.S.A. Trilogy, 118

Valéry, Paul, 4, 6, 28–29, 46, 65–66, 80, 165, 201
Van der Meersch, Maxence, 198
Variétés, 29
The Vatican Cellars, 113
Velásquez, Diego, 96
Vergil (Publius Vergilius Maro), 174
Verhaeren, Émile, 41
Verlaine, Paul, 40
Vico, Giambattista, 10
Victorianism, 42, 75, 174
Vielé-Griffin, Francis, 19
Vienna: A Poem, 122, 196
Views and Reviews, 71
"Villanelle" (Empson), 184, 186
Villers: see "Adam, Villiers de l'Isle"
Villon, François, 51
Vinci, Leonardo da, 157, 178

"The Vision of Judgment" (Byron), 153
Voices, 51
Voltaire (François-Marie Arouet), 32
Vorticism, 43–44

Waddell, Helen, 181
"The Wall" (Sartre), 183
Wallace, Edgar, 118
Walpole, Hugh, 75
Walton, Eda Lou, 154
The Wandering Scholars, 181
"Wanted: A New Communicative Language!" (Jolas), 58
"Wanted: A New Symbolical Language!" (Jolas), 58
"The War and the Intellectuals" (Bourne), 46
War and Peace, 73
"A War Diary" (Bourne), 46
Warren, Austin, 186–188, 195, 200
Warren, Robert Penn, 4
Washington, Martha, 87
The Waste Land, 24, 27–28, 66, 106
Watts-Dunton, Theodore, 54
The Wave, 53
Webb, Beatrice, 154
Webb, Sidney, 154
Webster, John, 34
Wellek, René, 186–188, 200
Weller, George, 194
Wells, H. G., 40, 42, 67, 72, 178
Wescott, Glenway, 46, 189
West, Nathanael, 92–93, 194
West, Rebecca, 43
Wharton, Edith, 2, 109–111, 195
Wheels, 51
"White Christmas" (Rodgers), 167
Whitman, Walt, 40–41, 45, 71, 157
Wilde, Oscar, 97
Wilder, Thornton, 50, 76
Wildman, Carl, 97
"The Wild Swans of Coole" (Yeats), 44
Williams, William Carlos, 51

Wilson, Edmund, 2–3, 64–67, 135–136, 191
Wimsatt, William K., 2
"Wine of Wyoming" (Hemingway), 98
Winesburg, Ohio, 92
The Wings of the Dove, 70
Winner Take Nothing, 97–99, 194
Winters, Yvor, 2, 13, 53, 60–61, 191
The Wolf at the Door, 196
Woolf, Leonard, 190
Woolf, Virginia, 4, 5, 11, 19, 23, 31–32, 42, 132, 189–190, 199–200
Wordsworth, William, 157
Work in Progress: see *Finnegans Wake*
The World from Below, 195
World's Fair of 1891, 41
World War I, 40, 43, 47, 85, 101, 126, 165

World War II: see "Second World War"
Wuthering Heights, 149

Yale University, 1, 62
Yarmolinsky, Avrahm, 195
The Years, 199
Yeats, William Butler, 19, 41, 44, 46, 65–66, 96, 153, 165, 176
Yeats: The Man and the Masks, 200
Young, Stark, 4
Young Lonigan, 102, 126
The Young Manhood of Studs Lonigan, 102–104, 126, 194
Youth, 53

Zola, Émile, 2, 6, 12, 75–76, 159–162, 118, 199